obsessed

obsessed

obsessed

ALLISON BRITZ

a memoir of my life with OCD

SIMON PULSE

New York   London   Toronto   Sydney   New Delhi

NOTE TO READERS:

Certain names and other characteristics have been changed. In some instances, those portrayed are composites. Conversations are re-created, and events are described, based on my memory and/or therapy notes.

SIMON PULSE

An imprint of Simon & Schuster Children's Publishing Division

1230 Avenue of the Americas, New York, New York 10020

First Simon Pulse hardcover edition September 2017

For information about special discounts for bulk purchases, please contact Simon & Schuster Special Sales at 1-866-506-1949 or business@simonandschuster.com.

The Simon & Schuster Speakers Bureau can bring authors to your live event. For more information or to book an event contact the Simon & Schuster Speakers Bureau at 1-866-248-3049 or visit our website at www.simonspeakers.com.

Designed by Steve Scott

The text of this book was set in ITC New Baskerville.

Manufactured in the United States of America

10 9 8 7 6 5 4

Library of Congress Cataloging-in-Publication Data

Names: Britz, Allison author.

Title: Obsessed : a memoir of my life with OCD / by Allison Britz.

Description: First Simon Pulse hardcover edition. |

New York : Simon Pulse, 2017. | Includes bibliographical references and index.

Identifiers: LCCN 2016048641 (print) | LCCN 2017025855 (eBook) |

ISBN 9781481489188 (hc) | ISBN 9781481489201 (eBook)

Subjects: LCSH: Britz, Allison—Mental health. |

Obsessive-compulsive disorder in adolescence—Patients—Biography.

Classification: LCC RJ506.O25 (eBook) | LCC RJ506.O25 B75 2017 (print) |

DDC 616.85/2270092 [B]—dc23

LC record available at https://lccn.loc.gov/2016048641

To GRB — for being you

obsessed

obsessed

PROLOGUE

Still crouching, I pull my hair dryer out from under the cabinet, untangling its cord as I bring it into the open. I begged my parents for weeks to get it for me for my birthday last year, explaining that I did, in fact, need a $150 hair dryer with four different heat levels and a retractable cord. Holding its white plastic, I am suddenly bashed in the back of the head and thrown forward. At the same time, the angry buzz of a swarm of bees fills my ears as the floor starts to shake violently. I brace myself against the toilet. The glass lights around my mirror tinkle. Jewelry, fingernail polish, toiletries are jostled out of their cabinet and fall loudly to the floor. The earth shifts powerfully, jaggedly underneath me. An earthquake. Or worse. My throat is tightening, my tongue swelling. There is a powerful, hot presence, a strong hand pressing forcefully against my throat. A gentle taste of blood. I can't breathe.

DO NOT TOUCH THAT.

It is livid. In pure reflex, choking, I throw my arms upward and topple over onto my back. *BAD!* it screams. *DEATH!* I cower from its radiation. I've never heard this voice before, but I know it is my monster, my savior. The source of my secret messages, the inspiration behind my insider discoveries. Anger is vibrating in waves across the bathroom.

I am on the floor, hands in the air, completely still. I should have stopped when I felt the twinge. But how could I have known? A tide of dark clouds closes in over the bathroom, and I let out a pathetic whimper as I shield my face. Outrage crackles through the air. It is furious. It won't be ignored.

You will not dry your hair, it commands.

I nod eagerly in understanding. "I won't. I won't, I won't, I won't." I will do anything it asks, now that I know its true form. "I promise."

CHAPTER 1

"I don't think the pigs smell me. I think they see me," Ms. Griffin says, reenacting last night's assigned reading from *Lord of the Flies*. She pretends to apply mud to her face and body like war paint and crouches down, ready for the hunt. Overweight in a way that reminds me pleasantly of my grandmother, with her frizzy, out-of-control hair flying in all directions, she scuttles in between the desks at the front of the room, a ruler raised high in the air as a spear.

In the fourth row, third chair back, I am using Lauren Madison's hair as a shield to stay out of Ms. Griffin's line of vision. I spend most English classes annoyed with Lauren's blond, conditioned locks—the way they tumble beautifully across my desk and how they smell like expensive shampoo and roses. Today, however, her mane provides a convenient wall to hide behind while I study for my upcoming sixth-period chemistry test. I am feverishly attempting to memorize the molecular formula of a long list of compounds, most of which I have never heard of outside a chemistry textbook. Head bent forward, pencil streaming across the page, I am writing and rewriting the formula for glucose as I simultaneously whisper it to myself.

"Allison, what about you?"

I look up from my mound of notes, mouth agape. $C_6H_{12}O_6$. $C_6H_{12}O_6$.

"Allison, hi. Yes, join us, please. Put away whatever else it is you're working on. What are your thoughts on the question?"

Blank stare.

"I asked what you think about the mounting tension between Roger and Jack?"

I continue to look at her, openmouthed. My subconscious clanks and grunts, struggling to shift to a new train of thought. *Lord of the Flies*. Focus. My mind is silent, my stomach tightening more with each second. Ms. Griffin, sweating slightly from her pretend spear hunt, locks eyes with me from behind her podium at the front of the class. I can see that she is enjoying this.

I am the girl who other students don't want in their classes. Brimming with anecdotes and opinions, I am the girl who raises her hand when the teacher asks, "Are there any questions?" I am the student, to the chorus of groans from my peers, who reminds the teacher when she forgot to pick up our homework assignment from the night before. The tense silence continues as I search my brain for anything that's not an atomic symbol. I glance at her, a plea for mercy, but she doesn't flinch. See if I rescue you next time no one is participating in your class discussion, I think moodily. Gradually, my classmates turn around to look at me. They're torn from their bored stupor by the fact that somehow Allison, the girl who was voted Most Intellectual in the eighth-grade yearbook, didn't do the previous night's assigned reading.

"Well, I . . . think . . ."

My eyes dart around the room, looking desperately for

4

assistance. I make eye contact with Greg Sauers, and he just shrugs at me. How did she even see me behind Lauren's hair?

"I think . . ."

"Okay, Samuelson High, it's Thursday, and you know what that means!" My hesitant mumbling is interrupted by an announcement crackling through the school's intercom system. A peppy female voice echoes against the whitewashed cinder-block walls. "Thursdays mean JV football, Bulldogs fans, and tonight we are facing none other than Hamilton High School." A low-toned "Boooooo" lilts through the hallways. "Make sure you come out and support your JV boys tonight at eight p.m.! As always, go, Bulldogs!" With her last syllables, the bell rings, and the entire class lurches into action. Saved by the intercom, I quickly gather my disarrayed chemistry notes into my binder and dodge through the crowded classroom, launching myself into the hallway to avoid Ms. Griffin. I make a mental note to myself to catch up on *Lord of the Flies* tonight. After that performance, Ms. Griffin will likely target me again in the future, if only for her own entertainment.

"Allison, hey!" The familiar soprano voice of my best friend, Sara, lofts over the chaotic hallway scene. In my rush to escape, I completely forgot to wait for her outside class like I always do. In the strict social hierarchy of Samuelson, many unspoken guidelines govern the student body. One of the most important: Never walk anywhere by yourself. In between classes, on the way to lunch, after school in the parking lot, have enough pride to never be seen alone. Sara is my best friend, of course, but also a convenient built-in walking partner.

"Dude, Ms. Griffin totally called you out. It's like she has some sort of radar or something. She *only* calls on me when I forget to do the reading," Sara complains. "It's as if she can see the guilt in our *eyes.*"

I let out an exasperated breath before she even finishes her sentence. Sara has been my closest friend since she sat next to me on the first day of summer camp when we were nine. She is pretty in a way that tells you she's been told it her entire life. Her raucous auburn curls and winged eyeliner are the antithesis to my simple blond bob and light mascara. Her Rolling Stones T-shirt clashes with my pink cardigan and pearls.

"Okay, first of all, you never do the reading, and second, I didn't *forget* to do the homework." I cast her a sidelong glance with a slight headshake for good measure, acting more annoyed than I am. "I have a chemistry test this afternoon and I was up all night studying, so I didn't have time to do the assignment. It's called prioritizing. I'll catch up on her reading after this test."

"All night? Get a grip, girl!" Sara exclaims with concern in her eyes, an edge of judgment in her voice. Since childhood, she has proclaimed it her mission to get me to "take the stick out." "Life is too short for this. You haven't been to one JV football game this year."

False. "Hello, I've been with you twice already! You know cross-country practice goes until seven and the football games start at eight. An hour isn't enough time to get home, shower, change. It's just not worth it. . . ."

"Yeah, yeah, I know. And you do the long loop on

Thursdays." Sara isn't on the cross-country team, but by now she knows our workout schedule by heart.

"*Exactly.* We do the long loop on Thursdays. Seven miles. I'm so exhausted when I get home. Sweaty, sore. Making it to a football game afterwards is just a lot for one night. Not to mention having to do homework after we get back at almost midnight." I'm trying to sound resolute, but it comes out more like a whine.

"Yeah, well . . ." She pauses and, glancing around to ensure secrecy, half whispers, "Let's just say you're not going to get anywhere with Sam with a social schedule like that." We look at each other, and she shrugs. "Look, he asked you out for ice cream, y'all ate some delicious treats together and laughed a bit. Then he texted you two consecutive days in a row. Two!" She stares at me intently, her pointer and middle fingers in the air as a visual aid. "Now it's been what, five days, including a weekend, since you've heard from him? You have to do something." She is emphatic, energized. If we were standing still, I know she would have stomped her foot. "He always goes to the Thursday football games—the whole basketball team does. Tonight after practice, drive home, take the fastest shower of your life, and then come over to my house. I'll do your hair and makeup and we'll get his attention."

Sara grabs my hand and beams at me, and suddenly, optimistically, I have changed my mind about the night ahead. I see myself sitting in front of a mirror, in a bathroom almost as familiar as my own, as she straightens my hair and gives me a lesson on bronzer. "Look"—she leans in and whispers from the side of her mouth—"I know you're nervous. I know it's scary. So let me help."

We make brief eye contact and she shows a small smile. My heart swells with gratitude for her and her genuine concern for my prom prospects. She doesn't know that I check my phone multiple times a minute hoping to see *Sam* appear on the screen. She has no idea that I chewed all my fingernails off last night while playing our ice-cream-date conversation on a loop in my head. Only I can feel how much his sudden silence is gnawing at my insides, but she can tell, just from being beside me, just from being my closest friend, that I need a little help.

It seems so recently that we were eating ice cream. After we chose flavors, after he paid (he paid!), I looked out the window at the rainy, dreary day and made a comment about how sad and ugly the weather was. He put his arm around me, looked me in the eye, our faces four inches apart, and said, "That's okay. You more than make up for it." His breath smelled like Juicy Fruit.

And now he's MIA.

For almost a week I have been placating myself with tales of broken cell phones or dead grandmas or any number of fluke accidents that might have prevented him from texting me. He is probably starting to grow fearful of just how much he cares about me, I've told myself. Our spark is too intense for his soft, sensitive skin.

But, as always, Sara speaks the truth: He is losing interest. It is time to act.

"Okay, yeah, fine. I'll come to your house as fast as I can

after practice. We can just be a little late for the game." I nudge her happily with my shoulder. "Gotta go to Civics," I say as I pivot ninety degrees to enter the nearby brick building.

"Have a good day!" she throws over her shoulder as we part ways. "And make sure you keep all those chemistry notes. I'm going to need to use them next year."

Nine hours later, I reach the top of the stairs and let my book bag fall onto the kitchen floor with a heavy thud. Every week we run that same seven-mile loop, and every week I question why I subject myself to a sport that feels like cruel and unusual punishment. Because it looks good on my résumé, I tell myself. Because it keeps me fit. Because that's where most of my friends are.

It's a relief to be home. I collapse into one of the chairs at my kitchen table. Our sprawling house is dark, lit only by the fading evening sun pushing weakly through the windows. My neighborhood, Blakely Farms, is one of the more affluent in town, and I wear our address like a badge of pride, despite my complete lack of involvement in our financial success. There is a swimming pool with a competitive swim team, a pond with an unnecessarily large fountain, playgrounds in every backyard.

Chemistry test and cross-country practice behind me, I am finally feeling the full burden of yesterday's all-nighter. I know I need to put some effort into my social life, to see and be seen. But I'm just so exhausted.

"Well, hey, sweetheart!" my mom drawls, walking down the hallway toward me. Her hair is still perfectly coiffed and sprayed from a day at the office, but she has changed into what she calls her comfy clothes and what the rest of the world calls a ten-year-old sweatpants set and fuzzy socks with grips on the bottom. A former army captain, she has yet to abandon both her regulation haircut and her strict attention to timeliness, rules, and regulations. As she walks across the kitchen, I almost hear her reciting to herself, *Left, left, left, right, left.* My mother is a corporate powerhouse, the family breadwinner. Sara calls her the Hillary Clinton of human resources. She is the VP of Everything and lives up to her reputation with an impressive collection of shoulder-padded pantsuits. She smiles at me and runs her hand under my chin as she passes. "You look tired—how late were you up last night?"

"Oh, thanks, Mom." I act offended, adjusting my seat to face her as she moves across the kitchen. "I was up all night."

"All night? Allison! You know that's not good for you." She is standing in front of the pantry, choosing tonight's dinner. "I don't like it when you do that. You need your rest."

"Well, I had a test today—what else was I supposed to do? Just fail? Not really an option, Mother."

I slump over loudly onto the kitchen table for effect. Cramming my face deep into my arm, I think about the enormous task that lies in my future: showering. It just seems like so much effort. All to drive to Sara's and spend way too much time getting ready for a boy who no longer seems to notice me. With hours between me and the conversation with Sara in the hallway, this football game seems less and less appealing. Are we just going to walk up to the basketball team in the stands like we're part of the gang? *Here I am with an hour's worth of makeup and a very padded bra—ask me to prom!*

My mom is humming as she pours spaghetti into a pot of boiling water on the stove. From the dark hideout inside my arms, I hear my cell phone vibrate deep within my over-packed book bag. A pang of annoyance, because I know it's Sara badgering me to hurry up. *Come on—there won't be any seats left near the b-ball team!* Or something mature like *You're so slooowww.* I don't move to check my phone, just to spite her, but then it buzzes again. Slowly, with individual, methodic, three-inch scoots, I move the chair across the linoleum toward my book bag while my mother casts annoyed looks at me from the other side of the kitchen. I dig around, moving aside binders and loose sheets of paper, and dislodge my cell phone from deep within a bottom corner.

Sara:

Just heard boys bball team is out of
town for tournament so Sam won't be at
JV game. Do u still want to go? Want to
come over and watch a movie instead?
Don't say ur tired.

Me:

Im tired.

Need to do homework and catch up on
reading

We will do something fun tomorrow
night, promise!! xox

A wave of relief sweeps over me, and I feel immediately guilty for being annoyed with her. She's just trying to help. Within five seconds, there's another buzz.

Sara:

Typical Allison. Sleep tight little bookworm!

I look up from my phone with a deep sigh. When did we lose the concept of a school night, I wonder, dragging my loaded book bag behind me down the hallway and up the stairs to my room. ("Don't take a long shower. I'm starting dinner!" my mom yells from the kitchen below.) I feel a quick blip of regret that I won't have the chance to sweep my potential future prom date off his feet. What if he meets another girl before I can convince him that he is still infatuated with me? What if Sara gets asked to prom and I don't?

After dropping my bag off in the den, I grab my own no-less-embarrassing version of comfy clothes from my room before heading down the hall to my bathroom. As I let the warm water rinse away the remnants of an arduous afternoon, I almost cry with the overwhelming relief that has swept through me at this last-minute change of plans. Of course, in the safety of the hypothetical, I would love the opportunity to woo my way back into Sam's good graces. In my daydreams, I walk toward him in the bleachers, chin high, chest out, and impress him with my wit, charm, and very well-straightened hair. Back in reality, however, I am a hesitant, wobbly colt. A girl who plans out our entire conversation before seeing him and still manages to get stuck on her words. The weirdo who has a list of brainstormed questions memorized and at the ready, in case I ever run into him and need to generate a conversation. (*So, how about those Atlanta Braves, right?*) I can't be witty or cute or flippant. Not with him! I can't even maintain eye contact for a complete sentence. Of course I want a date to prom, but entertaining a boy at a football game? In front of the whole basketball team? The thought makes me nauseous.

Loaded with a hearty spaghetti dinner and satiated after a few hours of homework, I settle into bed with my dog-eared copy of *Lord of the Flies*. I need to get to at least the end of chapter 5 to catch up with the class. Based on the thickness of the pages between my fingers, it should only take about thirty minutes. I picture Ms. Griffin's smug face at the front of the class this morning. It's like she has no idea that I have six other classes besides hers to deal with. And that intense *Les Misérables* assignment she had dumped on us a few weeks ago is only more proof of this. "Good night, big girl," my dad whispers, popping his head around the corner of my bedroom door. He uses the term "big girl" endearingly, like you would with a small child who is transitioning from a crib to a real bed. It has been his nickname for me my entire life. The way he says it sounds exactly like love. My dad is part hippie, part former army officer, and I know his biggest fear is that I might grow up to be a Republican. "Don't read too late."

"I won't, Dad. Just a few chapters." I smile at him in my doorway.

"Saw your light on late last night. Everything okay?"

"Yeah, just that chemistry test. No big deal. Glad it's over." The last words come out as the beginning of a long sigh.

He nods his head and gently taps the wooden door frame. "I sure am proud of you." An army brat who grew up in every corner of Texas, he has a rich, deep drawl, which leaks through against his will. Especially when he's trying to be serious.

We make eye contact but I look away quickly. Parent emotions. Dislike. I roll my eyes. "Yeah, thanks, Dad." I vaguely raise an eyebrow in his direction

He pauses there for a few moments, looking at me with a half smile. "Good night, sweetie."

"Good night," I mumble, already a few sentences into the book.

Ten pages later, I am lying flat, arms sprawled and eyes closed. Through my open window I barely register the guttural croaks of bullfrogs from the pond at the base of our cul-de-sac, the occasional hum of a passing car, the silence of a Thursday night in the suburbs.

Slowly, over minutes or hours, the calls of the bullfrogs morph into the gravelly voice of a middle-aged, white-coated doctor. My bed becomes the examining table, my sheets the thin paper hospital gown. The doctor is standing uncomfortably close to me, hand on my knee, gesturing at the dark images and shadows on the computer screen: "You have brain cancer, Allison. And I'm afraid there is nothing we can do." He points specifically at a golf-ball-shaped blur somewhere above one of my ears. I don't breathe, can't breathe, until my mother's wails shatter the humming silence of the fluorescent lights. Dizzy, nauseous, I slump over, crumbling onto the cold tile floor. When I lift myself up, I am in the parking lot of my high school. Shapes whirl past. There is a siren, the sound of screeching tires. Stumbling, disoriented, I begin to tell my classmates, who have surrounded me, the fateful news of my sickness, my imminent death. Their screams of sadness erupt with the force of a bomb, and I am immediately, violently thrown backward.

A flash goes off and I'm vomiting. It flashes again: the pinch of a needle. Swaths of my hair fall in a pile on the floor. Flash. My mother crumpled at my bedside. Flash. A prom dress with an oxygen tank. An IV dripping poison into my veins. I am gasping, crying. Thick black surgical stitches stretching savagely across my bald head. My mother and father, a dark room, the ragged breaths. "It's okay, sweetheart, you can let go now."

I am torn from sleep with a sharp breath in. An autumn breeze filters gently through my window along with the gray light of the early morning. My body is still sluggish with

15

sleep, but my mind and heart are awake, vibrating, racing with fear. I am crying, real ragged sobs of sorrow that shake my entire body. I clutch my quilt and wrap myself around it, latching onto it like a small child to its mother. A cyclone of grief and terror rages within me, and I force my face deeper into the pillows. *Terminal brain cancer.* The words shatter through me, causing an explosion of emotions. After everything I've done for my future, after how hard I've worked? I'm only fifteen! I have so much left to do! Prom, college, sex, a real job, marriage. I can't die yet. I haven't even gotten started. With each reason I list for not wanting to die, I am smacked with a gruesome image from the dream. I'm too young! Shaved head. So much left to do! A thick-needled IV taped to the inside bend of my arm.

I know I wasn't actually in the hospital or the parking lot, but that girl I saw was me. Is me. Somehow. I roll over onto my other side, leaving behind a soaked pillowcase. I'm here lying in bed. She's there in a paper exam gown. I'm awake. She lives in my dreams. But we are the same person. I know her.

A car horn blares outside. I am jolted from my thoughts and hurtle into a slumped sitting position. I rub at one of my wet eyes and let my arm fall listlessly back onto the bed. I stare without seeing at the wall, breathing slowly as thoughts filter into my brain. What just happened? My mind is silent in response.

I hear my mom's alarm go off down the hall. That means it's five forty-five a.m., only five minutes before my own alarm would blast me out of bed. She is moving around her

16

room. She turns on lights, opens the windows, warms up the shower. The comfortable, muted sounds of her morning routine shock me with bolts of terror and misery. My crying turns to bawling as I remember her falling apart in the doctor's office, the glaring shapes on the doomed MRI glinting off her tearstained chin. How is she supposed to continue after losing her only child? Imagining her pain and suffering is almost as bad as thinking about my own terrible destiny.

No dream has ever felt like this before. I'm choking violently on sobs. My tongue is clumsy and swollen, my mind at once panicked and groggy. Images from the dream pass like a slow-motion video reel through my head. My wailing friends in the parking lot, a prom night filled with nausea and needles, a new tombstone carved with 1989–2004. Gulping for air, fighting to breathe against a thick layer of mucus and tears, I burrow headfirst into my sheets, allowing my face to slide against the mattress and deep into a cocoon of blankets. Under the weight of multiple layers of cotton, my rapid breath begins to slow, and the small hideout quickly warms. In the darkness I am forced face-to-face with my thoughts, with the painful images that filter through the background of my mind. What happened last night looked like a dream and dressed like a dream, but from the knots in my stomach I know that it was much more than that. Something this powerful did not exist without purpose. This was not a dream. This was a message, a warning. I have brain cancer.

I lift my head a few inches off the mattress as this thought floats across my consciousness. I watch it move around weightlessly, a jellyfish in an illuminated aquarium. I evaluate it from afar like a newly discovered species. Something about the idea's sharp, ragged edges feels horribly right. An abandoned corner inside me is strangely fulfilled, as if it had been expecting something exactly this terrible to happen all along. As if it knew this life, this happiness, was all just too good to be true.

The truth of my brain cancer lies heavily on my inert body. I haven't tried to move, but I doubt that I could. I am frozen in my cocoon, stunned.

"It's all in my head. / I think about it over and over again."

My alarm. It is 5:50 a.m., and Nelly and Tim McGraw's current radio hit "Over and Over" knifes itself into my brain. I lurch to sit up but am forced back down by a taut layer of tangled blankets. I look around the darkness in confusion until I recognize the source of the noise and gradually relax back into the comfort of my bed, mindlessly following along with the radio. It's one of those songs you just can't escape. In the grocery store, in the car, in line at the pharmacy. I know every word. "'Cause it's all in my head / I think about it over and over again." I take two or three breaths before the thought clicks into place. I feel it snap together like two Legos. My heart thuds as I slowly repeat the song's chorus: *It's . . . all . . . in . . . my . . . head. . . .*

It knows about my cancer. The radio knows about my dream. It's warning me, about the illness *all in my head.* I dig my fingertips into my sheets. Overnight I was sent a premonition masquerading as a dream, and now I am being blasted

18

awake by a song that is clearly referencing the dark shadow on my brain. Clever. Very clever. This alarm is another barely veiled message (from who?) that there is something horribly wrong with me.

Smoothly, as if I had practice with this sort of maneuver, I slide myself out of the sheets, smack the top of my radio hard with my palm, and slide back through the small entry into my cave. In one fluid motion, my face is again covered in cotton, surrounded by a calm darkness, in less than three seconds. But the blast of outside air has shaken me a bit. As I get comfortable again, there's a slightly different hue to my thoughts. I have never felt such strong emotions in a dream or, for that matter, in my entire life. It seemed so real. And then there was the message from the radio. But, wriggling for a fresh air pocket in my cocoon, fighting against the cloud of warm breath that has gathered from my collective exhales, I think that maybe it was just a coincidence? Maybe I had a terrible, terrifying nightmare and then just so happened to wake up to a song by two wildly popular music artists. It is a major radio hit, after all. It's on all the time.

But *that* song? my brain screams in protest into the silence, with *that* chorus? What are the chances that it would be playing at the very moment my alarm is set to go off on the very morning I wake up from what I might go so far as to call a borderline paranormal experience? How much clearer do the messages need to be?

"Good morning, honey. Time to get up!" my mother coos as she pads down the hall toward my room. My entire body goes rigid. I can't let her see me. I'm sure my eyes are swollen, my face all red and blotchy. She will know immediately that I've been crying and swoop in close with a million questions. I stay buried deep under the blankets. There is a change in the air when she enters the room. "It's almost six o'clock, sweetie! Up, up, up!" She tickles the bottom of my feet.

"Mooooom," I moan, "I'm awake." My voice cracks unintentionally.

"Oh, honey, you sound very stuffed up! I'll make sure to put some allergy medicine out for you downstairs. Are you feeling okay? Do you need a tissue?" She pauses briefly, wiggling my calf through the thick comforter. With my extended silence, her tone changes. "You need to get up or you are going to be late. I'm not leaving this room until I see your smiling face out from under these covers." She claps a few times. "Now. Up." I continue to lie still, facedown in the sheets damp with my own tears. "Allison Marie. It's time to get up now. Five . . . four . . . three . . ." There is nothing more infuriating than when my mother starts a countdown. It makes me feel like I'm six years old and getting bullied into cleaning up a mess of toys.

"Mooom. Okaayyy." I mean to groan at her, but it comes out more like a snarling growl. "Go away. Please." A few seconds pass in awkward silence. "I don't need your step-by-step assistance, thank you." I can feel her presence as she stands quietly above me for a few moments. I rarely talk to her like this, and I know she is debating whether to make this into a parenting moment. After about ten seconds, and with what I imagine to be a shake of her head, she walks away down the hall.

CHAPTER 2

I haven't made a single mark on the blank sheet of notebook paper lying in front of me on my desk. I don't know for sure that I have brain cancer—there is a chance the dream was just a dream and the alarm was just an alarm—but the heavy feeling deep in my gut tells me the real truth. I look around at the students who will go on to live long, happy lives filled with graduations, weddings, children. They won't know the suffering, the injustice, of dying at fifteen. Dying before your life has even started.

In the distance, my Civics and Ethics teacher is halfway through an overly intricate flowchart of how a bill becomes a law. I would be impressed by his effort if he hadn't already drawn the same picture three times this school year. It is the crown jewel of his teaching repertoire, and it is losing its effect more quickly than he seems to know. Above him, running along the edge of the board, is a row of presidential faces and names. Stoic-looking old men in lacy shirts and stiff jackets. The history teacher's version of the alphabet.

Mr. Roberts is intently focused on ensuring that the lines of the arrows connecting the steps in his flowchart are straight. As his dutiful pupils, we are supposed to be following along, copying his work, again. For the fourth time. Half the class is scribbling away on procrastinated homework assignments while the rest are staring down into their laps, not even trying to hide that they're on their phones. The arrangement works. Mr. Roberts doesn't have to actually ever talk to his students, and we don't have to pretend like we're paying attention.

The silence is interrupted by the jarring ring of our classroom telephone. The phones rarely ring unless it is to call a student up to the office for one reason or another. Who would it be, who would it be? After carefully replacing the lid on his marker, Mr. Roberts shuffles calmly across the room toward the landline phone on his desk. Lifting the receiver off its base, he stares at it hesitantly, seemingly concerned about its cleanliness.

"Mmm, hello?" he inquires, a bit too loudly, holding the phone three inches from his face. Like the rest of the class, I am leaning toward him, eager to get the inside scoop on this exciting development. Sara will expect me to text her immediately if anyone interesting gets called to the office. "Yes, she is here today." It's a she! That eliminates half the class. "Yes. Yes." Twenty-five sets of eyes scan the female population. One of us is the chosen one, for better or worse. "Okay, I will send her." He places the phone down and plods back toward the board, oblivious to the rapt attention of his students. Picking up his pen to resume his drawing and without turning around, he says, "Allison, dear. Your presence is requested in the office. Only twenty minutes left in class. Best if you take your belongings with you." He continues along with his squeaky scribbles on the whiteboard without even looking at me.

In a single synchronized moment, the entire class swivels toward me with questioning eyes. I stare at the back of Mr.

Roberts's shirt without moving. "What did you do?" freckled Sean Morren asks eagerly from the desk beside me. I shrug. I have no idea. "Wow, I hope no one died." With a meaningful glance at him across the aisle, I gather my supplies in my bag and walk toward the classroom door with the eyes of all my classmates burning into the back of my head. The irony of Sean's comment threatens to pull a fresh set of tears down my cheeks as I quietly close the door behind me.

Maybe the school knows about my brain cancer too? I wonder as I trudge toward three sets of double doors that lead out of the building. Plodding down the hall, I can think of nothing but the slow, miserable decline into death that lies in my future. The prolonged chemo, the endless surgeries, all leading me toward the inevitable. I push my way out of the humanities building and am accosted by brilliant sunlight rushing forward from the October sky. A chorus of birds relaxes high in a towering oak tree, a few young squirrels scamper happily across the grass. Cowering away from the beaming light, I scowl at Mother Nature. I have just found out my life is coming to a gruesome end and she taunts me with the beauty of her creation. I deserve a thunderstorm. Or at the very least some dark and rumbling clouds.

Samuelson High School was built in the 1940s and has grown over the decades to accommodate the ever-increasing student population. At this point the school's sprawling campus includes ten separate buildings, each with its own dedicated academic subject, in addition to an administrative building, a library, and a gym. The large brick structures echo the seventies with their orange window trim and decorative geometric mosaics. All the buildings are connected by a series of covered, aged concrete pathways bordered with azaleas, daffodils, and patchy grass. I walk toward the main office, using my hand to shield my eyes from the shimmering morning sun. On any other day, my mind would be abuzz in a panicked effort to figure out why I am being called to the office. It could really only mean I'm in serious trouble or, like Sean said, someone has died. My grandma's face flashes quickly behind my eyes, followed by my other elderly relatives, in descending order. But today, and probably for the rest of my ill-fated life, my brain is consumed with my own sadness.

Eyes cast downward, I am watching my gold flip-flops swish past each other over the gray concrete path when I see my foot land on a crack in the sidewalk. In this exact instant, as if it has been triggered, I am forcefully swept up in the memory of a long-forgotten rhyme from elementary school: *Step on a crack, break your mother's back.* Although I haven't thought of this childhood chant for years, it is now glowing like a neon sign in my mind. My brain latches onto the idea and I freeze with my foot still directly on top of the crack. If stepping on a crack can break my mother's back, can it . . . can it also cause brain cancer?

The question hits my mind with a thud. Confused, I look up into the towering oak tree above me, my eyes scanning the sky for a hint. How can stepping on a crack affect my brain (or my mother)? The question feels awkward and nonsensical, but the idea has power. It refuses to leave. I examine my fingernails, squinting against the sun at the carnage I caused while studying for chemistry. Finding a tiny corner of skin, I peel, peel, peel it back until a dot of red blood appears. I wince and wipe it off on my jeans. The idea that cracks are related to cancer makes no rational sense, I tell myself, but the thought that maybe, just maybe, stepping on this crack could worsen my illness or speed my imminent demise is too frightening to ignore. This inspiration for the elementary-school rhyme appeared so randomly that it could be another sly message (from who?), like the dream and the alarm.

I feel a dull pain low and deep within my skull. The tumor. As I close my eyes against the ache, the words flash across my mind like a breaking story on the local news: *Cracks cause brain cancer.* And with them my head explodes in agony. I clamp my hands to my ears and collapse to the warm sidewalk. Through the radiating pain, I feel the idea repeat over and over: *Cracks cause brain cancer. Cracks cause brain cancer. Cracks cause brain cancer.* I am squatting now, attempting to gain composure in the face of what I assume is some sort of tumor attack. An explosive side effect of my terrible fate. *Cracks cause brain cancer.* My eyes are frantic, darting. Sirens blare in my ears, blocking my thoughts. I lean forward, trying to find a position to stop the chaotic tornado roaring within me. Nails screech down a chalkboard. *Cracks cause brain cancer.* Adjusting my stance, I see my gold flip-flop still planted on the original crack. As a sharp alarm sounds in my left ear, I shift my weight to my arms and forcefully extend my leg, pushing my foot off the sidewalk crack.

And with this movement the world falls immediately and

completely silent. The sharp pain and noises fade away into a vapor, disappearing as quickly and unexpectedly as they appeared. I lower myself into a sitting position, hang my head heavily between my knees. An ant crawls across the heel of my shoe, and with a long exhale I swirl a few early autumn leaves around on the ground. *Cracks cause brain cancer.*

I knew it.

"Allison, is that you?" I look up from my thoughts to see my friend and cross-country teammate Lindsey approaching with a concerned look on her face. *Crap.* "What are you doing? Are you okay?" Caught by complete surprise, I leap from my perch on the sidewalk and frantically scan the horizon, searching for a plausible excuse.

"I . . ." Why am I on the ground? Alone. In the middle of third period.

"Oh my gosh, you have dirt all over you! What happened?"

"I . . . *fell!*" Classic. "I was just walking along and got all tripped up on my flip-flops here," I say, gesturing at the golden culprits. "I'm okay now, though. No worries." I nod at her to show just how okay I am.

"I guess it's fine to laugh at you, then, since you're not actually hurt, right?" she teases with a smile. "Why aren't you in class?" she asks, extending her arm to help me up. Her vibrant red hair is on fire in the sunlight.

I accept her hand and we both groan as she pulls me to my feet. "I got called down to the office during Civics," I explain, wiping off pieces of gravel and dirt stuck to my jeans. "I'm headed there now."

"Oh, me too! I think it's for some award. Ms. Michaels was telling me about it yesterday." She stares at me, smiles, and tightens her ponytail. "I'll walk with you." My eyes look up at the long sidewalk ahead of us. Crack after crack after crack after crack.

"No, no," I say a bit too quickly and loudly. "I mean"—she looks at me—"I just have to . . . wait here. I'm . . . waiting for someone." *Sidewalk cracks cause cancer. Sidewalk cracks cause cancer.*

"Who are you waiting for?"

"My friend," I say over my thoughts. Lindsey's continued blank stare tells me she isn't satisfied. "Who is in the bathroom," I overemphasize, pointing over my shoulder to the brick building on the slight hill behind us. "I'm waiting for her . . . while . . . she is in there." My eyes dart around campus for ideas, inspiration, distractions. I am floundering. Lindsey's eyebrows crease at me. "It might be a while. Her stomach, you know. No need to wait with me."

"Oh. Um, okay," Lindsey says as she shoots me an offended glance and turns to continue walking toward the office. "Well, bye, then. See you in the office?" Her questioning voice trails off and she begins to move away.

"Yep! Bye! Be right there!" I stretch my best Miss America smile across my face and wave at her until she has turned the corner out of sight. As she enters the main office, my shoulders fall and the smile drops off my face. Left in peace, Lindsey no longer a threat, my mind is once again flooded with the ominous message: *Cracks cause brain cancer.* I can feel the thought's importance. And with a certainty I've

27

never known before, deep in my gut, I feel the danger. I survey the sidewalk that lies ahead of me. Each crack is a rogue cell poised to mutate, a dangerous carcinogen waiting to pounce.

Ten full minutes after the initial message, I am still standing in the same place on the path. Behind me lie dozens of cracks pockmarking the route back to class, while the path to the office looks just as treacherous. A minefield of cancerous cracks. Moving in either direction, it seems, is to tempt fate. I am surrounded.

As I eye the obstacles, a glimmer of an idea flits into my consciousness. If this recent message is correct and cracks cause brain cancer, then maybe avoiding them altogether can help cure it? I tilt my head in questioning, but I can feel the thought gaining power, a snowball growing as it rolls downhill. If stepping on a crack means certain death, then avoiding a crack must mean certain life. Every action has an equal and opposite reaction! (Thank you, Isaac Newton.) I nod to myself, knowing I'm on the right track, and allow an almost imperceptible smile to pull at my cheeks for the first time today. If I can avoid all the cracks on the sidewalk, I can stop the progression of my cancer. Or maybe even cure it!

I've discovered the truth: Cracks may cause cancer, but avoiding them helps cure it. And I'm free! Free at last! Bolstered with renewed confidence at the promise of safety ahead, I delicately proceed toward the office, avoiding all the cracks in the path along the way. Relief sweeps through me as I step over one crack, two cracks, three. I don't know why or how cracks are connected to cancer, but I do know that escaping them brings me a welcome swell of calm. For the first time since waking up from my dream this morning, I feel in control of my future. I have an escape route. As I open the doors to the main office, I look over my right shoulder at the concrete path leading down from Mr. Roberts's classroom and feel a wave of pride for having discovered the relationship between sidewalk cracks and brain cancer. I'm taking this situation into my own hands.

The administrative office building smells like printer paper and cleaning products. As I walk through the lobby, my eyes scan the familiar whitewashed walls covered in plaques and pictures from throughout the school's history. The air is filled with a chorus of ringing phones, copy machines, and polite female voices. I smile shyly at a grumpy-faced woman in a sweatshirt featuring a litter of kittens in a basket with a giant bow. She glares at me through thick red-rimmed reading glasses.

"Hi, I'm here to . . . Well, I was called up . . ."

"Hey there, Allison. Did you get lost?" Our school principal, Mr. Castillo, greets me from the other side of the office. "You kind of missed the party, but come on, come on, I can tell you about it in my office." With a second glance at the kitten sweatshirt, I hurry after him down a long hallway. He is wearing a tweed jacket with elbow pads like a misplaced European fox hunter. We pass the mysterious teachers' lounge, adorned somewhat sparsely with a microwave and mismatched couches from the 1970s. The grainy TV in the corner is blaring *The Price Is Right*. I imagine Ms. Griffin in there eating leftovers with saggy Mr. Roberts, giggling about a pop quiz she has planned for the afternoon.

"Have you ever heard of the Young Artists Program?" Mr. Castillo asks as he ushers me into his office and gestures to one of the chairs across from his desk. I shake my head, surveying the contents of his bookshelf, and he continues. "Here are the packets I provided the other students." He hands me a navy folder embossed with golden letters that is thick with papers and brochures as he settles into his presidential oversized desk chair. "The Young Artists Program is a way to recognize high school art students of exceptional ability and promise. Each honors and Advanced Placement teacher in the state recommends one student from each grade who they feel excels." His gray hair is thick but receding. As he talks, his bald forehead emphasizes his thick bushy brows and friendly blue eyes. "You have been nominated by Ms. Michaels in the individual-piece category as well as for your overall portfolio." He looks at me and, smiling widely, smacks his hand on his leg. "Congratulations! I hope you know what an honor it is to even be nominated. And twice!" His eyes grin at me across an imposing wooden desk.

"Oh, wow, that's so . . . great! Thank you!" I have never heard of the Young Artists Program, but Mr. Castillo's excited expression tells me I am expected to act interested. I love art class and I love Ms. Michaels. My heart thinks about a small pump of happiness, but it's quieted quickly by my brain. There is no point in getting excited. I can avoid cracks all I want, but from the lump in my gut I know I'm still dying.

"Yes, yes, well, additionally, the administration of each high school is permitted to select a handful of students who they feel best represent the . . . what was it?" He looks down his nose through his glasses at the sheet of paper on his desk. "The 'artistic vitality and spirit' of their school." He sticks out his lips and nods, seemingly approving of the wording. "This year, you have been selected to represent the sophomore class of Samuelson." He pauses, perhaps for effect, perhaps waiting for a response.

"Oh, nice. Wow. I don't know what to—"

"The program spans the summer," he says, interrupting me. "Each student must . . ."

Mr. Castillo continues his explanation as my eyes glide around his office. I've never been in here before. His desk is cluttered and crowded with six-inch-high stacks of paper. The wood-paneled walls boast framed pictures of Mr. Castillo with a former student who went on to play in the NFL, along with a large signed jersey. The thick dark curtains and over-sized leather chairs make me feel like I'm in a cigar lounge rather than the office of a high school principal. Looking down, I notice my chair is sitting on a small throw rug while my flip-flopped feet are stretched out in front of me onto the black-and-white floor. They are extended casually, cross-ing over multiple tiles, rolled slightly to the side against the cool surface. The picture freezes in my mind like a Polaroid and the world stops. Mr. Castillo's voice disappears into the background and my entire being is focused on the two limbs that seem to have once again doomed me to death. Looking at my feet on the floor, I don't see my bright pink painted toenails or the wear on the edges of my favorite shoes. I see the grout-filled spaces between the individual tiles. I see cracks. Hundreds, thousands of cracks. Vertical, horizontal.

They are everywhere. Frantic, I scramble up onto the aged leather chair, into a tight ball, my legs multiple feet above the dangerous floor. My heart pounds in a spasm of panic as I look out over the sea of cancer below. How do I know which cracks are the dangerous ones? I've only been paying attention to the gaps between concrete slabs. But now, here we have the sidewalk crack's close cousin: cracks in tile floors. My brain begins spinning, whizzing with questions. What about the spaces between planks in hardwood floors? And what about the cracks *within* each sidewalk slab—the natural cracks caused by years of exposure to the elements? I have been provided no specifics along with my anonymous inspiration, and my mind is now feasting on the possibilities. Looking down at the tiled floor, I nod to myself, knowing the truth. From now on, all cracks are created equal.

"This is genuinely something to be proud of, Allison. I encourage you to seize this opportunity and make the most of it. We are very proud of you."

I hear his words but cannot bring myself to speak. My mind is tangled within itself and overwhelmed by the size of my new discovery and all its implications. I look down at my fingernails and fidget with an inflamed, angry hangnail.

"Allison? Is everything all right?" I glance up at him. He is inclining his head toward me meaningfully. The overhead lights reflect off his forehead.

"What? Yes. Yes, yes. I'm sorry, Mr. Castillo." I see his eyes shift obviously to my feet, which are planted safely, and clearly inappropriately, on the leather cushion. Sheepishly, I slide my legs down from the chair, careful to ensure they rest safely on the small rug below, protected by its fabric from the cracks beneath it. "I'm just exhausted. With practice, studying. You know me, just working too hard." I humor him with a chuckle and smile across the desk. "Thank you for thinking of me for this opportunity." I need to get out of this office. I need to get away from the sea of cracks. Without looking away from him or dropping my smile, I quietly gather my book bag and purse from the floor and pull them closer to my feet. "I'm so excited to learn more about the program." In one awkward motion, I lift my bags, stand, and turn toward the door. I step to the edge of the small protective carpet. "It seems like it will be such a good learning experience," I throw back at him over my shoulder. There is a three-foot chasm of cracks between the safety of the throw rug and the thin carpet of the hallway. "Please tell Ms. Michaels that I appreciate the nomination." It seems close enough to jump, but I know that my loaded book bag is going to weigh me down significantly. Behind me, Mr. Castillo is clearing his throat to speak again. I can feel him rising in his seat, about to call me back to one of his leather chairs. Dipped into a slight crouch, I rock back and with a little jump push off hard with my right foot. I land cleanly, if clumsily, in the hallway and, still falling forward, pull Mr. Castillo's door closed behind me. It slams louder than I intend. "Thank you again!" I yell through the window in his door with a wave. He is half standing behind his desk, one eyebrow raised. I scurry into the hallway and clench my teeth as I walk as fast as possible out of the building.

The warm southern air rushes into my lungs. Even in the

first few days of October, the sun carries on with the strength of summer. I've placed both my feet safely in two adjacent sidewalk squares with the doors of the main office behind me. At the same time that I breathe a sigh of relief, I shudder with embarrassment thinking about Mr. Castillo's face as I jumped out of his office.

From a small courtyard ahead, six different breezeways snake off in multiple directions. I look closely at the concrete, scouring the surface for hints of cracks or crevices. It's a minefield. Not only are there the obvious cracks between slabs, but each square is littered with additional veins of danger. The concrete has given in to the years of rain, snow, and sun— each square buckling into multiple pieces over the decades. I move back and forth on my toes, imagining the best path through the obstacles. Carefully, slowly, I lean forward, placing the toes of my left foot into the corner of the square in front of me. I hop four feet to the right, landing flat-footed in a large, crack-free slab. I continue skipping and hopping through the breezeway, tongue out for added power of concentration, slowly picking up speed and confidence.

And then the bell rings.

I know from experience that I have about thirty seconds before I am consumed in a tsunami of bodies. The entire school of more than two thousand students is getting ready to pour out of their classrooms onto this very pathway. I move as fast as I dare through the treacherous sidewalk, but the specter of cancer emanating from the cracks keeps me from getting too much farther. I must resign to my fate. Brace for impact.

34

I hear the crowd before I see it. A swell of chattering students funneling through one main corridor. I plant my feet sternly in place and mentally map out my coming steps. It flashes across my mind that I will be walking alone to class, an enormous social faux pas. Mildly terrified as the mass sweeps me haphazardly toward the innumerable sidewalk cracks ahead, I am also strangely energized by the challenge. It's me against cancer, and losing is not an option. Jostled and pushed from all directions, I am consumed by the living, breathing herd. I fold seamlessly, anonymously into the crowd. Behind a wall of bodies, I can barely see upcoming cracks until they are immediately upon me. I find myself jumping frantically from side to side, darting diagonally, then horizontally, through the knots of students. I smash into arms, book bags, metal poles, ignoring the blatant mean stares shot at me from every direction. About a hundred feet down the path, I leap dramatically, and what I hope is gracefully, through an opening in the crowd to reach the doors of the foreign-languages building. Landing perfectly on the toes of my right foot, I stretch out my arms, envisioning myself in *Swan Lake*. A full orchestra twinkles in the background. I hold the pose for a moment, lost in my thoughts, until my airborne leg is slammed hard by a passing trombone. The symphony in my head crashes to a halt, and I collide with the glass doors of the building.

In all my time at Samuelson, I have never thought to examine the floors of the academic buildings. Until today. The air-conditioning dries the small beads of sweat on my forehead, and I crouch down to look closely at the stone floors, running my hand over their surface, feeling for a seam, a crease, a source of illness. Wiping my hand around the floor, I soon gather a small, unappealing pile of dust, hair, and paper scraps. "What the hell, Allison?" Steven Woodlock jars my shoulder hard with his leg as he passes. "Get out of the way!" I look up at him with a hurt scowl, but he is already disappearing down the hall. My hand is covered in a thin layer of floor residue. I gag when I see an old Band-Aid dangling from my pinky.

The bustling crowd around me thins, signaling that I only have a few more moments before the final bell rings. I stand up with a triumphant smile and good news: There are no cracks in the school hallway floors. It seems to be one long contiguous slab of speckled gray rock. I walk freely down the hall, ignoring my throbbing trombone injury, smiling to myself at this pleasant surprise.

I am in the doorway to Señora Ramirez's room just as the bell rings. About half the class is already seated, but many are still unpacking their binders or chatting with friends. The room bursts with color, passion, excitement. She has a mannequin in the corner wearing lipstick and a flamenco dress and three Dora the Explorer piñatas hanging from the ceiling. The entire back wall is covered with last week's homework assignments: drawings of our bedrooms labeled with that week's themed vocabulary. She is playing loud pop music with lyrics recorded in Spanish. The room bubbles with positive energy.

I catch my foot halfway through its first step into the room. Tile floors. The same danger that covered Mr. Castillo's office

36

sprawls threateningly across the Spanish classroom. How have I never noticed this horrible tile in all the time I've been a student here? In the school's forty-year history, am I really the only one to know the truth about—

"Siéntate, por favor, Allison." Señora Ramirez beams at me from in front of the dry-erase board and gestures toward my open desk in the second row. She is slightly pudgy but in an endearing, maternal way: the kind of body that looks like it would give really good hugs.

The tiles are squares, about six inches on each side. I eyeball my flip-flop against it. There is no way I can step flat-footed without encountering a crack. I will have to tiptoe. I nod to myself, envisioning the path to my desk. *"¿Señorita? ¿Estás bien?"* I jerk my head up. Her hand resting casually on her hip, Señora Ramirez is looking at me with gentle concern as I sway in the doorway. The rest of the class only stares. I crack the knuckles in my fingers and take a deep breath.

Placing my toes in the center of a square about three feet into the room, I glide forward with my eyes searching for the next foothold. Balancing on the ball of my right foot, I thrust my arms to the side like a tightrope walker and aim the toes of my left foot at a safe spot ahead. I am again in a dramatic dance number, the spotlight highlighting my perfect form against a curtained backdrop. In my head I pirouette to my desk to the approving applause of my classmates. Everyone is smiling and clapping because not only have I discovered the truth about cracks but also I'm just so darn graceful.

A coughing fit from the back row draws my eyes upward to reality and the crooked lines of occupied desks. The entire room is staring at me. Some look confused, some look interested. I glance at Señora Ramirez. She, too, is watching me. She steps toward me and tries to say something but stops herself when we make eye contact. Heat builds under my collar as I balance between tiptoed feet spread across the tiles. I am roasting under the pressure of their attention. I have to say something. A distraction, a cover.

"I'm sore!" I blurt out into the silence, the words bursting out of me. "Sore from cross-country practice!" I quickly bend down and grimace, placing my hand on my hamstring with a quick glance at my audience. I am a specimen. A curious sideshow. I add a bit of a limp to my next steps, a slight hop and a pained expression. "Walking on my tiptoes really helps!" I make a show of gritting my teeth and point down at my legs, just to reinforce the message. Reaching my desk, I flop into my seat and massage my calves. "Maybe I'm dehydrated? I'll get a Gatorade after class. That should help." Eddie Chester turns completely around in his desk and peers at me through narrowed eyes. He looks first at my calves, then at me, and, with a final furrow of his eyebrows, turns around to Señora Ramirez, who has begun her lesson. My cheeks flush a deep shade of crimson.

What am I doing? A sinking feeling opens in my heart and I allow myself to fall into it and curl up in self-pity. What started as a horrible nightmare last night has today somehow mutated into an irrational fear of cracks. I open my Spanish binder and flip to last night's homework assignment. Every day, I reason, thousands of students traipse carefree across Samuelson's crack-laden campus, and yet there is no cancer epidemic ravaging the school. I have been stepping on cracks, both large and small, for more than a year now and have not yet contracted any sort of disease. At least not as far as I know. It doesn't even make any sense! What do cracks have to do with cancer? Frustrated, embarrassed, I slide down into my desk and stew for the rest of class. I hear nothing Señora Ramirez says.

The class bell draws me from my stupor. I stay seated until the room has cleared out—no need to perform for my classmates if I don't have to. As the room empties, I lift myself onto my tiptoes, pushing up off my metal desk. The maze of cracks lying before me asks, *What now?* I imagine myself walking flat-footed out of the classroom and into the hallway. No stares, no raised brows. The thought triggers a deep rumbling, and I suddenly hear the muted beeping of hospital monitors, the hushed weeping in the hallway. My mother caresses the thick bandages wrapped around my head. I press hard on the nurse's button for more morphine.

"Allison, do you need something?"

I whip around to see Señora Ramirez sitting at her desk in the corner of the room. I had no idea she was still here.

"Nope! No, just packing up," I say with a start. "I'm leaving now." I grab my book bag. *"¡Adios!"* Thoughts of revolution quashed, I maneuver the tile floor in tiptoed leaps and jump into the safety of the hallway.

•   •   •

Because my locker is so close to the gym, I am always the first member of the cross-country team in the girls' locker room after school by at least five minutes. Located in the oldest section of campus, the locker rooms have no AC and even less air flow. The humid, thick air calms me as I sit down with my gym bag on a long wooden bench. The heat has a sedative effect on my worn brain. My tensed muscles relax for the first time all day. I breathe in, eyes closed, and enjoy the silence of the empty room. These thoughts, these messages—I can tell they are not my own creations. They appear like foreign parcels in my psyche, arriving clearly and forcefully from an outside sender. Is it God? Mother Nature? Balled-up paper towels litter the floor near the sinks. There is a faint dripping in a shower around the corner. Who is trying to protect me?

The locker-room door swings open, and my silence is shattered by wild conversation. Maddie's face lights up when she sees me. "Hey, girl! How was your day?" she asks, setting her gym bag beside me on the bench. She unzips the top and begins unloading her sneakers, socks, and sports bra at the same time she slips off her sandals.

I shake my head and pretend to mentally run through the day's events. "Eh, you know, the usual. Just another Friday."

CHAPTER 3

"Why are you walking like that?" Sara asks, annoyance dripping from her voice. Her eyes are scanning the hallway, taking in the sidelong glances and open stares as we stride toward our next class.

"Walking like what?" I leap diagonally, arms thrown outward, into the concrete square directly in front of her. She slams into my back with a grunt.

"Walking like . . . *this!*" She gestures at me and then zigzags her hands wildly in the air. "Like you're playing some sort of crazy hopscotch or something. Walk straight. Stop being weird. You were doing this last week too."

She is really not happy with me, but, strangely, I don't care. "Oh, I've just got blisters from practice," I say as I slide my left foot into an open space back on my side of the pathway. "It hurts when I put my foot down a certain way. Helps to kind of tiptoe." I point generally at my heel, the site of the fake blister.

"You just look like a crazy person. Maybe find a Band-Aid? People are going to start looking at you. . . . At us." She shifts her cross-body bag self-consciously. Sara has always been attuned to our social standing. Where we sit at lunch, who talks to us at football games. I care, in the general sense of not wanting to be an outcast, but for most of our lives I've simply followed her lead. She finagles the invites to the cool-kid parties, and I happily plod along behind her as we maneuver long, dark driveways leading to big basements and out-of-town parents. Sara is the glimmering, sparkling headliner, a perfectly developed, closely curated representation of high school popularity. My job is to look nice, dress well, and not say anything too weird. Don't talk about school or books.

I nod my head, pretending to take her advice. I have been evading cracks for almost four full days and I can tell a difference in my brain. It feels lighter. The tumor is shrinking. I am healing myself. Each step over a crack is one of cancer's soldiers killed.

Sara mumbles a quiet good-bye, more a multisyllable grunt than words, and veers toward her next class. She doesn't turn around when I yell, "Text me later!" Her mess of curls disappears into the crowd.

The school cafeteria is located in the heart of campus in a cavernous building that is also home to the auditorium and band room. The enormous brick structure could pass as a cathedral if there were anything remotely attractive about it. Its sprawling ceilings tower fifty feet above my head, the chipping green and orange exterior paint from decades past reminding me how old this school actually is, how many tens of thousands of students, some now much older than my parents, have lived out their high school years passing through these exact doors. There is the smell of pizza and chocolate chip cookies. The roar of voices, tension and excitement. A long, white, hand-painted banner screaming HOME OF THE BULLDOGS! hangs above the never-ending row

42

of burgeoning trophy cases, tagged here and there with permanent-marker graffiti.

The student population rotates through the lunchroom in three "rounds" between eleven a.m. and one p.m. every day. In August, I hugged my friends and cross-country teammates Jenny and Rebecca with glee when we discovered we were in the same lunch round. It was a relief to know I would have someone to eat with all year. The only thing worse than walking alone is sitting alone.

The cafeteria has a pulsing, raging heart. When you enter, you become part of the storm. And it's also one of the most dangerous locations on campus. Not only is the entire floor the same evil that spans all the classrooms, but the walls are covered in green and white ceramic subway tiles. I almost sense the beams of cancer radiating from the cracks surrounding me. They emit a constant, low-toned static.

The entrance is clogged and chaotic. The first lunch round is shuffling past the line of trash cans on their way to class while the second round is stampeding forward toward forty minutes of freedom. With a shove from behind, my face is smashed into someone's navy book bag. I teeter perilously on my tiptoes, trying to maintain a safe footing, swaying at the mercy of the mass around me. I catch occasional glances of my feet through the sea of book bags and bodies, but I have no control over them as I am pushed, pulled, and knocked by the crowd. I know I am stepping on cracks. I can feel them searing my toes. I can hear the cells in my brain pop-pop-popping into malignancies. The crowd thins, and, spat out into a space between two lunch tables, I come to a flat-footed stop. I stand frozen, breathing and recovering, as the tumor in my brain reinflates. My cells are the giant exploding bubbles in a pot of boiling water.

The noise of the cafeteria echoes off the tile walls and back again. Looking down at my shoes, each planted across multiple cracks, I am slammed with an intense pain deep in my head that screams outward through my ears. The soles of my sneakers burn against the carcinogens. A slow, creeping feeling of doom rolls over the horizon. Alone, trembling between crowded lunch tables, I'm filled with a heavy dread. Looking at the cracks, it's horribly obvious: I just brought the cancer back. I am suddenly furious at myself, furious at my clumsy feet and gangly legs. I have ruined everything.

The students sitting at the surrounding lunch tables begin to turn around and look at me. I haven't moved positions since I lurched out of the crowd, and, wrapped in my own riddle, I have no sense of how long it has been. Ten seconds, a minute, two, five? Strangely, it's not their curious stares or craned necks that draw me from my thoughts, but instead the quieting of their usually all-consuming chatter. The loud laughter and raucous conversations thin out quickly as more and more heads pop up to look at me. The muscles in my body tighten under the weight of their eyes. Everything inside me is screaming to save myself. From the gossip. From the rumors. (*Did you* see *Allison at lunch yesterday?*) Out of reflex my legs twitch, ready to move. Escape, escape! But I am trapped. To move and to stay are both equally dangerous. Remaining here, I risk pumping more cancer evil into myself. I risk more embarrassment, more

44

stares. But to leave? To leave is cracks, steps, the unknown. Book bags, accidents, the unpredictable.

I look up, intentionally avoiding the eyes of anyone around me, and scan the cafeteria for inspiration. Fifty feet across the room, Rebecca is waving at me from our usual table near the soda machines. I glance away without acknowledging her. Heat radiates up my legs from the cracks. My head throbs against the hard kernel of cells taking shape in my temporal lobe. What do I do? Where is my protector? Frantic, I look around the cafeteria as if the being sending me secret messages might be winking at me from the corner. My previous moments of divine inspiration just appeared in my mind on their own. The dream, the alarm, the cracks. But, right now, everything is silent. I have no guidance, no cleverly hidden messages. I tilt my head back so I am looking toward the ceiling and close my eyes. Opening my palms to the sky, I stretch my arms out wide, imitating the worshippers on Sunday morning televangelist broadcasts. Something about it feels unexplainably right. I hope it is a sufficiently pitiful plea for help. *Protector, please. Guide me.*

And in the back of my mind, with my eyes closed, my face turned toward the ceiling, I hear it. If avoiding cracks can help prevent cancer, there must be something else, some other action, that also has an unknown meaning or power. Like a crack, it may seem arbitrary, but it wields a hidden magic. There have to be more secrets waiting to be discovered. I hold my plea stance like a yoga position, asking patiently for more. People shuffle by me on both sides, squeezing between my outstretched arms and the students eating at the cafeteria tables. "Um, what's going on?" a girl says to my left. From the seat directly beside me: "Is she praying?"

Am I praying? I ask myself.

Silence.

I lean my head as far back as it will go and stretch my arms out completely to my side, palms up. I am begging for a message.

It hits me. It's like I have discovered something I already know. I immediately understand that the idea is perfect: It is not only avoiding cracks when you walk that matters, but also how many steps it takes for you to reach your destination. If where you place your foot is important, clearly how many times you do it is just as meaningful. While still significant, avoiding cracks is only one part of the overall equation. I need to think bigger! If, after I step on a crack, I can still reach my final destination within the "correct" or "safe" number of steps, then the danger is negated. It is all so obvious.

With a relieved sigh, I open my eyes and drop the pose. I have a way to escape my misstep and its attached death sentence. I have been given a second chance. But how do I know the safe number of steps? Where do I find this magical number? How will I—

42.

The number appears in my brain. Its arrival sounds mechanical, like it was fed to me by the machines that spit out tickets in parking garages. The outline of the number blocks out all other thoughts. I know this is my safe number.

I surface from my discovery to the burn of a heavy, newly

familiar heat: the pointed stares of my classmates. I have just put on a show for at least a hundred students. "That girl is in our English class!" No one moves. They are waiting for me to say something, to explain myself. Eyes fixed, mouths open. "Is that Allison?" I have nothing to hide behind, no veil of an excuse.

With a blank face, eyes down, I pivot on my back leg and move to tiptoe out of the cafeteria. Alarms blare as I move my leg, *42* flashing behind my eyes. *COUNT IT!* The message is a silent explosion, an angry voice over a police megaphone. My protector is screaming at me.

One, I say to myself, as I place the toes of my left foot in an open tile. Shifting my weight, I move my—

OUT LOUD!

"Two," I say as I set my foot down. "Three, four." The entire cafeteria continues to roar, but the two tables near the windows sit in awed silence, listening to me count.

LOUDER!

"Five!" I yell. "Six!" I place one foot in front of the other, methodically counting my steps, attracting more attention with each one. Bobbing up and down on my tiptoes, I've screamed my way to twelve before reaching the edge of the tiled floor.

Safely in the hallway, I run to the women's restroom, still counting aloud, and slam myself into a stall. It smells like cigarettes and urine. The tears start as I slide the metal lock into place. Winded, leaning lightly against the stall, I can feel where their stares had burned my skin. Kelsey Jameson was actually laughing. And Maisey and Madeline. I spent the night at Kelsey's house last month. We stayed up all night talking about prom, college, the future. Eating pizza and Cheetos. *Bitch.*

I dab my face with a wad of toilet paper. My phone vibrates:

Rebecca:

Hey is everything ok?

What just happened?

Me:

Yeah, fine.

Completely forgot about homework for next class . . . gotta do it real quick

I wonder how much she and Jenny could see from our seats as a wave of embarrassment sweeps through me.

I stare through my tears at the back of the stall door. I know Kelsey is whispering with her lunch table. How many people will she tell by the end of the day? And what will she say? I can see her gossiping in the parking lot after school. *She was like, counting, or something.* A chorus of gasps. *But not even counting—like, yelling! And tiptoeing? It was so weird.* Sara is going to hear about this at some point today for sure.

I hit the toilet paper dispenser with a clenched fist. The noise it makes rings off the cinder-block walls so nicely that I hit it again. Harder. A new emotion is flowing through my gut, pumping upward with a power I haven't known before. Anger. It doesn't matter if they stared! I roar to myself. They're the ones who are crazy. Walking on cracks all the time. They don't know. They don't *even know* what they are doing to themselves! I nod my head in agreement as the edges of my outburst slowly wear down.

Fist unclenched, I pick at the top layer of paint on the bathroom wall. What they saw or thought didn't matter. It only matters that now I have the full picture. Now I might be safe.

I use a handful of toilet paper to wipe my nose and bend down quickly to look under the walls of the stall. I'm alone. Thank goodness. I open the door and tiptoe out. The bathroom is painted a sickly 1970s orange. There is a single fluorescent light hanging from the unfinished ceiling and exposed pipes. Three dingy mirrors sit above three pedestal sinks. I dab at the eyeliner and mascara puddles under my eyes. If I looked pretty enough, smiled big enough, I had thought this morning, maybe no one would mind that I tiptoed and skipped and jumped through campus. Clearly, that was wrong.

The heavy wooden door swings open, and Latisha Simones saunters into the bathroom, humming. She beams at me with a huge wave.

"Heeyyy! Happy Monday!" Her face immediately drops when she sees I've been crying. "Girl! What is wrong! I know you ain't cryin' in here by yourself."

I smile at her before I can stop myself. Tisha runs the

four hundred meters, so I see her around the track and locker room every day. She has always been so unexplainably nice to me. "No, I'm fine! I just kind of made a fool of myself at lunch. I'm being an idiot." I shake my head. "It's not a big deal. I don't know why I'm crying."

She tilts her head sympathetically. "We've all had those days, baby. Trust me, I've definitely had mine." She crouches down so her eyes are in my line of vision. "Tomorrow will be better. You know that." We hold eye contact until I nod at her. "Good. I gotta pee. See you this afternoon at practice. And smile! Don't let that shiny hair go to waste!"

She shuts the door to a bathroom stall and resumes humming. With a lighter heart and the remnants of an involuntary small grin, I reach for the bathroom door. Lunch is over and it's fifth period. I am headed to precalculus, my most challenging class. The only real threat to my almost perfect GPA. I hold on to the door handle without moving. Where do I find my safe number? In the cafeteria it just, well, appeared. I wait quietly.

57.

It floats down into my mind like a gift with a parachute.

I swing open the bathroom door with a new outlook. I've made a few embarrassing mistakes, but I'm fighting cancer. I am the holder of insider information about the true nature of human physiology. It's not going to be easy. And, like Tisha said, it will always be better tomorrow.

I count my steps out loud all the way to precalculus. I arrive proud of my life-saving efforts, and with twelve steps to spare.

• • •

The bell rings to end sixth-period chemistry, and the room shuffles into action. I linger, packing up my notes and textbook, waiting for my safe number to appear in my mind. As I pretend to fuss with the binders in my bag, it arrives. *68.*

"Come on, slowpoke." Jenny is waiting for me at the door and points at her wrist. We have to get all the way to the gym on the other side of campus for dance class. "Would you hurry *up?*"

"Coming, coming . . . ," I mumble as I stand from my desk. "One, two, three," I count my tiptoe steps toward her across the classroom. Jenny is in almost all my classes and also a member of the cross-country team. Although she is a much faster runner than I am, I do better than her in school. We are both close friends and fierce rivals.

"So, did you finish your homework?" she asks.

"What homework? Twelve, thirteen, fourteen—"

"The homework you forgot to do. The reason why you skipped lunch with me and Rebecca?" Her voice questions and assaults me. She is clearly annoyed.

"Oh, yeah. I finished it. Thanks. Twenty, twenty-one . . ." There is an uncomfortable silence. I know what's coming.

"Why are you counting?"

There it is. And I'm ready for her. "Well, there are about two thousand steps in one mile. I just want to see how far we walk every day between classes. Don't you think Coach would be interested?"

"Um, I guess so. Isn't that what a pedometer is for?" She pauses, looks at me, and continues before I can reply. "So, last night I was talking to Sara, and I told her . . ."

Jenny continues her monologue as we maneuver through campus. "Thirty-eight, thirty-nine." She wants a new pair of boots for her birthday. "Forty-two, forty-three." But it's just so hard to find good brown boots, you know? "Forty-nine, fifty." Especially in this little town.

"Fifty-one." I stop.

Jenny walks a few paces before noticing. "What's wrong? What are you doing?"

I look up at her. I only have sixty-eight safe steps, and I'm already at fifty-one. Looking down the path, we are much farther than seventeen steps from the dance studio. I can't keep going without a plan. "I forgot my . . . calculator! In Ms. Matthews's class. I have to go back and get it."

"Your calculator? Just go back after school! You'll be late for dance?" Students jostle between us and she is forcefully carried away with the crowd. I know she's going to be mad that she had to walk alone the rest of the way to class.

"Tell Ms. Stern I'll be right there!" I yell down the breezeway.

I need to be alone for this. I have seventeen steps left to get me what looks to be about the distance of a football field. It seems unlikely, even impossible, but I have no other choice.

The path is crowded. It is the peak of class-change traffic, and I am being buffeted and nudged by the rabid mass flowing around me. With an emphatic jump I lunge forward and land about five feet down the path. My flailing arms swing wide and barely miss smacking a girl I don't know in the head. She glares at me and keeps walking. I lunge again, moving another five feet. Fifteen steps left.

52

I am exhausted as my steps dwindle to five, then four. It is hopeless. I am nowhere near the dance studio. The class bell rang long ago, and I am completely alone outside on the concrete pathway. I extend my front leg out and then wiggle it forward against the pavement until I am in a near split. I plant my hands on the ground and scoot my back leg forward to meet my front. Three steps left. A stream of sweat begins to trickle down the side of my face onto my neck. I am moving slowly, the weight of the day adding to gravity's effects.

I extend myself into another almost split and then drag my back leg up to meet my front. Two steps left. My shoulders sag and I feel myself giving in to self-pity. Where is all of this coming from? A week ago—four days ago!—I knew nothing of cancer cracks or brain tumors. I halfheartedly kick my leg out for another split and find myself sobbing.

None of this makes any sense. Why are there safe-step allotments? Why do cracks cause cancer? My friends, my teachers. They are noticing. They are staring. I don't *want* to count my steps, I don't *want* to avoid cracks, but how can I not? This is brain cancer!

I crumble from my split onto the concrete and allow the sobs to take control. Confusion, fear, frustration pour out of me. Wiping my nose on my arm, I lie down on the concrete. The warm surface is soothing against my cheek. I almost forget that I'm—

"Allison?" There are brown loafers about six inches in front of my eyes. Frayed denim. I lift my head a few inches to look up, and framed against the sun is a letterman jacket and tousled brown hair. Sam. "Is everything okay?"

I lurch my torso up from the concrete, snot and tears covering my face. "Me? Oh, hi! Yes! Of course." My voice breaks slightly as I try to tamp down the raging tears. "I, well . . ." I look back down and quickly wipe my cheeks across my sleeve. It only creates a bigger mess, I can tell by the mascara now smeared on my arm. Gritty dirt mingles with the thick wetness on my face, and I smile blankly up at him. How can I explain this? His green eyes question me, waiting for a response. My mind racing, I open my mouth without a plan, hoping for the best. "You know, I think I have low blood sugar." Ah, yes. Well done. "When I don't eat or something, I just fall like this out of nowhere. I'm so glad you found me." I look up at him again, a dainty maiden rescued by a preppy, basketball-playing knight. "It's never happened at school before." I half giggle, half exhale as I try to dab away the more obvious drops of sweat between my eyebrows and along my hairline.

"You should really get that checked out, Al." I blush at the nickname. No one else has ever called me that. His arm is extended down toward me, but I can't see his face against the sun's glare. I hold his hand as he pulls me to my feet. He smells so good.

I smile at him. "Probably should!" An awkward, forced laugh. We look at each other for a few moments and I give a small shrug. Ask me to ice cream, I will him. Invite me to your basketball game tonight.

We make eye contact for a full three seconds. He opens his mouth, moves to talk, and then closes it, tearing his eyes from mine. "Well, gotta run to class," he says as he gestures his arm to the right and, with a whip of his neck, flicks his hair out of his face.

"Yeah, yeah. Me too." I fidget with the corner of my binder. "See ya around!"

He walks away from me down the pathway and I can finally relax. I let out a long, stale sigh and realize I've been holding my breath. I don't move. Can't move. I only have two safe steps left. Out of my peripheral vision, I see Sam pause as he rounds the corner and glances back at me, frozen in place with dirt on my forehead. My smile remains plastered on my face, my waving hand still suspended in the air. It tingles where he touched me to help me up, his fingerprints glowing coolly on my skin.

I want to cry. I have to cry. Again. My chest shakes, my breath catches in my throat, but there is nothing there. I know that tears would help, at least a little bit. But I'm empty.

I need more steps.

When I accidentally stepped on a crack, I was saved by introducing a second, more difficult requirement—reaching my destination in a certain number of steps. *If you obey this new thought, then you are forgiven for stepping on that crack.* It was like a trade! I gave my protector something else it wanted, and I gained back my health. I feel a tentative edge of comfort as I realize this is my way out. I can barter for more steps. I look around for ideas. What would my protector want? It needs to be meaningful. I want to demonstrate true sacrifice. Show him that I'm not just trying to gain more steps, but also thanking him for his protection and warnings.

I scan my body: shoes, legs, shorts, arms, lunch bag.

Lunch bag. I've already eaten most of the contents but there are still grapes and pretzels inside I have saved to have as a snack before cross-country practice. As my stomach sends a pang of hunger through me, I know I have found the answer. I whisper out loud: "I won't eat my afternoon snack if I can walk safely to dance class."

A window of hope opens wide within me. I have another tool, another weapon to fight against cancer. My glimmering happiness tells me my protector approves. Still avoiding cracks, I walk casually toward the dance studio, counting out loud, with a new safe number. I roll the top of my lunch bag down tightly and shove it into my book bag.

Sara:

Is everything ok?

Me:

Yeah, I'm fine. Why do you ask?

Sara:

I ran into Sam. He asked me if there is something wrong with you . . . like mentally . . .

CHAPTER 4

Later in the week, I spend all morning rubbing the edges of my brown paper lunch bag between my thumb and forefinger, continually reminding myself how much leverage I have left for the day. The Ziplocs of food all stare at one another silently. It's Russian roulette: Who will be sacrificed next?

I have eaten almost nothing in two days. With my new-found bartering tool, I trade away food with abandon. It's as if my mind knows, lunch bag in hand and dinner on the horizon, that I have about ten get-out-of-cancer-free cards. My feet are looser, my gaze less focused. *Oops, a crack. There goes my ham sandwich.* I lose my Fritos when I run out of steps after fourth period and my string cheese when I trip onto a crack on the way into lunch. Each mistake is muffled by the bubble wrap padding of bartering away individual servings of food. Each loss sharpens the pangs of hunger that color my every movement, but the pain is comforting. It is the side effect of being cancer-free.

My body is physically drained. As I walk about campus, I teeter on the edge of consciousness, tempted toward a warm cloud of sleep and darkness. My tongue drags across ragged, chapped lips. Gorging myself at the water fountain, I fill my stomach to its brim, briefly tricking it into drowned submission.

I can't focus in any of my classes. Not today, not this week. I spend a significant amount of time at the beginning of each period ensuring that my feet are positioned perfectly to avoid the ragged cracks in the aged classroom floors: the white tips of my sneakers frozen on pointe like clumsy, double-knotted ballet slippers. I check on them frequently to make sure they haven't shifted. My thoughts are consumed with food: what's in my lunch bag, what I've already given up. How many more mistakes can I make, how many more lives are left in my brown paper bag? Over and over, against the drone of a teacher's lesson, I run through my remaining options as if trying to remember a phone number. Carrots, Jell-O, Nutri-Grain bar. Carrots, Jell-O, Nutri-Grain bar. Carrots, Jell-O, Nutri-Grain bar. My stomach growls loudly against my ribs. Listing them makes them real, it reminds me there is hope. My hands have a slight tremor and my head is fuzzy, but I still have a chance. Carrots, Jell-O, Nutri-Grain bar. There are still some options. One of those could eventually make it to my stomach.

I settle onto the long wooden bench in the women's locker room. It's the treasured solitary minutes of warm, humid silence between afternoon classes and practice. For the first time today, I have a few seconds to myself. Since lurching into first period at eight forty-five this morning, I have been surrounded by a tornado of other students—their words, their laughter, their haphazard steps all mixing with and confusing my own thoughts. I've been blindly, passionately avoiding cracks and donating food to find redemption for my missteps. Balancing the continuous buzz of anxiety with my searing hunger, I am exhausted.

I sigh into the silence. Out of context, standing on their own, these secret connections in my mind look like randomly created Mad Libs. Insert creative noun here ("cracks"), insert scary consequence here ("brain cancer"). In a quiet, cobwebbed corner of my mind, I laugh at their absurdity. They honestly make no sense. I look at these rules, newly chiseled on my brain like the Ten Commandments, and, for a moment, I falter. My mind presses hard on the brakes of what feels like a runaway train. *How* do cracks cause cancer? Is that really possible? Wouldn't everyone in the world be dead by now? And who am I sacrificing food to?

The questions bounce around my mind, each one seeming to make a better point than the one that came before. What makes a number of steps "safe"? And who is deciding what the right number is? My mind digests the questions for a few moments, chewing on their rationality. Cracks are just cracks. No one is communicating with me. It was a harmless dream followed by a harmless song on the radio. A feeling is swelling in me, the crest of a wave of clarity rising up from within. A hopefulness. I lift my head slightly at the rays of sunshine poking through four days of clouds.

But what *if?* My mind stomps, shattering my thoughts. What if cracks are dangerous? What if counting my steps is the thin wall between me and death? What if someone is protecting me and these sacrifices are all that keep me safe?

What if I die of brain cancer?

And with this thought I'm submerged immediately in the cold, murky sea of my dream. I'm in my inevitable future. At first, in the weeks after the diagnosis, things would be okay.

We would be powerfully optimistic, put on plastered smiles in the hopes of a miracle. They would enroll me in medical trials, adjust my medications, pump me with poison. But by my sixteenth birthday, the silver SUV with an enormous red bow I've always imagined is replaced by a beeping plastic hospital bed. They shove it into my room under bouquets of well-wishes and dozens of balloons. I lose weight and my hair. My father buys me a wig, but it never gets taken out of the bag. There isn't time. Feeding tubes, last good-byes, my mom's tears staining my quilt as she cries herself to sleep at my bedside. My grandfathers, my father, my uncles and cousins strain under the weight of my casket. Bob Dylan's "Forever Young" leads my devastated parents out of the church into a harsh, lonely world without their only child. My breath quakes with the sound of a metal shovel hitting soil in front of my new tombstone.

Cracks cause cancer. I need to count my steps. You can trade a fatal mistake for food and be forgiven. Something inside me knows. This is right. It has to be.

A tightness in my chest returns, the sharp edge of being on alert at all times. The fear, in its strange familiar way, is comforting. I grab and hold on to this renewed feeling of conviction, of knowing the truth.

"Oh, heyyyyy!" Maddie bellows between opened arms from the doorway of the locker room. Her beaming smile moves toward me as she leads a group of jabbering girls forward. "Ready for the long loop? Gotta love Thursdays." She flops her book bag down on the bench beside me. I look at her blankly as a thought drags itself into my brain. It's

Thursday? A long pause. If it's Thursday, why hasn't Sara texted me about the JV game? She has badgered me about going to the JV games every Thursday since the first week of freshman year. Of course she's noticed my counting and the "blisters" that have kept me tiptoeing through school for a week. But, until this moment, it had not occurred to me that it might impact our friendship. That she might find someone else to go to the JV games with.

"Are you okay?" Maddie is stooped down in front of me, peering into my eyes. "You look out of it. Are you sick?" She is in the middle of putting up her wild hair and mumbles through multiple bobby pins stashed between her lips.

"Sick? What?" I loll my head to my left shoulder and lurch off the bench in an effort to literally escape her question. "I'm fine! Just exhausted. Studying, you know. It'll get ya." I tiptoe toward the nearby water fountain, pretend to take a sip, and stumble back toward my bag, keeping my eyes focused steadily downward. I am watching for cracks but also intentionally avoiding eye contact. Although Maddie is a few months younger than me, she is a wise old woman. I know she will see through my half-conscious mumblings and excuses. And she's the type who will make her opinions known. Loudly.

"Right, I guess I know what you mean." Her eyebrows crease together to go along with her changed tone of voice. "Maybe try to go to bed earlier? You need to rest. You're not a robot." I nod and busy myself with my gym bag. Maddie's eyes examine me for another ten seconds until she moves away toward the bathroom.

With a heavy sigh, I let my eyelids sink closed. Just a ten-minute nap. Right here, this bench. I need it so bad. The thought is satin against my face. I curl up on the wooden surface and—

"Wake up! What are you doing?!" Maddie nudges my shoulder with her socked toe. She glares at me with what could either be anger or concern. "Seriously! Get up—get changed. *Let's go.*"

I might vomit.

A few blurry minutes later, Maddie pulls me by the arm through two heavy metal doors. The cool afternoon breeze is a shock after the damp sauna of the locker room. Summer seems to have finally decided to give way to fall. From within my fog, I can tell it is a beautiful day. The campus is buzzing with activity, conversation, laughter. The football field is covered with groups of students hand-painting banners, Ford F-150s covered in green and gold crepe paper. The local radio station is blaring over the stadium loudspeakers. I stare at the scene and a realization dawns on me.

"Maddie," I call out to her black ponytail walking a few feet in front of me, "is it homecoming this weekend?"

"Um . . ." She looks toward the football field covered in students and banners and back at me. "Obviously?"

The loose stones of the parking lot crunch under my feet as we walk toward the football field and the four-hundred-meter track encircling it. Aside from prom and graduation, homecoming is one of the biggest events of the school year. And I somehow went the whole day, the whole week, without noticing. "What? Don't we have a banner?" We cut through a side entrance of the fenced-in track and follow the path of the one hundred meter dash toward the opposite end of the stadium. Every organization on campus—athletic teams, clubs, honor societies—has a banner in the homecoming parade. It's just what you do. I look out over the football field at the dozens of works-in-progress spread across the white-painted yardage lines. "Shouldn't we get started on one? You know I love painting the banner! Ours was so good last year, remember?"

She looks at me strangely for a few moments before replying, "We do have a banner." She inclines her head toward me and tilts it with meaning to the side. "We have been talking about it nonstop at practice. There was a sign-up sheet to help design and paint it that was passed around during stretches every day this week. There was also an e-mail *and* I texted you about it." She purses her lips, crosses her arms, and looks at me. She is waiting for an explanation.

I've been so out of it the past few days, so distracted by my own mind, I somehow missed all of this. I guess I remember seeing her text message, now that I think about it. I just didn't have room in my brain to care. Stepping over cracks, starving, stepping over cracks, starving . . .

Maddie looks me directly in the eyes for five silent seconds. "What is going on?"

I can feel the weight of my uneaten sack lunch in the gym bag on my shoulder. The crackling plastic bag of pretzels, the thick slices of wheat bread and honey-roasted ham. *What's going on? I'm saving myself from cancer, if you must know. Battling for my life.* The rest of the team has congregated on a small grassy area near the goal posts for pre-workout stretches. Jenny's cheery laugh filters above the chaotic noise as I see the group transition from calves to quads. I wonder how many cracks each of them stepped on today. How long will it be before their cells start mutating?

"Hello?" Maddie stares at me.

My eyes click back into reality. She is glaring at me with demanding eyes. I can't label the emotion on her face.

"What?" I don't remember her question.

Our eyes connect.

"Seriously? Allison!" she almost yells. "What is wrong with you? You haven't been yourself all week, but things have really gotten weird yesterday and today." Her hand moves up to her hip. "You've been lethargic. Jenny and Rebecca told me you haven't been eating anything at lunch. You're always counting?" She shifts her weight and her tone lightens. "It's all just kind of out of nowhere." A few seconds pass as she catches her breath. I see the muscles in her shoulders and cheeks relaxing. "This isn't okay." She gestures her hand up and down my body. "*You* aren't okay."

Somewhere inside me there is a small glimmer of appreciation for her concern. A tiny flame in a dank corner of my brain flickers in recognition of our friendship, but it is quickly blown out by a strong gust of pride. *I'm* not okay? *This*—I picture my shaking body—isn't okay? I'm carrying a full course load of honors classes, I'm a member of the cross-country team, and I'm actively fighting cancer. Maddie and her messy hair and crazy freckles. She has no idea what she is talking about. She'll be sorry one day.

I know I can't tell her that cracks cause cancer, that I'm starving myself for my health. Even though these thoughts are new, it's obvious they were a gift bestowed on me and only me. To share them seems disrespectful, somehow sacrilegious. I don't know their source, but I know they are special. Sacred.

"I'm. Fine," I say softly through clenched teeth and a sudden, powerful swell of anger. "Just tired—I told you. It's been a rough few days with school." I brush past her and allow my shoulder to clip hers so she is pushed roughly to the side. "We're going to miss stretches."

I walk away from her toward the chattering crowd near the end zone. I don't turn to see her face, but I know her openmouthed stare is watching my back the entire way. My cheeks flush with shame, or maybe sadness, as I replay our conversation. I've never had a temper. I rarely get mad, especially at my friends. The strong, almost immediate wave of anger that bubbled up with Maddie's questioning is completely out of character. But, I think, watching my feet plod across the closely shorn grass, it feels good.

Although we always stretch together, today I plant myself as far away from Jenny and Rebecca as possible. Busy talking with each other, neither of them notices me when I walk past. We are targeting hamstrings now, sitting on the ground leaning diagonally toward outstretched toes.

I press my face hard into my thigh, savoring the break from reality. On the grass, there are no cracks. In the dark of closed eyes, there is no Maddie. I switch to the other leg without looking up. I've still got two servings of dinner left if

65

I don't make any more mistakes. I extend my arms over my head as I come up from the stretch and look up to the sky. Two things to eat at dinner! It has been a good day.

Nodding to myself, I stand up at the sound of Coach Millings's whistle. Within the rustling crowd, I see Maddie huddled with Rebecca and Jenny. Ducking behind people and ponytails so they won't see me, I watch their conversation through the gaps between bodies. Maddie is speaking fast, gesturing her emotions. They're talking about me, obviously. I'm naive if I think they aren't in on this together, tracking my strange behaviors during nightly phone calls. Wouldn't I do the exact same thing if one of them started tiptoeing, counting, and not eating? Wouldn't I also get a bit of innocent excitement from the unfolding drama?

Blind momentum carries me through the first two miles of our run. I lodge myself in the middle of the pack and keep my head down. My safe number is *25,000*. "Three hundred twenty-two, three hundred twenty-three"—seems fair enough—"three hundred twenty-four." We tramp through the school campus down Peachtree Road, and eventually turn left into a rambling, sprawling subdivision that will act as our host for the next five miles.

Rolling Meadows is a solidly middle-class neighborhood in a solidly middle-class town. The houses are right out of the fifties and sixties, the glory years of the region's tobacco boom. Each yard is adorned with bird feeders, angel statues with upturned faces, American flags flapping beside the front door. An old man mowing his yard in suspenders stops to watch our herd. The sun glares off the bright metal of the playground slide.

Through the traffic, I can barely see the bounce of Maddie's hair ahead. She is usually my running partner for the first three or so miles, but today she is leading the pack. I wonder what she's already told Jenny and Rebecca. A memory of her concerned eyes filters across my mind, and I'm filled with a rush of warm shame. I squint against the afternoon sun as the group stampedes downhill. With each step, each contact with the pavement, I sense myself veering slightly farther to the right, to the right, to the right. A feeling of lightness. Pavement.

At first it is silent. Calm. The world nothing but dull white noise. It's the pain in my knee that draws me back to the surface. Like turning on a TV, I am suddenly blasted with color, noise, action. A ragged, ripping feeling across my leg mingles with the rapid conversation taking place above me. I'm lost in a confusion of black road and white sneakers.

A murmuring silhouette of ponytailed heads looks down at me and fires questions. "Are you okay?" "What happened?" "Did you trip?"

Slowly, with squinted eyes, I raise myself up to my elbows. I am shaky but remarkably more steady than moments before. Blood, dirt, and gravel mingle together across my kneecap. The sun is blotted out by the crowd of teammates huddled around me. I look up at the forms four feet above, unable to process anything but the shape of their heads against the blue afternoon sky.

"Allison?" It's Jenny. A hand with wiggling fingers

appears in front of my face. "Come on, girl." I am pulled to my feet with the assistance of multiple teammates. My head swims as my eyes adjust to the new altitude. With the change of angle, I feel the warm threads of blood spread down my shin from my knee. I'm on my feet, and twenty sets of eyes wait for a comment. My starved brain is fuzzy. I'm distracted by the tremor in my hand. My whole body feels paper thin. A strong wind could send me off above the trees. "Helllooo, Allison?" Jenny dips her head down so our eyes align. "You really don't look so good. Are you sure you just fell? Are you sick? You didn't eat anything at lunch." She fidgets with my T-shirt, dusting off the remnants of gravel and leaves.

Through the crowd around me, I notice a blond head bobbing quickly toward us. On my tiptoes, I see it's Anne Marie, the team captain and my personal hero. Not only is she the fastest runner in the county, but she also just found out she has a full scholarship to Duke University. Her boyfriend picks her up from practice in his candy-apple-red SUV with muddy, oversized tires. She is everything I could ever hope to be.

"Hey, ladies, what happened over here?" Despite being more than two miles into the run, she speaks clearly, as if we have been out on a Sunday stroll. The collective group gestures toward me, and Anne Marie shifts her beaming eyes up to my face. I gawk at her through a frozen smile. She's so pretty. The hot pink shoelaces on her running shoes match the stripes on her shorts, which match her sparkly nail polish. She has her hair pinned up in a messy, effortlessly perfect bun of curls. A few individual strands fall gently to her shoulders. Anne Marie, teach me your ways!

Over her shoulder, I can see Maddie staring at me behind crossed arms twenty feet up the road. Her glare sends me a wave of clarity. I need an excuse, a distraction. Now. "I tripped," I almost yell. "I think there must have been a stick or a rock. I felt my foot hit something." The words flop out of my mouth before I'm even aware that I've thought them. The whole team turns their heads to examine the completely clear road. "There was definitely something there." I hesitate as I see a few girls raise their eyebrows questioningly. "Some kid probably just put sticks in the road to trip us all up, you know? I've heard of people doing that before. . . ."

What? I know it's a terrible lie as soon as I say it, but it's my only escape. I've gotta go with it. Eyes on me. A few tentative nods and half smiles. Inside, I'm willing them to believe me, to take my excuse and not ask questions. Anne Marie looks at me with a strange expression until Jenny interrupts the lengthening silence.

"You probably just tripped over your own foot." She nudges me in the arm. "Wouldn't be the first time." The group laughs quietly in agreement, the tension fading. Freed from their intense gaze, I am furious with myself. Sticks in the road? Was that really the best I could do?

"Well, you should probably head back." Anne Marie grimaces at my knee. "But be careful. Take it slow. Check in with Coach before you leave." She pats me on the shoulder with a small smile before turning to the rest of the idle team. "All right, y'all, fun's over. Let's go!"

I pretend to jog back toward campus until the group has wound down the road out of sight, and then I slow to a walk.

Limping, my pride more hurt than my knee, I'm happy to be alone.

There were no sticks in the street—it was obvious that wasn't why I fell. It didn't even make any sense, I scold myself, shaking my head at the lame, ineffective excuse. Even if only a few people know I haven't been eating, this is the kind of story that, if heard by the wrong ears and spread by the right lips, could mutate into a powerful, irresistible rumor.

Let Jenny, Rebecca, and Maddie enjoy their gossip session in peace. At least if I don't see it, if I'm not following twenty feet behind them, I can pretend it's not happening. It's obvious that three of my closest friends are discussing my eating habits, my lethargy, my strange gait. I imagine them laughing as they recount how I leap across the sidewalk, gasping when Rebecca and Jenny say they haven't seen me eat lunch all week. But if I don't know for sure, if I don't see them chatting incessantly through a seven-mile run, it doesn't hurt as badly.

CHAPTER 5

I have become a finely tuned instrument. With more than a week's worth of practice under my belt, I float across the crack-laden sidewalks and classrooms of school like a well-practiced ballerina. I know each divot, each turn, each carcinogen lurking at the edges of concrete squares. My chest swells with a smug confidence. If this is all it takes to defy cancer, I could live forever.

"Fifty-nine!" I yell. "Sixty!" The roar of the cafeteria drowns out my counting as I cross the threshold of a massive pair of double doors. I survey the familiar tiled floor and move quickly toward our usual table in the far right corner. The Samuelson cafeteria is cavernous. Hundreds of voices bump into one another as they bounce from wall to wall. "Seventy-eight! Seventy-nine!" As I approach, Rebecca looks up, smiles at me, and nudges Jenny with her elbow. Jenny immediately puts down her sandwich and grins at me as well. They both stare intently as I walk toward them. "Eighty!" I sit down in my usual seat and park my book bag in the empty space to my right. Since August, we have sat in the same cafeteria seats. It's an unwritten, unspoken rule that you don't change lunch seats after the first day of school. It used to be a comfort to know that no matter what, I would always have this spot with my friends waiting for me. But today it feels like I'm walking toward the judge and the jury. I know they've got yesterday afternoon on their mind.

Jenny and Rebecca are still giving me the same anxious smiles from across the table when I look up from my book bag. Flanked by the soda machines, our tiny table seems isolated. I'm not sure if I should feel safe or cornered. They stare at me expectantly. "What's up with you guys?" I plop my brown lunch sack onto the table. "You're being kind of odd." I don't allow myself to think about what Maddie might have told them about our conversation yesterday.

"Odd?" Jenny looks to Rebecca. "Us?" Rebecca shrugs back at her with a small snort. There is something going on.

"How is your knee feeling?" Rebecca asks as she unrolls the top of her lunch bag and begins unloading filled Ziplocs. "It looked like you were bleeding pretty badly." Rebecca is a senior, the mother hen of the cross-country team. Painfully slow yet unwaveringly supportive, she attends every varsity race armed with banners and posters trailing green and gold streamers destined to decorate the finish line.

"Oh, it's fine! It looked a lot worse than it was, really." I pretend to rummage through my lunch, although I have already bartered all my food away for the day. With a shrug, I add, "Probably should have just kept running, to be honest." After rustling around in my paper bag, I make a show of pulling out my turkey sandwich and examining it, separating the bread and poking at the lettuce. "How was the rest of practice?" I force myself to block out a persistent mental image of the three of them running together, exchanging stories about me, followed by a late-night phone call with Sara.

"Same old, same old, I guess," Jenny responds as she crunches on a Cheeto. "Oh! Except, listen to this. . . ." She adjusts herself, a one-woman show always ready to perform. "So we're running, right. That really hilly part after you get to the stop sign." She pauses and looks at me until I nod back at her. "And guess who comes *tearing* around the corner in his Jeep . . ."

"*Brendan!*" Rebecca and Jenny half shout, half squeal in tandem. I gasp. Brendan. Michaels. Of all the days for me to miss practice!

Jenny continues her melodrama as she describes how Brendan Michaels squeals his tires as he pulls up beside his girlfriend, Anne Marie. "He really slams on the brakes. Like, I saw smoke come up from his tires. And he pulls out this red Gatorade and hands it to her."

"Oh my gosh. So cute."

"I know, seriously. So I'm running by, and she is saying something about how she's sweaty and he shouldn't kiss her. And then *he* says"—she lowers her voice—"'But, babe, I like you sweaty.'" We erupt in a storm of wild giggles that draws annoyed looks from the tables of students around us. Rebecca is choking on a carrot as we finally regain our composure.

"Could she be any more perfect?" I say with a sigh.

"Could *he* be any more perfect?" Rebecca comments.

A few seconds pass as we all nod silently in agreement.

I am moving my fingers around in a bag of Triscuits. I pick one out, bring it up to my face and examine it, then place it back in the bag and repeat. Breaking off substantial chunks of cracker, I arrange them on the table in front of me. The more crumbs, the more it looks like I've eaten.

Moving to trade Triscuits, I see Jenny and Rebecca exchange a glance. Rebecca nods at her, and I barely I hear her whisper, "Just do it."

"Can't you do it?"

"It was your idea!"

My insides immediately lock up, but I pretend that I don't notice their exchange. My body readies itself. Waiting for Jenny to speak, I am tense, alert, but continue to act engrossed in my Triscuit collection.

"Hey, Allison, um . . ." Jenny is nervous. Moving her eyes around the cafeteria, she seems suddenly and uncharacteristically serious. I look up at her with what I hope are my most innocent eyes. "So, well, it seems like maybe you have been having a hard time." She takes an awkwardly long breath, as if she is preparing for something. "Like, I don't know, you just don't eat as much anymore"—she looks at the crumbled Triscuits on the table and shifts in her seat—"and, you know, you fainted yesterday."

"I *tripped*! I told you! I have never fainted in my life!" I respond more quickly and loudly than I intend to.

"Right, yeah, that's what I meant! So, yeah, you tripped. And, I don't know, I just wanted to do something nice, so, um"—she moves her hands down to her lap—"I got you this cookie." She slides a freshly baked chocolate chip cookie wrapped in plastic from the school cafeteria across the table at me. "I know you love these cookies! I just thought, maybe, I don't know. I hope you like it."

Jenny looks down at her hands while Rebecca nods a silent *Good job* in her direction. They clearly planned this together. Maybe even during practice yesterday. I eye the cookie sitting a few feet in front of me. Every fiber of my body is taut as the cookie glares at me through its evil chocolate chips. I can't just *eat* a cookie. That's not how cancer prevention works. Safety is about planning, precision, sacrifice.

"Oh, thank you," I say, smiling, "but I'm fine. I have my lunch." I lift up my crumpled brown bag. "I don't need a cookie. You should have it!" I stretch my Miss America smile across my face and plaster it in place. A high-pitched siren is approaching from somewhere in the distance. A muscle in my right shoulder curls up into a knot. Jenny is completely unaware that I am begging her to reconsider.

"Allison, you haven't eaten any of your lunch. Not today, not yesterday. Please eat this cookie. It will really make me feel better to see you eat something." She reaches onto the table and pulls the cookie out of the wrapper. When she breaks it in half, melted chocolate oozes onto her fingers. "Yum, hot and fresh, just how you like." She moves the cookie in circles under my chin, and I think I feel its warmth on my skin.

It's true. I do love our cafeteria's gooey chocolate chip cookies. I used to spend at least five dollars a week satiating my appetite for midday treats. But things are different now. Today I have the whole picture. I know there is a mysterious, powerful connection between food and preventing cancer. I know I can't eat an unplanned cookie.

After a few seconds of goading, she puts the cookie back down on the table and trades a meaningful glance with

Rebecca. They're going to talk about this later. Probably with Maddie. I can see Jenny, thriving under the attentive gazes of our teammates, as she dramatically reenacts the scene during stretches before practice. For the next ten minutes she and Rebecca banter about the weekend's upcoming homecoming activities and leave me to my cracker crumbs. Far from their chipper voices, huddled into myself, I'm starving. There is nothing I want more in this world than to grab that cookie and snarf it down in two quick bites. But it's not worth it. I have no specific warning against it, but it's an outsider. An unexploded bomb at my feet.

"Allison, please?" I'm jerked from my thoughts. Jenny is staring at me, wide-eyed, across the table again, begging me with her body to respond, to comply. "It's just one cookie." She pushes it a little closer. "You're already skinny. You don't have to worry about that." She shifts it gently on top of its light plastic packaging.

It doesn't matter that I'm skinny. It matters that I'm *alive*.

"For me?" she whispers, an equal mix of pleading and concern.

Under the pressure of her eyes, I loosen a bit as I'm flooded with a warm rush of friendship. She must really care about me. Buying me a cookie, confronting me like this. Jenny Jordan, you're not so bad. But that doesn't change the situation, and it doesn't change the truth. I cannot eat the cookie.

"Look"—I pull myself out of my seated slump—"I already have my lunch. I'm really just not hungry. But thank you." I nod at her with a genuine smile. "That's really nice of you."

Jenny's facial expression begins to change as soon as she realizes I'm turning her down once more. As I talk, I can feel her toughening. She shakes her head at me in disappointment.

"Dude. I just spent a dollar on that for you." She gestures with frustration down at the table, her voice distinctly different from just seconds before. "Eat the freaking cookie." She forcefully slides it toward me so it stops directly beside my lunch bag. "I'm serious." She's jabbing her finger at it. "Eat!"

Jenny is the youngest of five daughters. She grew up out near the lake in a beautiful but crowded house filled with photo albums and various midsized pets. At home in decade-old hand-me-downs, she is loud, boisterous, some might say bossy. There is no beating around the bush with her. She is not going to let me off the hook without a fight.

"I'm not going to eat the cookie," I say in a flat voice, staring down at my picked-over nails.

"Why not?" I'm not looking at her, but I know her chin is jutted out and her arms are crossed against her enormous chest.

"I just don't want to. I have my own food, my own lunch."

"Yeah, well, you haven't eaten any of it. Not for days. Eat. The. Cookie." I stare at the dull glow of the lights filtering through the plastic covering of the soda machines. In the weeks we have spent sitting here, I've never noticed their quiet hum. Against the buzz of the giant machine, Jenny's incessant prodding screeches against my ears. "It's getting scary, honestly." I look up at Rebecca, who seems to be alarmed at the direction of the conversation. She is listening intently, obviously, but is pretending to be absorbed in her glowing cell-phone screen. "And don't expect me for one second to believe you actually tripped. . . . I know you haven't been eating, I know that you . . ."

Something inside me breaks, and an unexpectedly powerful wave of anger rushes forth. She has no idea what she is saying. Just eat the cookie, just walk normal, just act like you don't know we're all killing ourselves. I slam my palms in tandem on the table.

"I didn't ask you to buy me a cookie, did I, Jenny?" I'm surprised at the way my voice rolls forward like thunder, unfurling across the table. "Just like I didn't *ask* for your opinion on how I eat or whether I'm—how is it you put it?—'having a hard time.'" I mimic these last words in her high-pitched voice. Standing now, feet primed in tiptoed readiness, I growl, "Stop bothering me, Jenny Jordan. I didn't *ask* for your *help!*" I'm halfway through the sentence before I realize that I am screaming. It feels good. To yell, to release. "Leave me alone!" Slamming my books together, I quickly pack up, fighting the hot tears building in my eyes. I wipe loose snot on my hand and it spreads across my face. People are looking, gaping. I stand for a few moments, out of breath, taking in my audience. As I turn to go, I hear Jenny:

"It was only a cookie. . . ." And then, more gently: "I'm just worried about you."

Sobbing now, I tiptoe as quickly as possible out of the cafeteria and, once I reach the safer hallway, break into a run. I lurch past lines of lockers, past the wide door leading into the band room, and the hallway opens up to a small lobby. I push my way through the double doors at the back entrance of the building into the forceful sunshine. With most students either in lunch or in class, the breezeway is almost deserted.

I check my cell phone and there's a text:

Sara:

Is everything all right with you? Jenny
told me you fainted at practice . . . and
that you just yelled at her . . .

With a sigh, I shove the phone in my pocket. There are still twenty minutes left in lunch. In my rush to escape Jenny and Rebecca and, to some extent, school in general, I haven't had a chance to come up with the next step in my plan. Surrounded by cracks, dejected, and still crying, I can't (won't!) go back to the lunchroom. But, almost as important, I can't let anyone see my tearstained face. Nothing gets people talking like crying, especially when they can tell you're trying to hide it. With nowhere else to go, I walk behind the cafeteria building: the home to industrial-sized trash cans, delivery bays, and mysterious puddles of sludge. Although there are no cracks, I tiptoe gingerly across the pavement, avoiding broken bottles and indiscernible globs of trash.

The air seeping from the trash cans is sour, but at least I am alone. And hidden. I stand behind a brick partition, lean against its warmth, hoping that the cool breeze will help with the red swelling around my eyes. A line of enormous, archaic air-conditioning units clang loudly behind me. In my heart, I feel Jenny and Rebecca sitting at our cafeteria table, talking about me. *What in the world was* that *all about?* Rebecca asks, wide-eyed, finally looking up from her phone. Jenny is shaking her head, arms crossed.

I don't know if I'm embarrassed or angry. Am I crying because I'm ruining my relationships with my closest friends? Because my counting and tiptoeing are knocking down years of Sara's hard work for my reputation? Or am I angry? Angry that no one can mind their own business, angry that I'm the only one shouldered with this knowledge?

Yes. All of the above.

But at the same time that I'm feeling everything, I am also slipping hopelessly into nothingness. I don't pay attention in class. I'm not a good friend or teammate. All of a sudden, I am counting. And stepping. And trading food. And not much else.

The bell rings for class, and it seems both way too early and much too late. I straighten my back and take three deep breaths, girding myself for the afternoon ahead.

What's more important, your life or your reputation? I ask myself.

I don't respond as I pick at the loose edges of the brick wall.

What's more important, your life or your reputation?

"My *liiiife*," I groan out loud in frustration. With a heavy exhale, I know I'm doing the right thing. I adjust my book bag on my back and, dry-eyed, step out from hiding onto the main path.

It's a week after I yelled at Jenny and I'm sitting at the dinner table. Our kitchen, usually airy and spacious, is suddenly suffocating. I hum quietly to fill the air, to fill the void. We're a small family of three, so our dinners are typically short, quiet affairs, but tonight the silence is different. The room is tense. My parents' concern is palpable. I wince every time my mom cuts her eyes at my full plate. There is a self-conscious pang inside me with each of their loaded exchanged glances. The past week they have watched me warily from across the table, but tonight something in the air is different. So I sing. I hum. I tap my fingers on the tabletop to the beat of my own internal jam session. Never stop moving. You can't let them see you down. Since the dream, I have been spewing a forced, relentless wave of happiness on my parents. So far it has been a fairly effective disguise.

I am pushing my food around with my fork, hiding individual bites of meat within my mashed potatoes. Tonight I am only allowed to eat one item from my dinner, and I chose broccoli covered in cheese. Since last week, I've faced this same situation every night. The round wooden table, the steaming bowls of food, an earnest attempt at moving the servings around to make my plate look empty. Yesterday I was allowed corn on the cob, Tuesday was crescent rolls. Last Friday, it was milk. I know it is impossible that my parents haven't noticed my new appetite. I know that it's the source of the dark cloud hanging silently above the kitchen table. But there is nothing I can do. There is no way to hide my food under their attentive gaze, and there is no way I can eat it under the specter of disease.

"I ran into Coach Millings at the store today, Allison," my mom says, eyeing me across the dinner table. She sits up straight, looks pointedly at my dad and back at me. "She asked why you haven't been at practice this week. Said she hasn't heard from you in a few days." She shifts her weight in the seat. "She wants to know if it has anything to do with you fainting last week?"

Her words hit me like a truck. Now I know why they were being so weird. They planned for this conversation. It's an ambush.

"Why haven't you been at practice this week?"

"You fainted?"

"Why didn't you tell us?"

For a few seconds, the only sound is the ticking clock on the wall. My mind is whizzing, frantically searching for an excuse.

"I've been at math tutoring." The words leak out before I can stop them, before I even know they are coming. "I . . . I didn't want to tell you." I emphasize a look of embarrassment. "I've been struggling in precalculus. I really need tutoring before the midterm, so I've been working with Ms. Tisman after school every day this week. I just . . . I wanted to . . . I've never needed tutoring before, and I didn't want anyone to know." I look down at my hands and feel a swell of genuine tears. I've even convinced myself.

I pause for a few moments for effect, to illustrate how embarrassed I am that they have found out my secret precalculus deficiency. I'm both surprised by and proud of my performance. That was a really good lie out of thin air. I'm feeling confident.

"And I don't know why everyone keeps saying I fainted! I fell. Tripped over a root, or a stick or something. Everyone saw it. I even have a bruise to prove it!" I gesture vaguely at my knee and shake my head. "I'll make sure to talk to her about it tomorrow. I should have cleared it with her first anyway." I let out a sigh and clear my throat. "Mom, this broccoli and cheese is so good tonight. Better than usual. Did you do something different this time?"

Easily distracted, my mom straightens up, shoulders back, and smiles: "Look at you—very good, sweetheart!" She swells with pride at my palate. "It's Gouda. I usually use Gruyère."

"I knew it! Where did you get it from? Whole Foods?"

"No, actually, you know I got it at that little place down near . . ."

And just like that, the conversation sails off in another direction. The issues, the questions, the doubts are swept quickly under the rug, out of sight, and I joke and laugh my way through the rest of dinner with a full plate. I think it's the outcome that we were all hoping for.

CHAPTER 6

The first few minutes of the morning, in that warm purgatory between sleep and wakefulness, I forget that I am at war. My face is pulled against the cotton pillowcase, and my mind is at peace, gently floating along with the rhythm of my still-slow breaths. It's been more than two weeks since the nightmare, and in that time I have been hopping, counting, bartering. Explaining away my behaviors with veils of smiles and quick lies. I know others are catching on. Skeptical glances bounce off me as I count my way down the hallway. My friendships are ripping at their seams. My parents eye me cautiously, silently. The looks on their faces say enough.

But in these few minutes of half-conscious snoozing, all that weight is lifted. The tightness in my chest and the lump in my throat, holding back tears, are gone. Sometimes, if I move slowly enough, if my body doesn't find out I'm awake, I can extend this peace from my bed into the morning. I ride the wave of perfect equilibrium for as long as possible until I'm jarred into reality by the events of the day.

This morning I've got a strong hold on this rare mental peace. The planets are aligned, and as I walk down the hall, as I step into the shower, as I bathe away a night of sleep, my brain hums along in blessed silence. I keep my eyes closed against the light of the bathroom, the individual streams of water from the showerhead. I hope my brain will, like a caged bird, stay silent as long as it's in the dark. Running my fingers through my hair to rinse out the shampoo, I am hesitantly optimistic. The shower is so warm, my mind is so quiet. Maybe today will be different. I could eat lunch! I could sit at our table and talk with my friends over plastic bags of safety. I feel the crunch of the Cheez-Its, imagine the satisfying snap of a baby carrot. It's been so long. If I could somehow be really careful all day, maybe I would have extra food left over at dinner. My heart surges as I imagine my mom's face as she sees me clear my plate, possibly reach for seconds. Something about today feels right.

I pull open the shower curtain to a rush of humid air and reach for the hot pink towel hanging on the wall. My bathroom is an ode to my love for bright colors and my parents' unyielding tolerance for "letting Allison be Allison." Perhaps as a result of their own strict military upbringings, my parents have a strong dedication to letting me follow my every passing passion. Art supplies, encyclopedias, science kits, instruments—our house is a monument to information, to exploring your interests.

One day a few months ago, during summer vacation, I stumbled upon a brilliant idea: My bathroom walls could be a collage. Instead of their drab blue wallpaper with petite, tasteful flowers, the walls could host my very own art installation. I became consumed with my project, carefully curating a perfect balance of magazine cutouts, newspaper clippings, meaningful quotes, photographs of friends. After almost a week of single-minded focus, I revealed the piece to my parents. They eyed my handiwork with poorly concealed surprise. My mother looked like she might be sick, and my father told me it was beautiful.

It is this jubilant, enthusiastic display of color that greets me as I towel off. The edges of the cutouts and photos are peeling up at the edges after months of steam from the shower. In the center of the wall is a picture of me, Maddie, Jenny, Sara, and Rebecca, crowded together, falling on top of one another in giggles.

I smile to myself when I think about how Jenny and Rebecca will look at me as I tiptoe toward the lunch table later today. Rebecca will wave and Jenny will continue with whatever dramatic story she is in the middle of. Later in the afternoon, they will tell Maddie and Sara how I ate an entire turkey sandwich and a bag of chips. How I chatted with them just like the normal Allison. I let out a deep breath of relief. Still slightly damp, I crouch down in front of my bathroom sink to retrieve my hair dryer. It is the first step in an almost robotic morning ritual that I have performed every school day for most of my life. As my fingers grasp the plastic handle, I feel a twinge deep in my skull.

I freeze. I recognize that twinge. I know what it's signaling. But the bathroom is so warm and the morning is so peaceful. I'm going to eat lunch today, laugh with my friends like before. Eat a full dinner in front of my parents. Today is a good day, I tell myself, and so I ignore it.

Still crouching, I pull my hair dryer out from under the cabinet, untangling its cord as I bring it into the open. I begged my parents for weeks to get it for me for my birthday last year, explaining that I did, in fact, need a $150 hair dryer with four different heat levels and a retractable cord. Holding its white plastic, I am suddenly bashed in the back of the head and thrown forward. At the same time, the angry buzz of a swarm of bees fills my ears as the floor starts to shake violently. I brace myself against the toilet. The glass lights around my mirror tinkle. Jewelry, fingernail polish, toiletries are jostled out of their cabinet and fall loudly to the floor. The earth shifts powerfully, jaggedly, underneath me. An earthquake. Or worse. My throat is tightening, my tongue swelling. There is a powerful, hot presence, a strong hand pressing forcefully against my throat. A gentle taste of blood. I can't breathe.

DO NOT TOUCH THAT.

It is livid. In pure reflex, choking, I throw my arms upward and topple over onto my back. *BAD!* it screams. *DEATH!* I cower from its radiation. I've never heard this voice before, but I know it is my monster, my savior. The source of my secret messages, the inspiration behind my insider discoveries. Anger is vibrating in waves across the bathroom.

I am on the floor, hands in the air, completely still. I should have stopped when I felt the twinge. But how could I have known? A tide of dark clouds closes in over the bathroom, and I let out a pathetic whimper as I shield my face. Outrage crackles through the air. It is furious. It won't be ignored.

You will not dry your hair, it commands.

I nod eagerly in understanding. "I won't. I won't, I won't, I won't." I will do anything it asks, now that I know its true form. "I promise."

There is a release in pressure like the sound of an air mattress deflating, and the presence evaporates. The storm rolls out of view, and, just as rapidly as the dark descended, a calm, humid energy filters back into the bathroom. Curled on the floor, hands shielding my face, I feel the presence receding, but I lie still, frozen and whimpering. After a few moments it is clear that I am alone again. The tense static has been replaced by my mom's gentle humming floating up the stairs. The *tink* of the dishes being placed on the countertop. When the monster moved away, he took with him the noise, the panic, the frenzy. The room seems to have returned to normal. The same thick, hot air lingering from my shower. The same dripping faucet against the early-morning silence. I slowly return to a sitting position, stunned.

The white plastic hair dryer is leaning against the cabinet door where I dropped it. Vibrant, neon waves of cancer are pulsating off it, rippling across the bathroom. I scoot across the floor so my back is pressed against the bathtub, as far from the hair dryer as possible. Worry bleeds through me as I realize what this means. I have gone my whole life unknowingly exposing myself to the dangers of hair dryers. Imagine the damage I have been causing to my organs and cells! I look down at my stomach, at all the intestines I have been poisoning every morning for my entire life. I caress my arm absentmindedly, appreciative that, as far as I know, my body has yet to give in to my abuse.

Thanks to my protector, I've now been taught the truth about hair dryers. I've already done a lot of damage, I'm sure, but at least from now on I can be more careful. I'm filled with a cloud of gratitude for my monster. Even if he did just yell at me.

"Allison, honey. Oatmeal is ready!" A few seconds' pause. "Hurry before it's cold!"

My mom's voice pulls me from my thoughts and replants me into Tuesday morning. I grab my damp towel and crouch over the hair dryer on the floor. I can feel my protector watching me, making sure I've finally heard his warning loud and clear. Careful not to allow any of my skin to touch the plastic, I wrap the hair dryer completely in the towel, gingerly pick it up, and hurl it back under the sink to the crash of bottles of shampoo and lotion. I slam the cabinet doors behind it. Then I pick up the towel from the floor and rub my wet hair around in it hard, scratching at my scalp and ears. I don't know what I'm trying to shake loose from my brain, but it doesn't work. Unnerved, I head downstairs for breakfast with my mom.

I sit at the lunch table in sullen silence. Jenny and Rebecca largely ignore me, chattering on about drills at practice and the fact that Leslie Morrow is now dating Sean Morren. ("But her *hair!*" Jenny cries.) Looking down, slumped over, picking at my nails, I can hear them talking, and I can see Jenny's wild gestures, but it's like there is a thick wall of glass between us. Their happiness, their energy, is blocked from me, muted and unfamiliar.

"So, you"—Jenny lobs a piece of celery across me over the table—"are you actually coming to practice today?" She is talking through a mouthful of green, a giant wad of vegetable stored in her cheek.

I look up at her, surprised. I'm sitting across from her at the lunch table because it's what I do every day between twelve thirty and one fifteen, but I was under the impression we weren't on speaking terms. "Uh . . . yeah, I mean, probably." Of course I'm not going to practice. So I can faint? So I can count fifteen thousand steps? So I can be surrounded by dozens of wary, questioning eyes—the people who are closer than anyone to realizing there is something going on? Absolutely not. "I want to go. I just don't know if I can."

She raises her arms in a show of frustration and then theatrically flops them down loudly onto her legs. "Coach is really not going to be okay with this. You haven't even talked to her about it!" She is leaning her head forward, eyes wide. "You know she isn't going to let you race next Wednesday." Her mouth shifts to the side into a half frown. "That's just the rule. You can't miss practice and still race." She leans back and crosses her arms as if she has proven some sort of point. I know that she expects me to object, to be upset at the loss. And a few weeks ago that would have been the case. I can't miss a race! I'm trying to make varsity! But now the idea of pushing through 3.1 miles of sweat (and cracks) seems impossible. I can barely make it through a day at school.

"I know, I know. I'm going to go see her soon."

"*Soon?*" Her face is painted in disbelief. "What are you even *doing* after school anyway? Like, all your friends are at cross-country practice. Sara's at work. I just don't get where you could be."

It's not what I'm doing after school that matters. It's what I'm *not* doing. Not eating, not stepping on cracks, not getting cancer. Avoiding my hair dryer, counting my steps, starving. *Unlike you, Jenny Drama Queen Jordan, I have things to worry about. My health to protect.* A strong wave of annoyance builds within me. She doesn't understand. But how could she? Who would? I glance up at her, and she is staring intently at me, clearly waiting for a response.

"I've been at tutoring." I lie as easily as I tell the truth

"Tutoring? For this many days? What kind of tutoring?"

"Well, it was precal one day, then chemistry another. One of those afternoons I also talked to Ms. Griffin about the *Les Misérables* paper coming up." I pat my book bag. "Oh, and then I had a dentist appointment." I look her straight in the eyes. *Boom. Try to question that.*

She nods slightly and exchanges a glance with Rebecca. There's nothing she can do. "Well, you really need to talk to Coach. This is so unlike you."

"I know, I know. I'll talk to her this afternoon at practice."

"Oh, so you're coming now?" She pounces on this misstep like a hungry tiger. "You just said you might not be able to."

"Yeah, well, I was going to try to go see Ms. Matthews about chemistry again, but you're right." I look up at her and make eye contact, shrugging my shoulders. "I need to go to practice and explain to Coach."

There is no smile in her voice. "Mmm," she grunts gently, "good luck with that."

I lied. I skip cross-country practice again. I said I would talk to Coach Millings about my absences but I can't. There's just no way I can get away with it. While my parents, and maybe even my friends, might believe my lies about tutoring, Coach, a teacher herself, would be a lot harder to trick. What if I trip up on my lies? And what if she asks for a teacher's note? What if she doesn't believe me? I can't risk all the questions. I can't risk a blown cover. Plus, there's no point in going to practice. I can't run if I haven't eaten. I learned that lesson already.

Walking across campus alone, I think about my parents, about my mom and what she would say if she knew. Not just about skipping practice and lying about tutoring, but about the urgent messages from my protector and the gnawing sadness spreading in my stomach. Tears prick at the edges of my eyes, because I imagine her wrapping me in a hug and leading me out of this maze. But I'll never tell her. Or anyone. Something inside me knows it's not allowed.

Home hours before I should be, I'm standing in front of the kitchen pantry, its thick wooden door thrown open to reveal a messy, jumbled array of boxes and cans. I can't eat any of it, obviously. I would never dream of something so suicidal. But, like a moth to a flame, I'm drawn to the pantry in search of a snack, even if all I'm allowed to consume are my own repetitive thoughts. Perched on my tiptoes on two linoleum tiles, my eyes scan the shelves, reliving the long-gone days of gorging on pizza rolls and ramen noodles after school.

Surveying what seems like a lifetime of food, I feel the twinge. A sharp tingling starts in the back of my neck and travels quickly down my spine. Goose bumps crawl across my body. My chest tightens with familiarity. Eyes darting around the kitchen, I try to locate its source. This feeling means cancer, illness, death. I have to find it. I can't disobey. The afternoon sun glares through the window over the sink. The room sits silently, ominously, waiting.

The unmistakable rumbling of the monster shudders down the hall, shattering the silence of my empty house. The floor shakes. The windows rattle. *Emergency! Emergency!* My heart pounds. I frantically search the pantry, my eyes jumping from shelf to shelf. With my monster closing in, I am in that moment before a fist hits your face. Before you're pummeled underwater by a wave. In those few seconds of clarity before impact, my brain reels off options in panic: Is it the pretzels? *Yes.* Is it the Cheerios? *Yes.* The canned soup? *Yes.* His footsteps in the doorway. Saltine crackers? *Bad.* Russet potatoes? *Cancer.* Oatmeal? *Death.*

The demands fly out of the pantry like individual fastballs. I feel them angrily whizzing by my head. Launching themselves off the shelves, declaring their dangerous truths. I yank myself forcefully, shoulder first, out of their way, ducking under their threats. My momentum spins me, and I land in a crouching position with my back to the screaming food. The flashing red of emergency lights pulses in my brain. My monster is *here.* I can feel him. He is in the room. The air is thick, sour. My eyes swivel around the kitchen, loose and uncontrolled on their stems. I am frantic to find an outlet, an excuse, a target. Something to appease him. Anything. He wants sacrifices, tributes, gifts.

Do something! Keep looking. The twinge. There is more.

I stutter over myself. The fruit basket on the counter. Peaches. Oranges. *Death and dying.* Bananas. *Cancer.* My eyes snap across the room. My heart is pounding. Bees are buzzing. And my mind gorges itself as it maneuvers around the kitchen. A penny in a handful of change. *Brain tumor.* A blue pen lying politely next to the chunky eraser I use in art class. A crumpled, lone sock under the kitchen table. *Carcinoma. Death. Sadness, misery, pain.*

I slap my hands to my face, reflexively jerking away from the powerful, never-ending stream. The impact stings sharply across my skin, and with it the electricity of my monster instantly fades into the background. The grip around my chest loosens and the kitchen suddenly falls silent. My heart slows. Crouched on the kitchen floor, hands still covering my eyes, it feels like I've knocked myself back to center. I know that I am alone again.

With my hands to my face and my mind in darkness, I teeter on my tiptoes on the linoleum. My still-quaking breaths shake my body slightly, but something inside tells me I am safe. For now. I balance in a squatted ball position, comforted by the welcome silence.

The monster's presence was a warning. He was telling me I was too close. I take a deep breath, examining my new danger list, written on a long sheet of paper unfurling across my mind. I have the same feeling in my chest that I get when I've procrastinated studying for a test. So much information—

how will I hold it all? How will I avoid bananas? Pennies? Blue pens and erasers? They're everywhere.

Are you not grateful? I yell internally, intercepting my thoughts right as I think them. Do you not realize what you have been given? Without your protector you would be dying. A skin-covered skeleton in a hospital bed. A straight-A student who failed at the only real test: survival. I'm taken aback by my own scolding but nod gently to myself. I have a point.

I have no idea how long I have been crouching here on the floor, but the arches of my feet are shaking with fatigue. For the first time in a few days, I feel truly calm. I have more discoveries, more information on how to stay healthy. I roll through the list in my head, gaining confidence from each item. A warmth gathers in me as I realize that I am impenetrable. My monster is helping me build a wall around my city on a hill. Everyone else carries pennies in their pockets, eats bananas with their breakfast. Not me. I have a protector who loves me.

I may be safe from the cancers of the kitchen, but I'm also stranded. With my eyes covered, I cannot safely maneuver the crack-laden floor. But if I open my eyes, something inside me knows, the alarms will sound, the lasers will power up, and I will awaken the powerful stream of warnings. I will find out that more of my surroundings are deadly. While I want to (need to!) know the truth, my life is already consumed, completely overtaken, by cracks, counting, trading food. I know that I can't handle much more.

Squeezing my eyes shut, I drop my hands from my face,

moving my arms slowly so I don't attract danger's attention. Through my closed eyes, I can feel the waning late-afternoon light filtering through the kitchen windows. Apparently, I've been at this for a while. I point my head down and barely open my eyelids, creating a tiny slit obstructed almost completely by eyelashes. I focus intently on the floor ahead, searching out the almost-invisible linoleum cracks, and move methodically toward the kitchen door. I sneeze and momentarily open my eyes to find them staring at the kitchen trash can. *Trash cans cause cancer,* I'm told before I can even register that my eyes have popped open.

"Crap!" I scold myself out loud for the mistake and bring my hands up to my eyes once again, cupping them in semicircles on my temples like horse blinders. Frustrated, I count my way down the hallway, maneuvering the maze of cracks in the hardwood floor like a tightrope walker. Once I've cleared the danger zone and my feet are planted safely on carpet, I launch myself up the stairs, eager to reach my bedroom and bury my head deep in the darkness of my pillows, where my roaming eyes can't cause any more damage.

But as I turn the corner to my room, as I feel my hands fall beside my legs, my eyes remember the new game they learned downstairs. Stereo. Lamp. Piggy bank. Boom, boom, boom. Death sentences. A stuffed Build-A-Bear, my cross-country uniform thrown on the chair. Bulging tumors, terminal illness. There is no twinge this time, no sirens, no bees. This is my mind gone rogue. My eyes wander around the room, seizing randomly upon whatever they encounter.

Sucking my world away. Pearl earrings, my watch, the stack of yearbooks on the bookshelf. *Early death, cancer, lymphoma.*

Everything in my path is mowed down and moved to the expanding list of dangers. With my final step toward the safety of my bed, I see my cell phone perched on the edge of my nightstand. My mind reaches hungrily for this nugget of gold, its most valuable prisoner yet. As my heart sinks to the pit of my stomach, my body crawls under the protective covers of my bed. Cell phones cause cancer. Great.

CHAPTER 7

It takes a while for me to adjust to my newly burgeoning danger list. Just as when I first began avoiding cracks, I slide tentatively through life, eyeing my surroundings for traps sent by death. Hunched and counting, always counting, I pick my way through the chilly morning at school, constantly alert for approaching danger. So far no peaches, no pennies, no pretzels. No oatmeal, no stereos, no lamps. The list is so long I'm constantly running it through my mind like the ticker tape at the stock exchange, reminding myself of all the things that I'm supposed to be avoiding.

I tiptoe down the breezeway from class. I'm submerged in my thoughts but surface occasionally to tune in to Jenny and pretend to be part of the conversation. "It's just that I don't even really like Mexican food that much, you know?" She seems very upset, so I nod at her. "Why of *all* places is that where she chooses?" I'm not sure whether she hasn't noticed my counting or if she has decided not to care. Either way, I'm thankful. Jenny patters on as I tiptoe us to class. "Even that new Thai place would be better, and I don't like Asian food!"

"Jenny, not everyone wants to eat pizza for every meal like you. Fifty-eight, fifty-nine. And it's her *birthday party*, so she gets to choose the restaurant. Sixty, sixty-one."

"She should at least consider other people's opinions. It seems— Oh, hey, Tabby!" I look up to Tabitha Grey approaching us. A junior and a volleyball player, she has run for one student office or another in every election of her high school career. She waves at us enthusiastically.

"Hey, girls," Tabitha drawls as she slows. "Look, y'all, can't talk—I'm supposed to be gatherin' signatures." She flips through a wrinkled legal pad in her hand. "We're petitionin' Mr. Castillo to let juniors park their cars on campus their second semester." She whips out two blue pens and extends them toward us as she continues: "By then we're basically seniors anyway, right? Why continue to treat us like children?" She wiggles the notepad at us, and Jenny moves forward to sign first. "Y'all sophomores should care too! You'll be in my shoes next year, and you'll want to drive to school then, won't you?" As I watch Jenny scrawl her name in blue ink across the lined sheet of paper, my eyes narrow in on her hand. The pen from yesterday in the kitchen. I see it sitting quietly next to my white eraser. *Death.*

Blue pen. I can see the tube of dark ink through its clear plastic outside. Blue pen, blue pen, blue pen. The glaring sunlight somehow collects into one shining beam and aims itself like a spotlight on the second pen, dangling casually from Tabby's hand. There's the sound of individual sections of bubble wrap popping. It's my cells. A demanding pressure on the back of my right eye. Cancer. Jenny completes the last whirl of her name and mindlessly extends the notepad toward me without looking. "I can't believe they won't let you guys drive. You're almost seventeen, for goodness' sakes!"

Blue pen, blue pen, blue pen. Cancer. Blue pen. Blue

pen. Blue pen. Do something! Blue pen. Blue pen. Escape! Save yourself! What undoes the danger of a blue pen? What undoes a blue pen? I've got my head tilted away from my friends, looking back over my shoulder to keep the pen out of sight. My eyes zoom across the muddy grass and concrete pathways. Like counting my steps or bartering food, it needs to be powerful, meaningful. Essential to my life. Like breathing. Breath. Holding my breath. I will hold my breath any time I see a blue pen. *Yes!* Yes. That's it. I won't inhale any of its contaminants and I'll be safe. Bluepenbluepenbluepenbluepen. With my new solution in hand, I clamp my mouth shut and tighten my stomach to hold in the air. Turning back to the girls, I'm immediately attacked: BLUEPENBLUEPENBLUEPEN. Instinctively, I whip my arm up and place my hand, which is clinging to my still-full lunch bag, in front of my eyes, blocking the pen from my vision.

Jenny and Tabitha are talking, I assume. I don't know what they're doing. All there is is that pen. And this cancer in my brain. And trying to save myself. I take another deep breath, and even though the pen is blocked by my bag, I keep holding my breath, just in case. My eyes are glued open but unable to focus, a piercing siren echoing around my head. Tabby is still extending her right arm toward me with the pen in her hand. Like a laser, a death ray shoots out from its tip. Based on the pain in my stomach, it seems to be currently aimed directly at my large intestine.

"Are you going to sign or what?" Tabitha is gesturing impatiently at me with the pen, its cancer laser slicing across my body, while Jenny tries to hand me the petition.

"I'm going to sign. . . . I'm just . . ." I snatch the petition from Jenny, keeping my lunch bag held up awkwardly in the air with the other hand, blocking out Tabitha's pen. I pretend to look through the names to buy more time. My mouth is dry. I can't use blue pens. I don't know exactly why. Cancer. Death. *Bad.* "Do you have a different pen?" The words flow from my mouth like acid as they ride out on the stale exhale. I immediately take a small, sharp breath and hold it in.

Jenny and Tabby are both squinting at me. "What do you mean? I have *this* pen." Tabby holds up the blue pen that has been poisoning us for the past few minutes. "And she has *that* pen?" And when she gestures at Jenny with her arm, the cap of her pen briefly escapes my lunch bag cover and pokes violently into my line of vision. I flinch, cowering from its glare, and adjust the position of my hand. Good thing I've been holding my breath. They both stare at me as I hesitate. My brain is in a clamp. My skull is shrinking inward, being squeezed like a grape. I wonder if they can tell that my eyeballs are bulging.

"Seriously, come on, just sign already." She wiggles the blue pen at me forcefully and I see her shoulder rotating above the edge of the bag. "I told y'all, I'm in a hurry!"

I can feel the cancer billowing up from the pen into a dark mushroom cloud. My muscles tighten up and I realize my shoulders have raised up to my ears. Tabitha's hand moves the blue pen even closer to me with her impatience. I can't. I can't do this. I have to make a break for it. This pen is dangerous and I won't risk using it, not for Tabitha, not for Jenny. I must escape.

"Allison, what are you doing? I'm going to—"

"Hey! Wow! I have to . . . go! To . . . class." I lurch into motion and accidently bump hard into Tabitha with a grunt. There is the shuffling of feet and the adjusting of book bags as I move to get around them. I'm already turning away when I shove the petition back into Jenny's arms. "I have to go meet a teacher." And with my first step, I feel the cancer waves lessening. I pull myself from their grasp with the sound of ripping Velcro.

"Right now? It's class change—who could you be meeting?" Jenny has that same look, the *What the hell is going on?* look I know from across the lunch table.

"Ms. Matthews," I say, just as I realize that Jenny and I have her class together sixth period.

"Ms. Matthews?" she asks with surprise as I tiptoe away, my arm continually adjusting my lunch bag to blot out the pens in their hands. "Why are you meeting with her? We have her class in a few hours."

"I'm not sure? She just asked me to come see her." Jenny looks at me with concern and I shrug at her. "Sixty-two, sixty-three." Not one of my more creative excuses but it seems to have worked.

From behind me, a few moments of silence followed by Tabitha's voice: "That was kind of weird." And then: "Why is she counting?"

I skip lunch and instead go to my secret cove of enormous trash cans and air conditioners. It's not picturesque, I'll admit that, but it's quiet and peaceful. And all mine. I lean against the warm brick partition and finally allow myself to relax a little bit.

I think about Rebecca and Jenny waiting for me at the lunch table. My absence is just another notch for them to add in their something-is-seriously-wrong-with-Allison belt. Maybe I should make a better effort? Maybe I should tiptoe into lunch, slap on a smile, and spray them with happiness like I do my parents? But just the thought is exhausting. My heart gives a small flip as I picture myself at the lunch table, Jenny firing questions at me about cross-country practice, and my mysterious meeting with Ms. Matthews. It's not worth it. Easier to just stay away.

The next morning, the bell rings at the end of English class and I remain sitting in my desk. The other students in my row clamor past as I wait patiently for my safe number of steps to appear in my mind. In my seat, through the wall of moving bodies, I feel the familiar warmth of someone's concentrated stare. I glance up to see Sara standing hesitantly in the doorway, looking like she can't make up her mind about something. Every day this school year, at least until recently, she and I have walked to third period together, trading gossip and inside jokes. The past week, however, she has passed me small, folded notes with lame scribbled excuses right as English class ended, and then slipped out of the room without me before I've even heard my safe number of steps. I grin up at her. So she's not mad at me—I sigh to myself with relief. I guess I was imagining it. "Hold on, just one second!" I say to her through a wide smile. I pretend to adjust a few notes in my binder until the number *46* appears quietly in my mind. Step assignment in hand, I stand up slowly, careful to watch the position of my shoes, and tiptoe toward her. "One." I freeze midstep as we make eye contact. "Two . . ." I move to say something, but the words are trapped by the look on Sara's face. She shakes her head slightly, looks down at the floor, turns, and leaves the room.

I watch the empty doorway, stunned and alone in the middle of the deserted classroom. Message received.

But in her absence, in this week's long, lonely walks to third period, I've discovered how much more effective I am on my own. I count every step, I dodge every crack. Without Sara, I don't make any mistakes on the way to Civics and Ethics, and I've been able to save one, maybe two items of my lunch every day.

So it's become blatantly obvious that I need to start walking to all classes by myself. I can't try to carry on a conversation while also paying enough attention to my steps, my counting, my long list of dangers. In the social jungle of Samuelson, I know this is an abomination. But I am willing to sacrifice my reputation and social standing to protect myself, to protect my future. I take a deep breath in and feel proud of my responsible, mature decisions.

While Sara has made a voluntary and easy exit from my life, Jenny has continued to walk by my side every day. Even though I've been skipping both lunch and cross-country practice for days with weak attempts at an explanation, even though I screamed at her in front of a cafeteria of hundreds, even though I never stop counting, she is still here. But I'm about to fix that. I have five classes with Jenny. Without her to distract me on my walks, I could maybe start eating full meals.

The bell reverberates across campus and I step out from my hiding spot behind the brick wall. 57 appears in my mind, and I tiptoe across the filthy gravel back toward the main walkway, my mind busy concocting a plan to somehow get away from Jenny.

There is a gentle, lumpy squish near the ball of my foot. Something condenses in a horrible way under the sole of my sneaker. I lift my right foot, expecting to see a pile of dog poop, but it's a sock. A sodden, disgusting, dirty sock. My foot has squelched out a small puddle of brown water from the fabric onto the dark pavement. Gross. Someone probably dropped it on their way to the locker room. It's just around the corner. They're going to—

I'm slammed hard from behind and take two dumb-founded, tiptoed steps forward. Thirteen, fourteen. A sock. A sock. Sock. Sock. Sock. Sock, sock, sock. Socksocksocksock-sock. The world of grass and pathways, students and school buildings, swirls into a tornado around me, and I remember the crumpled sock underneath the kitchen table. The one that meant cancer, illness, death, pain. The one that told me that all socks cause disease, that they're a harbinger of tragedy.

My breath catches in my chest, and I grab on to it, hold-ing it in tightly. Don't breathe near socks. Crap. I'm so freak-ing clumsy. Sock. Sock. How can I fix this? How can I undo this? My foot is frozen, hovering six inches above the pavement. Droplets of death are clinging to the bottom of my shoe. Sock, sock, sock. I look around my mind. It's starting to panic from lack of oxygen. What can I give? My massive, upcoming English project on *Les Misérables* appears in my mind. We're supposed to read the more-than-a-thousand-page book and write a ten-page paper. And that's when I know. In order to make up for stepping on this sock, I'm not allowed to do my English reading for the *Les Mis* paper today. There's a small gurgle of a response inside me. Good, but it needs more. Something still feels off. Unsatisfied. I try again: I won't do my *Les Mis* reading for the rest of this *week*. The sharp pain in my head lessens significantly with the thought. Better. Definitely better. But it's like the game at the fair where you use the giant hammer to hit the platform and try to make the metal ball ring the enormous bell twenty feet up. It feels like I'm 75 percent there. One more try. This time with real spirit.

To make up for stepping on this sock, I won't do my *Les Misérables* reading for English class. Ever.

Finally the tension breaks and I'm somehow released. By now the breezeways are crowded, and I suddenly realize I'm standing in the middle of the pathway, hovering in a strange yoga position, engulfed in bodies and limbs and book bags.

Hours later, after working to build up my confidence throughout the afternoon, I watch the second hand on the clock as chemistry winds down. As the time nears, I ready myself: I'm perched on the edge of my seat, feet safely positioned, book bag already packed and zipped. I can see out of my peripheral vision that Jenny is still taking notes on the lesson. Her head is buried deep in her binder. Perfect.

With the bell, I leap from my desk and scuttle out of class, launching myself into the thick crowd while Jenny is still scribbling out the last few words on her notebook paper. I have a strong head start but immediately get stuck in the clogged hallway. The crowd is barely crawling forward, and I have to force my way between bodies to make progress.

Behind me, she whips through the double doors and I hear, "Allison, hey! Slow down!" Jenny's voice lilts above the heads of the crowd. I haven't made it very far, but I pretend not to hear her over my counting.

"Eight, nine, ten."

"Wait!"

"Twelve, thirteen." Step over a penny on the floor. "Fourteen, fifteen."

"HEY!" I've known Jenny for five years. Something in her voice grinds me to a stop. Eyes clamped closed, I let out a long, slow breath of air as the mass of students divides around me. She isn't going to let me avoid a confrontation. "You're in a hurry today!" she scolds me across the hallway, completely unaware of the slight layer of sweat slowly appearing on my forehead as she walks toward me. "I've been trying to talk to you all period! Did you not see my texts?"

"Crap! Sorry." My voice sounds remarkably steady as I feign annoyance. "I forgot my phone at home today." Honestly, since I discovered its truth, my cell has been dead and buried deep within layers of blankets in a trunk at home. I should be protected from it there. For now.

"Oh my gosh, that's the worst. How are you surviving?" She smacks her gum at me emphatically, her bright sparkly nails resting on her hip. *I can't walk with you. I can't walk with you. I can't walk with you.* "One day last week I forgot my phone at home and I literally went crazy. Like, actually nuts." *I can't walk with you.* "I called my mom from the office and asked her to bring it to me. She was so annoyed and said no. Even though we both know she's not actually *doing* anything at home anyway." Still talking, she begins moving slowly down the hall toward the tail end of the huge mass of students funneling out of the building. "Oh, so the reason I was texting you. I heard the JV football boys are going to be at the . . ." Her words drift off as she realizes I haven't followed her down the hall. Ten feet away, she notices my shifting eyes. With a quick glance, she takes in my tiptoes. I look at her blankly as I see pieces falling together in her mind. "Allison?" A pause. "What's wrong?" The fearful look in her eyes is infuriating. Is she scared *of* me or *for* me?

The words rumble around my mouth as a wave of heat creeps up my neck. She is staring at me. Her perfectly painted nails, her feet resting on cracks, her blow-dried hair. The way she carelessly eats her lunch without me in the crowded cafeteria. "I can't walk with you!" I scream, bursting with pent-up annoyance at her persistence. Why couldn't she just make it easy like Sara? She is still staring at me, and I look her directly in the eye, voice steady. "I can't walk with you."

Finally. It's done.

The entire world pauses as our eyes connect across the

chaotic hallway. Her face is frozen in a look of confusion, and she clutches her books tight to her chest. If I know Jenny, her stunned silence won't last for long. I need to leave.

I don't realize I am crying until I'm pushing through crowds of people. I turn to look at her again and we make eye contact, her eyes wide and questioning. She mouths something, but my eyes are welling with tears and I'm looking away, so I can't be exactly sure what she said.

As much as I want to count my miserable steps in silence, there is something comforting in Jenny's insistent loyalty, in her constant search for confrontation and answers. I don't know if it's that no one else is noticing what is happening or if they are too scared, or in Sara's case too embarrassed, to talk to me about it. I tell myself that I don't want Jenny's concern, I don't want her conversation interrupting my counting, I don't want her blunt questions and unflinching stares. But as I weave through tight knots of students in the pathway, I know that that's *all* I want. I want it more than anything, but it's not possible. Not if I want to live.

CHAPTER 8

I've never met an English paper I didn't like. So in the first weeks of school, when Ms. Griffin stood up in front of the class and began describing a colossal, two-month-long project on *Les Misérables*, I was delighted. Worth 25 percent of our final grade, it included not only detailed chapter outlines and character analyses but also a ten-page paper.

Ten pages! My eyes lit up at the suggestion. I had never written something that long before. It was so exciting! I rubbed my hands together like a plotting dictator. Ms. Griffin had no idea who she was dealing with. That night, looking closely over the sheet of paper that described the assignment, I carefully penciled self-imposed deadlines into my agenda to help organize my journey through the gloriously thick novel.

Now it's November eleventh and I stare down at the entry—*Les Mis paper due!!*—that I doodled happily in pink ink a few months ago and purse my lips. How things have changed.

I have one day before I reach the fateful due date, decorated with squiggles and smileys in my agenda, and I haven't started the paper. Haven't opened the book in at least two weeks.

More and more, I've found myself caught in situations like the pantry and my bedroom. Sometimes it's sirens and buzzing ears and the twinge. My monster rumbles in, proclaiming the truth from on high. But other times it's the exact opposite. A glitch in the system. I begin to call it rapid-fire labeling: the times where my eyes rattle like a machine gun and spew danger labels onto my surroundings. Post-it notes, belts, polyester. Coffee mugs, newspapers, my aging cat, Scratch. Every day, without warning, my eyes aim themselves at seemingly innocent objects, and I'm informed they cause cancer, illness, death. The ambushes come in all shapes and sizes. Sometimes it's just a few brief bursts. Sometimes it continues for minutes, calming only under the darkness of tightly squeezed eyelids. As a result, I am always on edge. I never know when the monster might rumble or my eyes might go on a shooting rampage.

I'm sitting at my desk in the den as I reread the worn sheet of paper with the English assignment. I've been staring at it so long I almost have it memorized. *What social evils do you think Victor Hugo is criticizing in* Les Misérables? *How does each of the main characters support your opinion? Please respond in ten double-spaced, typed pages.*

The words clatter around meaninglessly in my head. I am gazing blankly down at the wood grain of my desk. I've found that the most effective means of limiting the damage of the rapid-fire spasms is to keep my eyes focused on a broad, featureless area like a wall, floor, or table. While not foolproof (yesterday I labeled cardinals as the most dangerous bird when one flew across my vision as I stared purposefully out the window at the sky), it limits the buffet of possible losses. I know the first step in writing this paper is reviewing the material I was able to read before the sock. I need my *Les Misérables* book itself, but I don't trust myself to look for it. From recent experience, I know that as soon as I turn around to retrieve the book out of my bag, my eyes will feast. Lined with bookshelves, paintings, family pictures, this den would be my mind's dream. It would be a bloodbath.

I've lost so much over the past few weeks, I can't risk any of my remaining safe possessions. The only completely reliable method of not cursing everything I see is not seeing at all.

With closed eyes, I slide off the computer chair, down to the carpet, onto all fours. Feeling my way blindly across the floor, I wave my arms out in front of me, searching for my book bag. The carpet feels soft and lush under my palms, and I smooth my hands forward. With my right hand, I feel a strap, canvas, a zipper. Binders, notebook, novel. I grab the thick book and crawl quickly back to my desk behind still-closed eyes. In my chair, I flip through the stack of pages and feel for the one that's dog-eared. Based on the thickness of the pages I have left between my fingers, it seems like I'm about halfway through. But I don't remember the plot at all, really. There was a lady with a daughter and a guy with a weird name. Pretty sure they're in France. Everyone's poor. I'm going to need to reread most of it, or at least enough to bluff my way through a ten-page paper.

But to read I have to open my eyes. After a few minutes in the dark silence of my mind, I know that I don't have much of a choice. The paper is due tomorrow. I scoot tight against the desk, almost pinning myself in place. I pull up the hood of my sweatshirt to cover my entire head and tighten the drawstrings so my vision is limited to a small circular opening through the fabric.

First my left, then my right, I open my eyes, squinting as usual through tiny slits at a blurry world. Through the wall of eyelashes, I cautiously scan my surroundings. The room sits in innocent silence. The tabletop is exactly how I left it. To my surprise, there is no rumbling, no twinge, no darkening sky. It's just a Thursday afternoon and I'm about to write a paper on—

DESK, PAPER CLIPS, PENCILS.

The message attacks me. I jerk at its appearance as if it has exploded like a firework. No, no, not now, not now. *COMPUTER. DVR. TISSUES.* My brain moves faster than I can close my eyes, screaming instructions before I can react. *RUBBER BANDS. COMPUTER CHAIR. MY* LES MISÉRABLES *BOOK.*

"No!" I yell, slamming my head into my arms on the desk. The entire table shakes with impact. Pens and pencils fly out of my carefully sorted organizers. But it's too late. Blindly, I grab the cancerous paperback copy of *Les Mis* from my desk and throw it across the room with all my strength. It slams into the blinds and falls to the floor, waking up my dog, Layla, who slinks off to another room. Exhausted, I collapse into my own arms on the desk and, once again, allow the sobs to flow through me.

But it wasn't only the book, my mind whispers. It was also the computer and the DVR. The desk and the computer chair. I spring to my feet, launching myself away from danger, and slam my legs against the bottom of the desk in the process. Turning in circles, I see that I am surrounded. What have I done, what have I done, what have I done? Slowly, and then collapsing all at once, I sink to the carpet and fold into myself. The safest place is darkness. The less contact with the world, the better.

Seconds, minutes, hours pass. I have no concept of the time as I slip into an almost sleep—a transient place between REM and consciousness. In this comfortable limbo, I float between worlds. Half in the present, half surrounded by dreams. I sleep, I wake, I sleep, I wake. The afternoon spreads onward under the umbrella of my eyelids.

I'm jolted to life by the clanging of the garage door and the arrival of one of my parents from a day at work. It takes me a few minutes to rise into a sitting position. My dad is rustling in the kitchen. I can tell it is him by his footsteps. His keys hit the counter. His blazer folds on top of his kitchen chair.

"Heyyy, Dad!" I yell with a smile. Act happy.

"Hey, hon," he calls as he walks up the stairs. I know he is loosening his tie, undoing the buttons at his wrists. "How was your day? How did the—" He turns the corner into the den. "Why are you on the floor?" He takes a few steps closer and eyes the telltale wrinkles on my face and arms. "Have you been sleeping?"

"What? No. I've been reading. Studying." I rub hard at the indentations across my skin.

"On the floor?"

"Yeah." I scoff at him like it's a normal place to be. "I sit in chairs all day. I want to sit on the floor for a change." I wiggle around a little bit to show how comfortable I am.

He nods at me silently, creasing his eyebrows. "Okay, well, whatever works, I guess." He turns to go. "Have you seen your mother? Do you know what's for dinner?"

"No and no," I say down the hall. He grunts slightly and closes his bedroom door.

Sitting up, talking to my dad, I feel surprisingly clear-headed and refreshed, like maybe the nap has recalibrated something within me. The room is a little brighter, my mind a little calmer. I've had my eyes open the whole time I've been awake and haven't added anything to the danger list. I pick up the *Les Mis* assignment sheet. It is already six p.m. I have to get started. I read the paper topic again and take inventory. Sort through the bodies.

My computer is banned. When I glance up at it from the carpet, it looks no more dangerous than it has any other day of my life. It seems like if I just tapped the mouse, the screen would light up and I'd be welcomed with instant messages from Sara, Jenny, Maddie . . . Sam. But that will never happen again. It's not safe.

And without the computer, I won't be able to type this paper like the assignment requests. Problematic but not insurmountable, I reason with a shrug. I'm sensing no danger from my English binder and the notebook paper it contains. I'll just write it by hand, the old-fashioned way.

Perfect. One problem solved.

Pencils. I inhale deeply as the thought settles heavily on my brain. I see myself sitting empty-handed in precalculus, art, chemistry. How will I do my homework, take tests, pass

115

my classes? Write this paper? The consequences of this one are massive. I look down at the carpet and take a breath. Even now, in the moment, I know this will not just be a road-block in my life. It will be the Berlin Wall.

Blue pens were one of my first additions to the danger list. I look back on that day in the kitchen with a gentle twist of nostalgia. The good ol' days of avoiding cracks and trading food. Those blue pens were then quickly followed by pens of all kinds. Along with the colored pencils and calligraphy pens we use in art class. As far as I can tell, looking down at my upturned palms, I now have no writing utensils left to my name. I scratch my scalp and nod slightly, almost impressed with myself. You can't say I'm not thorough.

I scan my mind, looking for ideas on how to write the paper. I picture an old typewriter and hear the ding it makes after every line. Markers? Crayons? (Do I have any crayons?) I question myself, chewing on bad suggestions, searching the den with my eyes.

That pencil over there.

The voice comes in a whispered hiss like Parseltongue from my very own Voldemort. Not from any direction in particular, it could almost be my conscience.

I jerk my head up and find myself looking straight ahead at a yellow-painted No. 2 pencil sitting on the carpet under my desk. It must have fallen when I slammed the table earlier. This one? I ask internally.

Yes, that one.

It's safe?

Yes.

How?

It's a gift.

A gift? For me? Why? There is no response. I don't deserve a gift. I'm talking to myself as much as to the silent voice. Why is it safe? How is it safe?

My questioning thoughts go unanswered. The presence has evaporated.

"Huh," I grunt out loud. A gift. From my seat in the middle of the floor, it looks to be a relatively new pencil. Crawling slowly toward it, edging around my computer chair, I see it is razor sharp with a barely smudged eraser. It looks like all the other life-threatening pencils I've seen, but my protector would never mislead me. This pencil is safe. Monster approved.

I scoot backward, pencil clenched in my fist, and sit cross-legged on the carpet. The situation isn't as dire as it once seemed. I have notebook paper and a pencil, the basic necessities. At least for the task at hand.

The idea of no computer and no DVR is a dark, foreboding cloud on the horizon. Without allowing my mind to wander too far, I quickly realize that no computer means no Internet. Which means no e-mail, no instant messaging. No friends.

I cut this thought off immediately, slamming my mind closed. Now is not the time. I can figure out the Internet and computer, the obstacles built by my mind, later. I always do. I will be okay. Focus. On. The assignment.

I reach for my English binder and open it to a thick stack of pristine lined notebook paper. I stare at it, almost nervous to get too close. It could set off the alarms. I place my hand on the pile of paper in my binder, run it gently under my palm. As I just learned, there's no way to know when my eyes will start firing again. I shouldn't be sitting beside such a valuable resource, I tell myself. I can't be trusted.

I look at the nearly thousand-page copy of *Les Mis* lying near the window on the other side of the room. The blinds are slightly dented from their collision, and the book's paper cover is bent awkwardly against the floor. When I look at the book's thick, light brown pages, it seems completely unchanged, but I know it causes cancer. And it's already late. I don't have time to reread anything anyway. My neck pops as I adjust my position on the carpet. The fuzzy memories of the half of the book I read early on in the semester in the weeks before my trade are just going to have to be enough.

I've grown up writing papers on the computer. Copying, pasting, editing easily. With a pencil and paper, I soon find, there is no quick-fix editing. If you make a mistake or want to make a change, you have two choices: erase or rewrite.

Flinging wrinkled pieces of pink eraser across the carpet, I erase the majority of the second page of my paper. The tiny eraser does its job but is wearing down with alarming speed. This is the only safe pencil in the world. When this eraser runs out, I have a feeling I won't be able to use another one for a long time. I think briefly of the large white eraser I use in art class but remember that I banned it a few weeks ago. In frustration, I drag the pink stub of the pencil eraser against the paper harder, faster. Its quick deterioration only brings me closer to the edge but is also somehow incredibly satisfying. I bend my elbow, crouch down close to the paper, and put all my strength into the violent eraser storm. As I yank the pencil hard, something changes in the physics, and I rip a deep hole across the middle of the paper.

With a scoff of disgust, I shove the torn sheet aside and reach automatically toward my English binder for more paper.

And there it is. The rumble. The shaking of the floor, the anxious tinkling of the windowpanes.

Almost expecting it, I lift my face to the sky, showing my willingness to listen to my monster. I hope that if I am compliant, he won't get so angry. Maybe he'll be gentle. The thought arrives: *Notebook paper is like counting your steps. It is only safe if used in the correct amount.*

Interesting, I say to myself on the floor. That makes sense, I guess. Without having to ask, I know that the number of sheets of paper I can use will be assigned to me just like my safe-steps number is. It will float into my brain, an intruder masquerading as a thought.

I wait for a few moments, pulling on individual carpet fibers.

Ten.

Perfect! My heart jumps a little, and I almost smile as I reach toward my binder to unclip the allotment from the metal claws. Ten pieces for a ten-page paper. My earnest plea must have worked. I couldn't ask for a better situation. Counting out the sheets—six, seven, eight—I feel the twinge again and look up immediately.

It gestures invisibly at the two sheets of paper on the

floor. My first full written page and the second, ripped sheet covered in eraser shavings. The paper is torn vertically, a five-inch scar that splits it almost in two.

These? I eye the sheets on the floor, picking up the torn one lying near my foot. But this sheet is ripped . . . ?

No response.

I try again, shouting now inside my mind: But this one is ripped!

Nothing. I've been abandoned. When the monster is done talking, apparently, he gives no encore. I gingerly pick up the torn sheet of paper and place it in the pile with my first written page and the eight clean new sheets. I guess these are my ten pages. Tape hasn't been banned yet, at least not that I can remember. I'll make it work.

Without having read more than half the book, without dedicating any real thought to the paper, I am simply word vomiting. A meandering, pointless dissertation that is mostly a muddled, inaccurate plot summary of the first four hundred pages of the novel. I scribble and erase mindlessly as the evening minutes tick past. At ten thirty p.m., I have about five pages. I lift my hand to relieve a cramp and see that the previously sharp tip of the pencil has been worn to a soft curving nub.

I reach into a basket on the floor underneath my desk that holds all my random school supplies and find a small, portable pencil sharpener. As I move the pencil toward the sharpener, I know what's coming. There isn't a rumble or even a tremor, but it's inevitable.

No sharpening the pencil.

My shoulders collapse under the expected news, and I let out a long sigh. The only safe pencil in the world cannot be sharpened.

Ever? I ask tentatively.

Just this paper.

Okay, good, thank you. I pause for a moment. But why wouldn't you tell me this at the beginning? I would have been more careful. I could have conserved the lead. You tricked me!

My monster doesn't respond, of course, but I'm also talking to myself, venting. No one knows about my internal swirling storm other than me—and we talk about it regularly. I am the only one who can understand.

I continue writing, repeating the same weak points I made in the first half of the paper. My main goal is to cover ten pages, but their content is much less important. With each passing paragraph, the tip of the pencil rubs farther and farther into the wood. By page seven, I am pushing hard at an angle to get the lead onto the paper. I rotate the pencil every few words to try to find an edge of sharpness.

The eraser, completely flattened, now only smudges the lead around instead of erasing it. The lip of the metal surrounding the eraser catches the paper regularly, pocking my work with angry pulled divots. As I drag the dull pencil to write over barely erased words and sentences, the whole thing becomes a big gray mess. The last three pages are a collage of light scribbles, blurry eraser marks, and jagged holes. There is a general suggestion of writing, but nothing that could actually be read by anyone, including me.

I gather the crinkled, messy stack of papers together, pound a quick staple in the corner (since just a few hours ago I learned that paper clips cause cancer), and place it inside my English binder. It's not the most genius bit of work I've ever turned in, that's for sure. I won't get an A, I might not even get a B, but I finished it. Over conversations with my monster and with the world's only safe, but unsharpened, pencil, I got it done. Looking down at the tattered paper, I'm filled with a strange mix of both embarrassment and pride.

CHAPTER 9

I push myself up slowly from the carpet, elbows and knees popping against the silence of the room. My eyes meet the clock as I stand: 2:34 a.m. If I fall asleep immediately, I can get three hours of sleep before my alarm goes off.

I cross from the den to my bedroom in a few short steps and collapse into my bed fully clothed. I briefly hear my dermatologist in the back of my head: *Allison, I've told you this before—use this medicine on your skin* every *night*. Shut up, Dr. Rau. I rub my face hard against the pillowcase, smearing my day-old makeup across the fabric. The dirt digs deep into my pores. But my once-infuriating acne has recently slipped much farther down on my ladder of problems.

Lying in bed, I think about the *Les Mis* paper stashed in my book bag only a few feet away. What kind of grade will I get? I feel a tightness rising in my chest. It might be tears, or possibly panic. I picture Ms. Griffin's face as she pulls my mess from the pile of student papers. Her top lip curls up as she pulls the cap off her red pen with a pop.

With one last surge of energy, the fragile outline of my old self tries desperately to ring the bells of alarm. A giant circled F on an assignment worth 25 percent of my grade! I haven't even finished the book! The concern fights hard to be heard, but it's muted against my mind-numbing exhaustion and my soft cotton pillowcase. Who am I? What am I doing? Despite the urgency in my voice, I just can't bring myself to care. Soon a heavy fatigue takes over, and I roll to the side and adjust my pillows. Ms. Griffin, the torn paper, even Sara, drift like ghosts through my mind as I fall deeper into the soft cloud. It's like I'm floating, off into the—

Everything you are touching right now causes cancer.

Almost asleep, I'm swimming through a warm cottony—

EVERYTHING YOU ARE TOUCHING RIGHT NOW CAUSES CANCER.

I jerk awake and my legs shoot out straight and rigid. I hold my breath and don't move, the way I always imagined I would react if I were to discover a burglar in my room in the middle of the night. My eyes are staring wide at the ceiling, heart pounding. Everything I'm touching. A pause. Touching? I'm not touching anything—I'm in bed. Three breaths. I shift slightly and feel the cool top sheet rub against my arm. Maybe I am touching something. Still frozen, I mentally survey my body. I guess I'm touching this top sheet. I glance down my nose at it, trying to stay as still as possible. That means I'm also touching *this* sheet. I envision the beige fitted sheet covering my mattress. I'm touching the duvet, I'm touching my pillows, I'm touching my clothes.

I leap out of my cancer bed onto the carpet. Turning to look at it, I almost see dangerous rays emanating from where my body just was, like heat off a blacktop in the summer. I quickly strip off my clothes and throw them in a pile. Once I'm naked, a headache I didn't even realize I had disappears. The knots in my shoulder muscles loosen slightly. Glancing down at the clothes at my feet, I wonder if a regular washing machine is able to clean out cancer rays. Then

I make a mental note to avoid this set of pajamas in the future. I flail my arms to try to fling any remaining germs off me. Standing next to my bed, I am shivering in the cold night air. The covers were so warm, so comfortable. I crouch slightly, trying to keep as much of my body in contact with itself as possible.

Where do I go? Where is safe?

The blue rug.

The blue rug? I scan my room. The blue rug. A panic rises in me. I don't know what this means! Until I see it. Our upstairs hallway is decorated with two identical, cornflower-blue carpets. I can barely see the edge of the nearest rug through my doorway.

Like a gazelle, I leap toward the small carpet, arms and legs stretched in all directions, and reach it in two bounds. I feel better as soon as I'm standing on it. A tension in my neck releases now that I know I'm safe. It's not that the rest of the carpeted floor is dangerous, I think as I look out into the darkness, but instead that this specific carpet is *chosen*.

It isn't much bigger than a carry-on suitcase, about two feet by three feet. In the pitch-black hallway, I edge my bare foot around the carpet's perimeter, getting my bearings, as my dad snores loudly down the hall. Exhausted, I slowly lower myself into a sitting position and the rug feels warm against my skin. After a few minutes, and with a heavy sigh, I let my head fall forward against my chest. I need to at least try to get some sleep.

I gently feel for the edges of the carpet with my fingers

in the darkness and gather a small collection of dog hair in the process. Scooting, grunting, adjusting, I place myself diagonally on the rug to maximize space. To keep myself safe, to keep my sleepy limbs from wandering to the surrounding beige carpet, I wrap my arms around my legs and squeeze them against myself. Tightly.

My shoulder blades protest against holding on to my legs. I rotate, roll into a ball, lie still for ten minutes, get uncomfortable, rotate, and begin the whole process again. My head is aching, either from sleep deprivation or from resting on the hard floor. There is a small green dot glowing from something electronic in the den. The dog lets out a long, slow groan from downstairs.

At least I finished my paper. That has to be worth something, I soothe myself, as my fingers complain loudly against their grip on my shins. And at least I'm not sleeping in cancer sheets.

I'm jerked awake by my mom's alarm down the hall. Based on the drool on my arm, I apparently got at least a little bit of sleep. I hear my mom rustling in her bed, putting on her slippers, picking up her robe. I'm immediately on high alert, aware of her every movement, ready to dart if she comes too close to her bedroom door. I'm warm from sleep but quickly developing goose bumps all over my body. I can explain fainting and skipping practice and not eating, but *this*—I see myself curled in the fetal position, naked, on the hallway floor—is not something I can hide behind stories and lies. This would set off her maternal alarm.

As I hoped she would, she moves into her bathroom and closes the door and I relax a bit. I wait until I hear the shower turn on before gently rising up from my carpet. Rotating my neck, rolling my shoulders, I stretch out. My joints pop as I move toward my bedroom, a little less steadily than expected. Glancing back at the carpet, I don't know whether to feel gratitude or disdain.

I look down at my bed. All the danger, all the fear I felt so intensely last night is gone with the new morning. It looks and feels like my bed on any other day—no cancer sheets, no death rays. It is somehow different than it was in the exhausted hours of last night. Minutes pass and I stand there, observing the bed. It feels completely safe, even though it was so recently labeled as cancerous.

"Honey," my mom coos as she walks down the hall to wake me up, as she does every morning. "Haven't heard your alarm go off yet. Are you sure you set it?"

Oh no. Mom. Do something. Act normal. I leap without thinking into the bed, roll over, jerk the covers over my shoulders, and close my eyes.

"Sweetie." She turns the corner into my room. "Time to wake up! Up, up, up!" She moves toward me and sits on the edge of the bed. "Hi, you. Good morning!" She strokes my face. I hope she can't tell how hard I'm breathing. "How did you sleep?"

I stretch the way I do every morning. A deep, long stretch starting with my arms and moving down to my legs. I yawn, rub my eyes. "Really well." Another stretch and a groan. "I was so tired from writing that paper, I fell asleep right away."

"Oh, your paper, that's right. I hope you weren't up too late?"

"No, no." I pretend to yawn again. "Not too bad." I nuzzle my head down into my pillow and close my eyes.

She kisses the side of my head and stands up. "Okay, get in the shower. Don't diddle-dawdle. I'm making cinnamon rolls."

Listening to her walk downstairs, I stay still in bed, waiting for the rumble. The attack. The furious monster charging toward me to tell me that my bed causes cancer and I just doomed myself to a painful, short life. Braced against the empty room, I know there has to be a punishment. Last night these very sheets caused cancer. But, surprisingly, all I hear is my mom shifting cookware in the kitchen cabinets. The *Today* show blaring in the background. The heater pumping softly.

I shift around in the bed, rub my hands tentatively against the bottom sheet. My insides are calm. My head doesn't hurt. I have no bees in my ears. It doesn't make sense but . . . these sheets are benign. I'm filled with a wave of relief. Oh, thank goodness. I still have a bed.

But why? my mind insists, projecting itself into my happiness. How are the sheets and pillows safe now when they weren't last night? I'm questioning myself as much as my monster. I don't actually expect him to answer—he only talks when it suits him. Looking at the ceiling, I remember last night's ban on sharpening my pencil, which had only applied to the *Les Mis* paper. It was a temporary rule.

Maybe that's what's going on here. But that doesn't really

make sense, I insist to the air. How will I ever know? How will I keep track of the dangers if some things are permanent and some are temporary? How am I supposed to function if I never—

A rough shake of the floor. An earthquake created by anger. *Don't question me.*

I jerk back to attention like a disciplined soldier in boot camp. I nod once, stiffly, and return to staring at the ceiling, doing my best to stamp down the pushy thoughts in my mind.

After a few minutes, I stand up and walk to the bathroom.

The water of the shower, like always, is calming. My muscles ache from a night on the floor, and I know I have to turn in that horrible paper this morning. But the shower is nice. For now, I feel a little bit better.

Opening the curtain against the blaring lights and winter air, I feel a static in the room before I've even wiped the water from my eyes. Reaching for my towel, my fingertips are stung. Electrocuted. Shocked. By the same hot pink towel I used yesterday and the day before. Different from any message before, it is an electric *NO*. A physical notification of its danger.

I pull my arm back immediately and stumble toward the other side of the shower. The sensation still burns on my fingers, and I shake my hand hard to try to decontaminate it. I picture tiny splatters of cancer flying off the tips of my fingers and sticking to the wall.

I'm dripping and not sure what to do. But looking again

at the pink towel, I know the truth. Towels cause cancer. Not just this one, but all of them. I'm not surprised.

I do my best to wring my hair out before stepping onto the bath mat. I only use my left hand, because I can still feel the electric cancer germs burning on the fingertips of my right. Bouncing around slightly, I try to shake off as much loose water as possible, while scanning the bathroom for a towel alternative. It's warm in here now from all the steam, but I know that a world of icy air waits for me on the other side of the bathroom door. I reach down to pick up a crumpled T-shirt that I wore as pajamas earlier in the week. At least I could use it to dab off parts of my—

That's cheating.

I feel his sneer as much as I hear it. Of course it's cheating! I snap back at him. Anything that could be even remotely beneficial is off-limits. My monster is as committed to making my daily life more difficult as he is to protecting me from danger. I throw the cotton T-shirt back onto the floor and roll my eyes.

I'm quickly ashamed by my thoughts, my tone of annoyance. My protector is guarding me from cancer, from an early death. He was the one to tell me about counting steps, and bartering, and my computer and notebook paper and pencils. Without him, without his guidance, I would be the me in my dream. I'm swept with a wave of deep guilt and quickly usher the rogue emotions into a dark closet in the back of my brain. Glancing around furtively, I hope I hid them before my monster saw.

A puddle has formed under me on the bath mat. How

do I dry off without a towel? I can't use other fabric—that's cheating. But I'm sopping wet—I need *something*. What about a fan? I wait for a response, a rumble, a sign. I picture myself standing under the ceiling fan in my bedroom being blown dry. What about a fan? I ask again internally. The thick humidity of the bathroom is silent.

No response is a good response. I have a plan.

"Allison, breakfast!" my mom calls up from downstairs.

"Coming!" I yell down at her as I swing open the bathroom door. "Two minutes!"

It is a few seconds before I'm hit by the wall of freezing air. The searing cold almost punches the breath out of my lungs and my wet skin screams against its touch. I dart down the hallway, dribbling a trail into my bedroom. With the flip of a switch, my overhead light glares on, and the ceiling fan blasts into action.

Until this moment, I didn't know that the cold could actually make your teeth chatter. I thought that was something invented for slapstick childhood cartoons. But it's real. And it's uncontrollable. On its highest setting, the fan is jerking in violent circles on the ceiling, putting its full effort into cooling me down. I'm shivering wildly, but I rotate my body under the airflow until I look passably dry.

I throw on a sweatshirt and pajama pants from the floor, relishing their warm cotton. My dripping hair immediately soaks a large dark spot onto the shoulders of the sweatshirt.

My morning routine is so mechanical that I almost always arrive at the counter for breakfast in the same five-minute window. Right when Al Roker appears to tell me what's happening in my "neck of the woods."

"I thought you said you made cinnamon rolls?" I say to my mom as I enter the kitchen. There is a boring-looking bowl of Special K at my seat.

"I burned them, sorry. Just have cereal." She notices my crestfallen look. Breakfast is my main meal of the day, the meal my monster typically doesn't have time to steal from. I was looking forward to something hearty. "Oh, please, give me a break. I got distracted upstairs and didn't hear the oven beep. Eat your food. You will be fine." She has no idea. She sits down beside me and turns up the volume on the television.

Reaching past me for the milk, my mother glances at me with a start. "Oh, honey. You really should blow-dry your hair before you come down for breakfast. Or at least wrap it in a towel. You're dripping everywhere." She gently clenches a handful of my hair in her fist, and water falls loudly onto the linoleum. I curl my arms into my oversized sweatshirt for warmth and don't respond.

I'm watching the weather forecast glow at me from the television screen and chewing mindlessly on cereal. It's going to be cold today. Hopefully my hair dries before I have to go outside. Maybe I could wear a hat. Do I own a hat? My winding thoughts are interrupted by a growing sense of agitation. Anger, aggression, annoyance. I can feel the emotions strongly, but it's strange because they seem to be coming from outside me. I know and understand the message, but it isn't my own.

I ready myself against an attack, placing my hands flat against the kitchen counter. Thundering steps. The yelling. This weird feeling has to be a precursor to an angry warning message, like the twinge. My muscles are tight in anticipation, but after a few moments no thought has arrived.

The powerful sense of annoyance and frustration is getting stronger, though. Focusing in on the emotion, I realize it is billowing up from the kitchen barstool underneath me. Like the static from the towel, the cover of the seat is now electric against the bottom of my thighs.

I shoot up from the stool and jump to the floor, my torso knocking into my mom. I hear her grunt slightly, her cereal slosh onto the counter, but I'm staring at the blue-and-white fabric of the seat cover. Without words, it tells me it no longer wants to be sat on.

"What are you doing, honey?" My mom is watching me. Her voice is alarmed, her last words quaking slightly. "Is everything okay?" She reaches out toward me and holds on to my arm. "What's wrong?" She brings her other hand up and laces fingers with me. She's almost as scared of what's happening to me as I am.

The look on her face pulls me three steps closer to reality. Once I stood up, the fierce anger from the stool subsided. It is now only giving off gentle rays of discontent. The furniture version of a sidelong stare. I yank my eyes away from it.

"Oh, no, nothing!" I pivot on my toes toward her. Our eyes meet, and I let out an awkward half smile, half cough. "I just remembered that I have a little bit of homework I need to do before school. Thank you for breakfast!" I spoon in two more mouthfuls of cereal and kiss her on the cheek. She smiles at me, but it's not her real smile. It's not the all-healing maternal smile. It's forced, her cheeks straining under the effort, skin cracking rigidly at her wrinkles. Her eyes are questioning, eyebrows slightly raised. The smile is saying everything that she is trying to keep inside.

One of the kitchen chairs gives me an eyeless wink as I walk by. I flinch, pretend not to see it, and focus on avoiding cracks in the linoleum. I turn to the barstool at the counter and whisper, "You're welcome," as I leave the kitchen.

CHAPTER 10

Upstairs in my bathroom, I feel smug about my recent discovery. I must have some sort of secret telepathy. A way to communicate with furniture.

What I now know to be a cancer towel hangs nefariously from its hooked perch. An aura of death surrounds it, and I keep my arm as close to the opposite wall as possible as I reach for my makeup bag and open the top drawer of my cabinet to get my hairbrush, bobby pins, hair holders. Grabbing the handle of the brush, I feel the sizzle. The electric buzzing inherent in all things dangerous. I pull my hand back immediately, but it has already set something off. I have no time to react, to protect myself or my possessions. The top bursts off the volcano, and lava pours down toward me, sounding remarkably like a swarm of bees.

HAIRBRUSH. HAND SOAP. HAIR HOLDERS.

My eyes swing wildly around the bathroom.

MAKEUP. TOOTHBRUSH. TISSUES.

I lean against the cabinet and stare intently down at the bathroom counter, moving my face to within inches so my entire field of vision is taken up by the creamy white swirls of the granite. After a few moments my thoughts calm, and the bees swarm away into the distance.

Hairbrush, hand soap, hair holders, makeup, toothbrush, tissues. The losses whoosh quietly around my mind, like the debris from a tornado caught in a leftover wind.

Bent over, staring deeply into the white, I let out a long, slow breath.

I look up at myself in the mirror above the sink. My hair, having had about twenty minutes to drip-dry onto my sweatshirt, has formed into icy, wavy dreadlocks. Without a hairbrush, the fine blond strands have knotted together, clumped into tangles. The constellations of pimples across my forehead and chin glare against my pale, malnourished, shivering skin. Dark circles gleam under my eyes.

I give a slight shrug at my ugly reflection. Our eyes connect: Not much we can do about this, I guess. I'm trying to convince myself that it's not that bad, that I don't really need makeup, that I'm one of those girls who is naturally pretty. But the mirror ahead is screaming a drastically different story. I almost don't recognize myself.

In the hallway I ease slowly around the blue mat from last night. My bedroom at the end of the hall is an advertisement for Pottery Barn Teen, a jubilant explosion of color and pattern. The walls are plastered with posters, mostly of baby animals. I have decorated every inch of open wall space between them with handwritten notes from friends, snapshots, celebrity pictures ripped from *Teen People*. The bed, covered in a bright geometric comforter, is layered with pillows and a lifetime's worth of stuffed animals I can't yet bear to relocate to the attic. The huge stereo that used to sing me through my morning routine sits in dusty silence since its ban. It glares at me from the wall, a dark shadow in my otherwise comforting room.

My stomach is grumbling with hunger as I pull open

the double doors to my closet. All my school clothes hang quietly organized in front of me. With my mother's intense work schedule and my own demanding routine of school, practice, and homework, we don't see much of each other during the week. So, to make up for lost time we would spend about one Saturday afternoon a month at the mall in an age-old mother-daughter bonding ritual. Making our way through my favorite stores, she would often comment, "If all it takes to get your teenage daughter to hang out with you is to take her shopping, then why not! Sign me up!"

My wardrobe, and social standing, have benefitted tremendously from her opinion on this subject. My closet is filled with the finest haute couture a midsized town has to offer, and, as a result, the popular crowd at school has been forced to accept me, even if it's just as Sara's friend. *She's a bit shy and cares way too much about school, but look at those boots!*

I take comfort from surveying the collection in my closet. I know I look terrible, soggy and pale, but at least I can dress like myself. I pat my vanity and pride on the back with this one consolation.

It's mid-November. During breakfast, before the stool interrupted, the news told me it was going to be in the low fifties. Flipping through the lineup, I choose a pink cable knit and reach to pull it off its plastic hanger. It's one of my favorite and most expensive sweaters, and this is the first time this year it has been cold enough to warrant wearing it. I specifically remember Melanie Cutten, the notorious leader of Samuelson's own mean girls, complimenting me on it last winter. It seems like the right thing to balance out the rest of my appearance.

I've never not brushed my hair after the shower. I'm vaguely, if not morbidly, curious what it will look like in a few hours. As I grab the sleeve of the sweater and pull with my left hand, I work to unravel a dreadlock with my right.

I'm overtaken by a wave of chills that sweeps through my distracted thoughts. The floor shakes violently, and I brace myself against the closet door. Suddenly, strong hands in rubber gloves grip tightly around my throat. I see a dead body swarmed by flies in an old, abandoned shed. My mother's face as her car slams into a tree. Overtaken with the violent visions searing through my mind, I stumble backward a few steps and the montage immediately stops. The room and my brain fall perfectly silent, and the poisonous static evaporates.

What was *that?* I stand frozen in the middle of the carpet, listening to my heart thud against my ribs. In the back of my mind, I'm almost annoyed at myself for bothering to try to stop my monster from labeling more items. It's not like I have much of value left.

After a few seconds, it's clear the presence is gone. Still shaken, I take a step forward and once again grasp the sleeve of the sweater to pull it off its hanger. Feeling its wool in my hand, I'm slammed from my bedroom into complete darkness. My dad is begging for his life as he's shot in the head. A sweaty, tattooed arm with a bloody dagger rises above me, poised to strike. I throw up my arms against the attacker, let out a painful scream, and crumple to the ground.

I'm dazed on the carpet, back in my room. The images

have disappeared with my fall. Death and tragedy are replaced by the universal beige carpet, the familiar posters and pictures on my wall. I don't move. Swallowing hard against a lump of leftover fear, I'm shaken by all the things I just saw. Each story or warning was filled with terrible, unthinkable violence. Basically a summary of my worst fears. Besides their gore, they all had one other common denominator: contact with the pink sweater that is now swaying four feet above my head.

I can feel the cable knit hanging ominously above me. It is staring, waiting to be acknowledged. With squinted eyes, I slowly move my head to look at what I used to think was one of my favorite items of clothing. Anger is glowing from its threads, its frustration emanating outward in waves. I close my eyes and raise my face to it, in a gesture of both respect and submission. I listen for its emotions, holding open my mind in welcome.

A few seconds pass and I sense it preparing, clearing its throat. A pause. It is furious, it declares into the silence, for having been ignored all summer and fall. Folded up, hidden away in the corner of a dark drawer for months at a time, while striped V-neck T-shirt and blue jeans—it somehow nods to the clothes at the front of the closet—got to spend the entire year in the comfortable closet. *I hate you!* it screams. *Those images were a warning,* it threatens wordlessly. *Wear me again and there will be blood.*

From below, I raise my eyebrows at this direct threat. The sweater is . . . jealous? I rub my palms against the carpet, and as my heart slows, I kind of understand the sentiment.

I wouldn't want to be stored in a drawer nine months out of the year either. But did it have to come to this? It's not my fault there are four seasons.

Rubbing my forehead gently, keeping a safe distance from the row of clothes in my closet, I look closely at each individual hanging piece. It feels like the sweater is the only one with an attitude problem. Without much additional thought, I go to the other side of the closet and pick a silent, gray, long-sleeve shirt, who seems to be a little more understanding.

CHAPTER 11

Today is the third day I've shown up to school with no makeup and tangled hair. The past few days I have feigned illness to explain my ragged, damp mane and bare face. Other students, even Ms. Matthews, have inquired about my health. "Oh my gosh, you look terrible! Are you sick?" I was so nauseous this morning, I say, no time for primping and makeup. Must be that bug, you know? The one going around.

I scuttle between classes, head down, trying to hide my face of gleaming pimples behind my wall of tangled hair. I'm embarrassed and ashamed to my core. My toothbrush has also been banned. I purse my lips against fuzzy teeth and rancid breath.

It's like everyone in the school has heard about me. Maybe not by name, but as the anorexic cross-country runner, or the crazy sophomore, or the girl who counts her steps out loud. I feel it in all the sidelong glances as I tiptoe down the hallway. The slightly squinted eyes and raised eyebrows that say, *What happened to her?* or *Oh, so the rumors are true.*

Each questioning stare is a tiny dagger, and with each stab wound I get more worked up. This is absolutely ridiculous. I *look* absolutely ridiculous. I'm a sideshow attraction. A wet, dripping, pale, ugly monster. I flinch at the last word. A wet, dripping, pale, ugly freak.

But do I really have a choice? Am I just supposed to wear

cancer makeup and brush my hair like it was simply another step in my normal morning routine? Not possible.

The school day is divided into seven class periods and a lunch round. Because each of my classes has its own enormous textbook and dedicated binder, I visit my locker three times a day. Once before first period, once during lunch, once after school. In the morning I put away the binders and textbooks I used for homework and load up my book bag with the things I will need for my morning classes. At lunch I trade my four morning classes for the materials I will need for the coming afternoon. With this system, I'm never carrying more than three or four textbooks and binders at one time, ensuring the weight of my backpack is manageable for my scrawny body.

As I kneel at my locker, unloading the books and binders out of my bag from last night's homework, my knotty hair falls forward over my shoulder. It turns out that in its natural dried state—no towel, no hair dryer, no brush—my hair is a flat, gnarled nest. It begins the morning in wet dreadlocks and progresses through a series of unappealing stages before reaching the final limp, tangled state it's in now.

Over the summer, Sara and I squealed at each other on the phone when we realized our lockers would be close to each other. It didn't make up for being apart for lunch, but it was better than nothing. At least we would get to see each other multiple times a day.

But now, months later, I'm packing my book bag as quickly as possible to avoid running into her. Having lockers near each other, once a cause for celebration, has become one of the main stressors of my school day. I miss her, I miss our inside jokes, I miss her texts. But letting her see me again with no makeup and ratty hair isn't going to help my cause. With her focus on finding an older guy and getting invited to upperclassman parties, I know that this is something she just won't understand, nor tolerate. Both Friday and yesterday, I've felt her glancing at me from her locker, surrounded by a gaggle of whispering girls.

She can't see me today. A third day without makeup, a third day with raucous tangles. I got flustered picking a shirt from my closet this morning and ended up settling on a misshapen turtleneck that I quickly found out is much too small. It's clear I'm not sick. That excuse can only work for so long. This is the new me.

As I hurriedly try to pack up my materials, my schoolbooks and binders angrily voice their dislike of my locker. I will fail all my classes, they threaten, if they have to spend one more minute cooped up in a metal cage. And so, looking over my shoulder for Sara, I quickly shove two additional textbooks into my backpack and wrestle the zipper closed. Like a turtle with an oversized shell, I struggle to my feet under its weight. Moving slowly to maintain my balance, I bend over and wrap my arms around the remaining two-foot-tall stack of grumbling binders and books. Lifting, straining my quads, I clumsily stand upright, about twenty pounds heavier. Once I've pushed the doors open with my back, I wobble down the sidewalk, tiptoeing and counting.

I skip lunch again. I've already bartered away almost all my food for the day and I don't feel like roasting under

Jenny's and Rebecca's suspicious gazes. And how would I explain this enormous stack of books? Note to self: Come up with a good lie.

I follow my newly familiar path past the cafeteria, keeping my head tilted away from the entrance so no one will see my bare face. I'm trembling. Starving. The bowl of cereal I had for breakfast does nothing against a month of not eating lunch or dinner. The weight of the stack of books in my arms pulls me quickly down the stairs and I slam out of the building through the double doors. I half lurch, half tiptoe to my favorite place. My hiding spot behind the cafeteria.

Safe behind the brick partition, I tear open my lunch bag and pull out the bag of cucumbers I am allowed to eat for lunch. It's freezing today. My skin turns a gentle red against the dry November wind. Stuffing two slices of cucumber in my mouth at once, I think of my mother. I could hear her chopping the cucumber this morning while I was getting dressed. Strangely, surrounded by trash cans on an overcast afternoon, I feel a surge of love for her. Quietly, day in, day out, she makes my breakfast, lunch, and dinner. Never complaining, only interested in taking care of her daughter. Popping another slice of cucumber into my mouth, I feel the heavy bagged lunch under my arm. My mom's love-filled creation. In the back of my mind, I recall her explaining her lunch-building philosophy to me one morning as I crunched on a bowl of cereal: "I make either a ham or turkey sandwich, then throw in something salty, something crunchy, and something sweet!" (Warm smile.) My heart surges. My mother! My darling mother! She puts so much effort into these brown bags, and I just . . . I just throw it away? Surely getting rid of something she put so much time and effort into can only lead to tragedy. Throwing her lunch away is basically my telling the world, telling my protector, that I don't care about her. This lunch is a piece of her, and I need to treat it with the respect it deserves.

With that, my passionate speech ends and my mind is silent. I know that I've stumbled onto something important. Its weight sits comfortingly on my heart. I pull my lunch bag out from under my arm and, with a small smile, zip it gently into my book bag.

I arrive early to precalculus, having left my peaceful hideaway as soon as the bell sounded to end lunch. My skin is chapped from the cold air, my nose running slightly. A few steps into the warm classroom, I look up from my counting to find myself directly in front of Sara's desk. I smile at her, out of reflex and naive optimism. For a moment I forget I'm the new me. The pimples. The gnarly hair. The constant counting. Briefly, she's just Sara and I'm just Allison, and my heart leaps as I think that she might have a good tidbit of news for me about Sam. But as we make eye contact, as I feel her examine my undecorated face and tangled hair, as her lips turn down into a frown, I'm yanked back to the present. She pulls her head back in mock disgust, gesturing at the pile in my arms. "Why don't you get a storage locker for all that crap, Allison?" She looks around to make sure the few other students in the room are listening. "Or at least a hairbrush."

• • •

Usually, both of my parents leave the house for work within thirty minutes of me getting up. And I've always appreciated this time alone in the morning. Before my nightmare, it meant I could get away with wearing more or less whatever I wanted to school. That halter top my mom would buy me *only* if I wore it with a sweater? These rules don't apply when there is no one to enforce them. Recently, too, my parents' schedule has allowed me to keep my new views on hair dryers, brushes, makeup, and a growing portion of my school clothes a secret. My parents see me in my early-morning pajamas and my late-afternoon running clothes (which I change into before they get home at night), but never in my actual school-day glory.

It's about eight fifteen a.m., and I'm counting gently to myself as I inch my way across the downstairs hallway. I'm startled when I look up from my toes to see my mom sitting at the kitchen table.

"Hi, hon!" she calls without looking up.

"Uhhh, hey, Mom." I freeze in my steps. "Shouldn't you be at work?"

"I have a dentist appointment at nine. I figured I would drive you to school, then head on over there." She is intently flipping through a magazine and hasn't seen me yet. Holding my breath, I take a few tentative steps back, carefully eyeing the nearby cracks. I need to escape. I can't let her see me. "I figured it would be a nice treat for you to not have to walk, especially in this cold." My mom looks up. And on seeing me, her face immediately changes.

"Allison!" She closes her magazine with a sigh. "You're supposed to be ready! It's eight twenty! We need to go!"

"I am ready?" I glance at her as I walk over to my book bag and the enormous pile of books resting on the kitchen floor beside it.

"This is you ready for school? Wet hair? You didn't even brush it. No makeup. Yeah, right, I think I know you better than this. Now go finish up."

I look at her directly, a rogue tendril of frozen hair glued across my chin. "I. Am. Ready." With a grunt, I throw my book bag onto my back.

"Allison Marie. You cannot go to school with wet hair. Go dry it. Now. And do it quickly." She snaps her fingers at me to draw my attention from adjusting my book bag and points down the hallway toward the stairs. Then she looks at her wristwatch. "Seriously, no more than five minutes. Bring your brush in the car, and you can fix your hair on the way to school."

An icy drop of water falls from my hair and runs down my back. Chills spread across my skin, and I feel anger bubbling rapidly to the surface. Why is she here? I just want to go to school. I just want to be left alone. She has no idea what she is doing. She doesn't know the truth.

"Mom, my hair is fine like it is. I'm ready to go now. Please."

"Allison, it's November, for goodness' sakes. You'll freeze. Just go blow-dry it." She can sense my mounting agitation but misjudges its source. "We're not in that big of a rush. I'll wait, don't worry."

As she is talking, I bend over and lurch the foot-high stack of books into my arms. I lean backward slightly under their weight. After a few moments I find my balance and toddle away from her toward the door to the garage.

"And those books! Honey! Go upstairs and get an extra tote bag. You can't just carry that around like that. It's not good for you. Why do you have so many books? This is ridiculous." She is moving toward me now, arms outstretched, Mom mode activated. "Here, let me get a grocery bag to put all of them in." She is touching my binders, trying to separate them into different stacks. Pulling my book bag off me, she is chattering about overworked students and our aching backs.

With her every motion, or maybe her very existence, my anger rises by a few degrees. My blood is boiling, not at her specifically but at the situation. I don't need her nosing around my life. I have too many secrets and there is too much at risk. She is digging through the pantry for a thick paper grocery bag. I can tell she is still speed-talking, but I don't hear anything through the low buzzing in my ears. I don't want her asking questions. I don't want her interfering. I don't want help!

"Leave me alone!" I scream at the side of her face as she tries to move my English binder from my hands into a brown grocery bag. My fingers clench under the stack of books and I shake the huge book bag on my back violently from side to side. "It's time to *go!*" This is a full-blown temper tantrum. "My hair is *fine*. My books are *fine*." A thread of spit flies across my face. I can feel my skin burning red. *"Get away from me!"* I've only ever screamed at my mother like this

148

through the safety of my bedroom door. I glance up at her under heavy breaths. Her face is expressionless.

There is a full ten seconds of thick silence. My breathing calms as I keep staring down at my book pile. When she finally moves, it is slowly, as if I'm a rabid animal. My mom stares at me. There isn't anger in her face but something else. What is that look? It's not one I've seen before. She licks her lips and nods her head, gathering herself before responding. "That is an inappropriate way to talk to me." I can feel her skin inches from mine, her body heat pouring out from under her suit blazer. "I'm going to blame this on working too hard and exhaustion. I know you're always up late doing homework." We look at each other, but her eyes don't have their usual smile. "But if this ever happens again, *ever*, there will be serious consequences." She turns away from me toward the stairs to the garage. "Let's go."

I galumph slowly behind her. I hear her get into the car, the engine roaring to life. If only she knew everything I'm doing every second of every day to keep myself safe. Then she would get it. Then she wouldn't ask so many questions. But there's no way for her *to* know, I acknowledge begrudgingly, finally reaching the bottom of the stairs. I'm always sneaking around, lying, hiding. I can't expect her to see through walls. But she's my *mom*, I protest to myself. I want her to just be able to feel it. I want her mom sense to tell her something is off. I haven't been eating. I look like a deranged homeless person. Has she really not noticed?

The ride to school is tense, the air so tight it's almost painful. My mom doesn't turn on the radio. The only noise

149

is the occasional whir of a passing car. I know she was only trying to help with her suggestions of drying my hair and paper bags for my books. She was just being a mom. But my life is constantly teetering on the sharpened point of a blade. Each interruption, each outsider with her warm cafeteria cookies and paper bags could be the one who pushes me over, out of equilibrium, into death.

I don't feel bad for yelling at her. I hope she learned her lesson.

CHAPTER 12

It shouldn't really come as a surprise. If I had allowed my mind to look forward, if I had room in my brain to plan ahead, I would have known it would come to this eventually. In a week, my monster has eaten my closet. What started as a few militant sweaters has become a full-blown rebellion. The pink cable knit sowed the seeds of revolution with its point about having been inhumanely stored for the spring and summer months. In droves, with mean looks and enthusiastic middle fingers in the air, the rest of my closet joined its ranks. They had standards. They deserved better. As each of them marched to the dark side, they whispered their consequences: *Wear me and your mother will die.* A vivid image of a rainy day, a mound of freshly packed dirt at the foot of her tombstone. *Wear me and your father will be in a car accident.* A searing picture of my dad's head smashed against the steering wheel, blood leaking down his face and pooling onto his khakis. The airbag didn't deploy.

I stare at the closet doors. There is a low mumble coming from within, but I can't hear any specific messages. I sit quietly in my room for a few minutes, listening to their grumbles, sinking deeper into my own shell. All my clothes are dangerous. I'm awoken by the sound of my dad's garage door banging open. It is the signal in my morning routine that I should already be done getting dressed and close to leaving the house. I'm going to be late. Again. But how do I get dressed? I have no safe clothes. My entire closet is banned.

A complete silence settles into the house now that my dad is well on his way up the driveway. With a long sigh, I slump over, unable to sit upright under the weight of my thoughts. How did I get here? The past weeks have congealed into a thick block, a blur of confusion. Now with pale skin and thinning hair, I barely remember the person who used to live in this room. The collage of posters, photos, and letters plastered across my bedroom walls seem so foreign. The eight-by-ten photo for the yearbook of the cross-country team posing in our bright white jerseys in the blazing sun. The note Sara wrote me with a drawing of Ms. Griffin dancing around in front of the class. The smiling girl who carefully and lovingly covered these walls no longer exists. I am a stranger in my own bedroom.

Wandering to the edge of my thoughts, I find my eyes settled on the large bureau at the foot of my bed. It is topped with picture frames, my banned piggy bank and jewelry box, stacks of books. As imposing as it is heavy, the massive dresser holds eight horizontal drawers. Eureka.

On my knees in front of the dresser, I eagerly dig through the bottom drawer, which spills outward as soon as I open it. Old sports jerseys, matching pajama sets, T-shirts from long-forgotten soccer tournaments. With mounting excitement, I shove my hands deep into the packed drawer. It's a treasure trove! Each of the eight drawers is bursting with a rainbow of opportunity. Pants, shirts, sweatshirts. A small light glimmers within me. Maybe this will be okay. Maybe I can make this work.

I smile smugly to myself as I remember all the times my mother has begged me to clean out this dresser. "There's just so much crap in there," she would say. "Send it to Goodwill. Give yourself some breathing room."

Twenty minutes later, I am standing in the middle of a knee-high mound of clothes. It turns out my mom might have been right. Quantity does not mean quality. I am enveloped by piles of paint-stained tank tops and torn running shirts. Ragged flannel pants and gym shorts from elementary school. I am surrounded by clothes, but I have nothing to wear. At least not in public. Sorting through the mound, I cringe as I think about Sara's reaction to any of them. I see her whispering with her friends at her locker, "What *is* that shirt?" I blush as I imagine their giggling stares against the back of my head while I wobble down the hallway under my pile of books.

I look at the clock. It's 8:50. I'm already late for art. If I don't get to school soon, my parents will get an automated phone call at work that I've missed a class, and that is not something I want to deal with. Just pick something. Staring down at the pile, it's like choosing between two evils. Death by guillotine or electric chair? Neither, thank you.

Pick something! I yell at myself. With a small start, I blindly shove my arm down into the pile and grab on to a sleeve. And with a light tug I pull an oversized gray sweatshirt out from the masses. Holding it up, I see it has a large red cartoon horse racing across the front. I crinkle my nose.

This sweatshirt isn't even mine. It's my friend McKenzie's. I vaguely remember wearing it home from a sleepover at her house once. Apparently I never returned it. Looking down at the pile, I spot a pair of red sweatpants and grab them as well. At least I could match.

I look in the mirror next to my bureau. There is a jagged rip across the right knee of the red pants. My entire kneecap is exposed, the fabric flapping lightly against itself. The sweatshirt is fine . . . if wearing cartoon animals to school when you're fifteen is fine. Dark circles echo under my eyes, contrasting with my pale, almost translucent skin. I don't know how long it's been since I brushed my mangled, dripping hair. It's already soaked cold, dark puddles into the shoulders of my sweatshirt.

I slide into the last five minutes of art and hope that Ms. Michaels never noticed I was missing. As the class bell rings, she walks by and silently slips a detention notice in front of me but doesn't mark me absent. I exhale with relief. The way today is going, I have to consider it a victory.

Tiptoeing my way to second period and creeping into Ms. Griffin's room, I try my best to go unnoticed. I am cowering: shoulders forcefully curled forward, head tilted down so my nest of hair covers my face. I bring my gaze up a few inches, looking ahead at the crack-filled tile floor, and find myself suddenly locking eyes with Sara. She jumps in her desk in surprise, gaping at me in horror, or maybe disgust. Her eyes drill into my scalp while I'm looking down, stepping gently between cracks on the floor. My neck burns. She only turns around as Ms. Griffin clears her throat to begin class.

"Okay, everyone, okay. It's the day you've been waiting for." She holds up a thick stack of stapled papers. "I've graded your *Les Mis* essays." The room bursts into whispers and groans. She begins walking around the classroom, handing out the papers in the order they appear in the pile. "Overall, I was pleased with your efforts. But I was surprised by the lack of thesis statements, given how much we have focused on them this year." She squeezes between desks. "I can see that some of you did not take my advice and left your reading for the last minute." The class fills with guilty murmurings. "Trust me, it showed." She weaves through the rows of desks, leaving behind stunned smiles, blank faces, silent curse words.

A slight nausea rises as I remember the torn paper, the dull pencil, the messy eraser. The long night that followed on the blue mat in the hallway. I'm picking nervously at my nail when I feel her body at my side. Ms. Griffin looks down at me, taking in my sweatshirt, my tower of books, my damp hair. She lays the paper facedown on my desk and taps it gently with two fingers before walking away, continuing her lecture to the class.

I stare at it for a few moments before slowly turning it over, rolling up the edges slightly so my neighbors can't see my grade. In thick red marker across the top is an enormous circled C-minus. Scrawled beside it she has written, *Illegible. Please type.*

A C-minus? A dusty corner of my brain leaps to life. I've never gotten a grade like this! Much less in English class. My mind is whizzing about, suddenly remembering that I care intensely about school. About my GPA. About college! I flip through the pages, scanning her comments, her grammar corrections. On the last page, in the same aggressive red pen, she has written, *Come see me after class.* Underlined three times.

The bell rings and I remain seated. Other students shuffle by me while I wait to be fed my safe number. When I look up, Ms. Griffin is gesturing me toward her desk.

"Miss Allison. How are you today?"

I force a smile. "I'm doing well, thanks! You know, just the usual." I shrug at her.

She nods at me gently and pushes her chair back from her desk. "Allison, we've known each other for how long now? Three months, four?" I shrug again. "Your *Les Mis* paper . . ." She opens her mouth, closes it, seems to rethink her words. "Your *Les Mis* paper . . . it didn't seem like your normal work." She looks at me and I look straight back at her. I have an explanation, but not one that she would understand. With my silence she continues: "I can tell you didn't finish the reading. You didn't really even attempt to answer the question. It's not typed. It's ripped? The last three pages . . ." She stops as I begin to squirm on my tiptoes. I can no longer make eye contact. My heart is pounding as I pretend to be very interested in a poster over her head. "Allison. Sweetie." Staring at the poster. "Allison?"

It's her gentle tone that breaks down the wall, and I suck in hard on my cheeks, trying to mentally stop the tears. I stare at the poster intently until my chin stops quivering and the wetness welling in my eyes soaks back in. When I look down at her, she is still sitting patiently, her left eyebrow slightly raised. "I know, I know." I look up at the ceiling again, willing away the emotions. "I'm sorry. I just, I didn't plan ahead. I got stressed at the last minute and I don't know, I panicked. My computer was broken. I didn't know what to do. I'm sorry." My arms are aching against the weight of my books. I've got goose bumps.

She lets out a long sigh and leans back in her chair, nodding. "I understand that things happen. You have competing priorities. This just isn't what I expected from you, Allison." We look at each other across her desk. "You should have talked to me. We could have worked something out." I choke on my breath at this comment. Highly doubtful, Ms. Griffin. This is a little bit outside your wheelhouse. Mine, too, for that matter. I can see in her eyes that she is genuinely trying to connect with me, to extend a life raft. But we live in different worlds. Her soft voice and questioning expression are comforting, but I know there is nothing she could have done to help me. I'm in this fight alone.

"Promise me you will come to me if something like this happens again." I nod at her, tight-lipped, and almost laugh to myself. No chance in hell.

Although I got control of my tears in front of Ms. Griffin, a thick lump sits heavily in my throat as I tiptoe alone to Civics and Ethics. I set my pile of books down at my desk in the classroom and immediately return to the hallway to use the restroom. I just need to take a few deep breaths.

I'm back from the bathroom only a few seconds after the bell rings. The class is milling about, the sound of chairs

157

scraping across the floor, zipping book bags. I navigate my way toward my desk and see what looks like a giant mound of trash beside my chair. Moving closer, I crane my neck and extend my tiptoes, trying to see what exactly it is. With held breath, as I get within a few steps of my seat, I realize it is just the stack of binders and books that I can't put back in my locker. But I don't recognize the pile that became my full-time companion just three days ago. What started as a stack of binders and textbooks has somehow mutated into a leaning tower of trash. Atop the inside core of school materials there are now dozens of used, crumpled paper towels, tissues, folded sheets of notebook paper.

I look back over the past few weeks and vaguely remember adding some of these treasures to the pile. I've known the truth about trash cans from almost the beginning, and since I started carrying around my stack of school supplies, I've added another damp, crumpled paper towel ball to the pile every time I've used the school bathroom. Including the one I have dutifully brought back with me in my fist from my most recent visit.

In addition to the paper products, there are also multiple bags of food. My ham sandwich from earlier this week, a mysterious bag of dried carrots, an uneaten Fruit Roll-Up. Sitting down in my seat, I see a flattened bag of chips inside my chemistry textbook. A mashed brownie squelching out between two binders.

I've been saving my lunches ever since my emotional revelation behind the cafeteria the other day. Instead of simply leaving my brown bag somewhere on campus, I squirrel away each individual banned item from my lunch into my backpack as a gesture to my mother. I stash a fruit cup in the front zip-up pocket, Tootsie Rolls between the notebook paper in my English binder.

Although I have been intentionally collecting food and paper towels, it is only now, long into my new hobby, that I see what my tower of books has grown into. Somehow it has expanded in height and girth. It looks like the deluded collection of a homeless person who mumbles the day away on a dirty city street. Looking down at the pile, I get a faint hint of terrible stench. The smell of a rotting ham sandwich.

Every student in the county is entered into the pool to be enrolled in driver's education on their fifteenth birthday. In late November, my name is drawn and the official letter sent. A major life milestone for my classmates, the on-the-road portion of driver's education is an important step toward adulthood and independence, an event to be celebrated. To me, however, it is a minefield of potential new discoveries and epiphanies. The best way to keep my mind at bay is silence, routine, staring at large blank spaces for hours at a time, hiding behind brick walls beside Dumpsters. The open road, strangers, a car. It's going to be a disaster.

Driving lessons take place either in the dark early morning before first period or in the setting sun after school. Since my parents think I am attending indoor track practice every afternoon (cross-country ended in late October), I show up to my first driving class on a frosty November morning. I am wearing red, white, and blue flannel pants and a tattered T-shirt from a long-past soccer tournament.

Although I don't quite need to wear a bra yet, the feel of the straps against my skin gives me a boost of confidence. Their outlines through my shirt prove that I am, in fact, a girl. This morning, to my complete embarrassment, all the contents of my "intimates" drawer—underwear, bras, tank tops—were banned. I sit in the front seat of my mom's car, self-consciously crossing my arms tight against my chest.

My mom pulls up in front of the school administration building behind a black Ford Crown Victoria, a generic version of the patrol cars used by local police. Compared to my mom's sleek sedan, it looks like a boat. A very slow boat.

I push open the passenger door and tiptoe over to a tall man who I assume is the instructor talking to another female student around my age. An icy blast of wind whips itself across the open parking lot, and I jerk convulsively inward, grabbing my thin, torn T-shirt against my skin. The gust pushes against my clothes, forcing them to wrap around me, exposing my bony silhouette. For the first time, I realize how skinny I've become. I can see my ribs protruding through the thin cotton. My thighs are only skin wrapped against rattling bones.

"Well, doggone, girl! It's winter! Where is your jacket?" The tall man, noticing the other student's distraction, says as he looks over toward me too. His entire face is lit up as he waves me over, his mouth spread into a gap-toothed smile.

"I've been trying to tell her that all morning!" My mom's voice pipes up anxiously from behind me. "All month, actually." She is walking quickly toward us, the door to her car still ajar, and extends two jackets in her hands. I turn and look longingly at the fleece in her left and the wool pea coat in her right, but they're not safe. They're from the closet. A furious static is billowing like smoke from their fabric. I can see it searing into her skin. A lump pops to life in her left breast, and as she moves closer to me, their poison begins to sting against my skin as well. An immediate, fierce anger rises from my stomach with the peppy edge of my mom's voice and her inability to just leave me *alone*. Mind her own business.

I swing quickly on my toes to face her. "Mom, I told you." My teeth are gritted, my hands clenching in fists against my legs. I can smell my own sour, rancid breath as it puffs into clouds in the air in front of my face. It's been more than a week since I've brushed my teeth. Bees buzz furiously in my ears and I close my eyes against their noise, trying to concentrate. My legs are shaking under my pajama pants. From either frost or fury.

"Come on, honey. It's literally freezing outside. Please. Take a jacket."

"I said, *no jacket*." The words shoot out of my mouth, fueled by the pent-up emotions of the morning: losing my intimates drawer, shivering under dripping, frozen hair. "Why don't you *listen* to me?" I'm screaming, my arms pushed rigidly down to my sides with clenched fists. I pause to catch my breath. *Well?* I ask her with my eyes, daring her to try to respond. My mom's face is stunned, her eyes opened wider than I have ever seen them. "Go to work." I whip back in the other direction, leaving my mom to gape at me from behind and find my teacher and the other student trying to hide the surprise on their faces. They both smile at me hesitantly, the way you look at someone who has just screamed at her mother in front of strangers. The way you stare at a girl wearing a holey T-shirt when there is frost on the ground.

As I hear my mom's car pulling out of the school parking lot, the tall man straightens his back, claps his hands together, and takes a deep breath. "Well, I'm Mr. Stowe. Your driver's education teacher." He smiles at us both like it's a sunny spring day. I wrap my arms tightly around my chest and look down at the ground. As he shows us the outside of the car, as we test the tires and adjust the mirrors, he tells us about his fifteen years of experience, his passion for teaching. "There ain't nothing better than preparing young people for a life on the road. It's my calling, I'll tell ya. It's the Lord's will."

We pile in the cumbersome car, Mr. Stowe talking incessantly. The other student, whose name I now know as Maria, takes the wheel first. I contentedly settle into the backseat, eager to put off my first encounter with the unknown. Mr. Stowe, I quickly find, is buoyantly happy and deeply religious. Before we have left the parking space, as we test the windshield wipers and the turn signal, I have been invited to attend his weekly Sunday school class at the local United Methodist Church. As Maria eases her way around the deserted parking lot, he flips on the Christian rock station and hums along happily.

Halfway through the lesson, we stop at a McDonald's for a breakfast break. Comfortable in the restaurant's warmth,

I stare up at the illuminated menu. I half expect angels to break into a chorus of "hallelujah." Look at all this food! And I haven't traded anything yet this morning.

With the greasy wrapped meal loaded onto my tray, I walk quickly to the small table Mr. Stowe and Maria have found in the back of the crowded restaurant. This is the most food I will have eaten in weeks. Before I even reach our table, my Egg McMuffin is unwrapped, its melted cheese stuck deliciously to the buttered bread. I tear into it, ravenous for calories, as I sit down in my seat. I bend the hash brown into my mouth in one bite. Heaven. Reaching back for the sandwich, mouth still full of fried potatoes, I see Mr. Stowe's extended hand, feel his patient eyes on my bulging cheeks. We make eye contact and he wiggles his fingers at me. I see he is already holding hands with Maria. Oh.

I place my greasy fingers in his palm and he swiftly drops his head. "Dear Lord, thank you for Maria and Allison. Thank you for creating them in your image. Thank you for making them exactly who you want them to be. Please keep us safe on the road, and safe in your heart. Amen." He lifts his head with a deep inhale. I've been staring at the bald patch on the top of his head the whole time, stunned. I look at Maria and she gives me a slight shrug.

He launches into conversation, moving on from the prayer like bowing your head in a crowded McDonald's is a normal thing to do. "Now, the most important thing for y'all to take away from our time together is, of course, driving safety. But I hope you will also learn a little something about the Lord, our Savior."

● ● ●

Driver's ed is a two-week course. Three days into my time with Maria and Mr. Stowe, I find myself looking forward to our early, quiet hours in the warm car. Maybe it's the muffled Christian-music station in the background, or Mr. Stowe's soothing voice guiding me through the empty morning roads, but my brain is perfectly, if unexpectedly, silent. There are no warning messages about the road or the car. White lines, traffic lights. There are so many opportunities for my monster to pounce, but for some reason he continues to sleep. I feel no bees swarming in from the distance, hear no screaming alarms. It is the first time I've felt even the slightest bit like myself since my nightmare.

For the first few days, I only hear Mr. Stowe's voice, not his words. I know he is talking about religion or Sunday school or, worse, the rules of the road, so I block it all out. But his deep accent and gentle tone alone are enough to lull me into peace. Looking out the window, relaxing in the privacy of the backseat, listening to him talk makes me feel normal. Just a girl in driver's ed. Just a girl with no thoughts, watching the world pass by.

My family is by no means religious. Growing up, we went to church to appease my grandparents, who lived nearby, but this habit stopped around the time I entered middle school. I don't remember much about church or Christianity other than the hard wooden pews and thick red hymnals. My grandma's firm but gentle hand on my leg when I was making too much noise. Church is something other people do on Sunday mornings while my mom and I are running errands and

164

eating Panera. Mr. Stowe's monologues about Jesus and the Lord's will and an assortment of other buzzwords I have only heard while flipping channels past televangelists are strange to me. I nod along politely to his sermons, more focused on enjoying my time in the upholstered backseat. His view on the world, the central reason for his existence, is foreign to me. But interesting.

It's Thursday and sunny. Despite the still-chilly temperatures, and the usual goose bumps running rampant under my thin sweater and pajama pants, I'm feeling an edge of happiness today. I look down at the cat cartoons that decorate my pajama pants and, for some reason, feel the small tickle of a smile. Mr. Stowe is lecturing at no one in particular. He doesn't seem to mind if we are listening.

"I sure wouldn't want to be a youngster these days, I'll tell ya." He fidgets with the loose tassel on his well-worn leather loafers. "I always say to the kids in my youth ministry—be yourself! God made you this way. You are perfect in his image. And if the Lord likes you the way you are, then you should stay just like that! It's God's will, you know?" He looks at Maria, who glances at him and gives a small nod.

"All these magazines, TV shows. They say, be this! Be skinny! Be immoral! But, no, that's not the only way. I'm telling you, girls. God made you like you are for a reason. You gotta honor that." He looks down and rubs his ankle as if in thought. "Oh, Maria! Turn left here." He lurches forward. "Turn signal." The car tilts around the bend, and I lean with it. "Well done! Very good!" I straighten up as we merge onto Peachtree Road and drive past the place where I fainted. That whole experience feels so far away.

I rest my arm against the door and look out the window without seeing anything, Mr. Stowe's words echoing around my mind. What does he mean, everything is God's will? What does he mean, we are perfect in his image? It's almost another language, but I find myself drawn to it. It's comforting. Maybe there is no monster inside me. Maybe I'm exactly as I should be. If God makes everything perfect, maybe these messages, these thoughts, are also perfect? Maybe they're from him?

That's it. The world around me melts away, and my entire body focuses on this thought. I feel something inside me hum to life. That's it. Clearly. The voices. The monster. The warnings. It's God. These are his messages, I am his vessel. I sit in the backseat, eyes wide with this realization, and everything suddenly makes sense. I immediately stop picking at the bloody hangnail on my thumb and instead smooth it down gently with my index finger. God is trying to tell me the truth. He wants to protect me, and he wants me, in turn, to protect others. To carry out his mission. Looking out the car window, I realize that I am not cursed or crazy. I'm *chosen*. I am special. My heart and ego swell with this knowledge. God wants my help. God needs me.

That night, I find our unused family Bible on the bookshelf, crack the spine, and begin reading it with fervor. I start reading it every day. Like my number of safe steps, each time I perch in front of the Bible I am told either how many pages I need to cover or for how many minutes I need to read. I delve into the book in earnest, concentrating on each word, attempting to learn as much about my newly discovered protector as possible.

Each morning of driver's ed, we hold hands and bow our heads over a small table of wonderfully filling fast food. Mr. Stowe gives thanks for me and Maria, asks God to guide us through our days. As I raise my head and open my eyes, I feel a warm, strong presence on my shoulder. My protector telling me he cares. Inspired by Mr. Stowe, I begin to make a conscious effort to pray more, to show my gratitude for another day cancer-free. I pray at breakfast, lunch, and dinner. I pray when I drink. I pray when I see anything that is banned, asking for protection from its evil death rays.

Soon, though, my mumbling, disorganized efforts don't seem to be enough. God is getting antsy. He wants more. I spend all of my lunch period on Tuesday behind the cafeteria creating a long, formulaic prayer that feels complicated enough to make my protector happy. I think of my favorite football players and their joyous celebrations after winning touchdowns. They point at the sky, they fall to their knees, they bow their heads in public, unashamed to show their gratitude. I want something like that. Anyone can say the words. I want to take it a step further.

Envisioning muscled NFL players in the end zone, I decide that after each prayer I must touch my heart with my fist, pound on it twice, then extend my arm completely in the air and point toward heaven. This is how I will show my true dedication. This is how my protector will know I am thankful.

CHAPTER 13

The kitchen air is thick with the spice of jambalaya, one of my favorite meals. I'm sitting in my usual seat, looking at the steaming pot in the center of the table. Unlike most dinners, jambalaya is served in a bowl by itself, no sides, no bread. Based on my successes and failures this afternoon, I am allowed to eat one side dish tonight. Looking at the bowl in front of me, I decide this means I can only eat one individual ingredient out of the jambalaya. I choose the sausage.

My parents join me at the table, and we begin serving ourselves in heaping spoonfuls. My mom is looking at my dad. They're talking intensely, but I'm not listening.

"Jeffrey, I just don't think that's right. It doesn't make sense." My mom is shaking her head.

"Look, I understand, but there's not much . . ."

With my forehead pressed against clasped hands, I'm halfway through my scripted prayer when I hear them stop talking. I know they're looking at me, but I continue, eyes closed, until a heartfelt "Amen." In the darkness, I hesitate, holding my fist in front of my heart. I feel my parents' eyes on me, a few furtive, concerned glances at each other. Are you thankful for your protector? I ask myself. Of course I am. He is the reason I am alive!

Then you must show him.

After a second of pause, I pound my fist hard against my chest twice and defiantly extend my arm toward the ceiling.

It feels good, knowing that I have just pleased the creator of the universe. But, at the same time, a cold panic bleeds through me as I think about my parents. I open my eyes, my arm still wavering, pointing, in the air and look straight down at my bowl. With my other hand, I mull through the rice and veggies, stabbing at the chunks of sausage.

The room is silent. They're still staring at me. This prayer formula is perfect, obviously, but impossible to conceal. Until this moment, I've been able to hide my new religiosity from everyone. My mom clears her throat.

"Allison, honey, are you . . . did you just . . . pray?" she asks timidly.

"Why don't you leave me *alone*?"

I feel my mom's head jerk back in surprise. My father continues to chew silently but lifts his eyes toward me, raising his eyebrows.

"Young lady, watch your tone. You—"

"Mom, I'm serious. *Stop*." I'm shaking with anger, or embarrassment. These furious outbursts have been our main form of interaction for a few weeks. I know they are inappropriate, but they're also highly effective. They stun my mom into submission.

My parents exchange a long, meaningful stare. Forks scrape gently against our bowls. No one speaks for the rest of the meal.

I wiggle slightly to adjust the position of my knees. After thirty minutes, even the plush carpet has started to dig uncomfortably into my skin. I'm crouched, shins against the floor, reading the mammoth blue Bible that has become one of my closest companions. My stomach rages with hunger, complaining about the too-few pieces of sausage I fed it at dinner. It is two thirty a.m., and I am wide awake, camped out on the floor of the den. The jarring overhead light casts my shadow over the Bible's pristine, open pages. I am under strict instructions to read until at least three forty-five a.m.

Through the darkness I hear shifting around the curve of the hallway, and my muscles lock. My parents spent the rest of the evening after dinner whispering loudly behind their bedroom door. I know they were talking about me. Torn between my only-child need to please my parents and my duty to please my protector, I sat sheepishly in the den, scratching out an attempt at homework with the world's only safe pencil. I want to show my respect to God, I just wish my parents didn't have to see.

With the sound of an opening door, I close my eyes against the possibility of discovery. How will I explain this? My heart pounds in panic. Down the hall I hear mumbles. "What's that light?" My dad.

I keep my eyes glued to the black-lettered page. As the noises grow closer, I feel him and see him in the doorway. He is rubbing his face or head. Now his shoulders. His neck cracks. The floor creaks. "Allison," he croaks through hours of sleep, "what are you doing?"

I keep my eyes focused on the words. I have to read until three forty-five. A terror rises in me as I realize my dad may send me to bed before I can finish my assignment. I have to read until three forty-five. Or else. "Dad, hi." I look up at him with what I hope to be a casual glance. "Yeah, I'm studying. Doing homework." I nod at him in silence until he clears his throat and squints at me through the foreign light. He cranes forward a bit, examines me and my big blue book.

He knows it's a Bible. I know it's a Bible. I'm reading the Bible. At two thirty a.m.

"Just . . . go to bed. Soon." He continues to look at me until I nod at him. Exhaling meaningfully while rubbing his goatee against his palm, he lingers for a moment. He gestures slightly, opens his mouth to speak, then turns back down the darkness of the hallway. Readjusting, I look back to my book, not sure what to feel about being let off the hook.

Later in the week, I come home to a brand-new tote bag lying innocently on my bed. I run my hand over it, examining the beige, flowered fabric and beaded accents. It's really pretty, and, looking inside, I discover it's from one of my favorite stores. For a moment I think that maybe it's a gift from God. But then I know. My mom. She saw me carrying my book pile a few weeks ago when she drove me to school. I'm sure she's noticed its growth (and stench) as it sits innocently beside my book bag on the kitchen floor each night. My heart floods with warmth. I've been so mean to her, so terrible. She probably knows I'll yell at her if she gets too close, if she even looks like she might ask a question. So she left the bag here for me to find it on my own.

The next morning, I gleefully pack my new bag with

about half my stack of books and throw it over my shoulder. Without the full weight in my arms, I feel like I'm walking on air. I bounce across campus with relief.

With the additional space that the new tote bag provides, I have much-needed room to store the leftover items from my lunches. Behind the cafeteria each day, I reverently move the individual Ziplocs from my brown paper lunch into my tote bag and backpack. Moldy blueberries, squished to a pulp under pounds of books, leak through the front pocket of my book bag. Four cheese sticks get stuck inside my math binder. There are muffins, rotten bananas, discolored turkey sandwiches. A snack pack of Jell-O bursts open under a textbook, staining all my school papers with a red, sugary tint. Soon a cloud of smell follows me through school. A sharp, ragged odor, violent to the nose. It's the scent of rotting lunch food and my mother's safety.

I trudge up my driveway after school. Shivering uncontrollably, I want to break into a run and launch myself into my warm house. But I don't have enough energy. I can't move any faster. This morning I was ecstatic to find a thick, safe sweatshirt hiding in the back of one of my drawers. Unfortunately, I was forced to match it with a tiny pair of running shorts designed for the depths of summer. Their flimsy mesh fabric has a slit deep up my thigh, encouraging airflow. Throughout the day I've noticed my chapped, exposed kneecaps turning a threatening shade of blue. I stop momentarily at our black iron mailbox, which is surrounded by a wilted, frozen flower bed. Leafing through the pile of mail as I near the front door, I find a thick, bright-pink envelope addressed to me. The handwriting is a swirly cursive. For a moment I can't be sure that it's actually my name through all the loops and curls. My fingers are clumsy with cold as I try to rip open the envelope, and when I finally get it, thick glitter flies out into a small cloud, getting in my mouth and lilting through the air across the front yard. I'm looking down at a square invitation covered in sparkles. The edges are cut to look like lace and a faint air of perfume wafts up from the paper.

You are cordially invited to

the birthday party of Melanie Cutten

January 7th

Cocktail attire requested

Melanie Cutten! *The* Melanie Cutten! My heart leaps in excitement. A sophomore who looks and acts eighteen, she is the undeniable queen bee. The auburn-haired, double-D-ed, designer-jean-clad leader of the pack. As stuck-up as she is beautiful. And *I'm* invited to her birthday party?

The winter breeze blows the remaining glitter off into the grass and I stare blankly at the delicate invitation in my hand. It briefly occurs to me that this could be a mean joke. The popular kids invite the weird girl to a party and then dump dog food on her head so she runs home in tears. But, no, I think. She must have made her invitation list before things . . . happened to me. Before there was any hint that I might show up to school in pajamas and no makeup. Carrying two bags full of rotting lunch food.

My frozen fingers fumble with the front door keys, finally getting the cold metal into the lock on the third try. I tiptoe straight to the kitchen, loudly drop my school supplies to the floor, and resume my inspection of the invitation, which I've found includes a small RSVP card. There are two options, each with a blank beside it for an answer: *Yes! I would love to help Melanie celebrate her sixteenth birthday!* or *No, I hate fun and don't want to come to the party.* Right. There is clearly only one correct answer to this question. I reach instinctively for a pen on the counter to draw a giant check mark beside the *Yes!* but recoil my hand at the last second. No pens. With a sigh, I bend down to my book bag and rummage around in it, looking for my safe pencil. I'm arm-deep in the bag when I feel its dull point and wrap it in my hand. As I'm standing up, I hear enemy planes overhead. Their buzzing, similar to an angry hive, is distant but quickly flying closer. Soon their rumble is partnered with the whistle of falling bombs, and the floor thunders violently under my feet. *You. May. Not. Go.* The bombs smash into the ground, shaking the house. Each explosion an exclamation point: *No parties! Cancer! Cancer! Cancer!* As loud and terrifying as the noises are, as hard as the explosions shake the earth, I stand perfectly still and calmly let the invitation flutter out of my hand to the floor.

Now that I know that my thoughts are direct messages from God, I have no reason to fear them. They're not coming from a mysterious monster or some other unimaginable demon in my brain. It's the *Lord*. The great *I Am*, the alpha and omega, and all the other things I've learned from my intense Bible reading. He's got the whole world in his hands, as the song from my childhood says, but I'm his favorite. And if God says I shouldn't go to Melanie's party, then that's that. No questions asked.

I bow my head, recite the prayer formula, pound my chest twice, and point toward the sky.

I let out a deep sigh. By now I'm used to this kind of disappointment. It doesn't sting the way it used to. And, looking down at the invitation on the linoleum, she specifically asks for cocktail attire. I don't think anything from my bureau would be deemed appropriate. Sara will be there. And the giggling girls who follow her around now. And Jenny and Rebecca. And Kelsey Jameson, the girl who laughed at me in the cafeteria. It's all probably for the best, I tell myself. At least I was invited.

This week is final exams, a ten-foot-high wall between me and Christmas break. With a groan and all of my strength, I lurch my book bag up onto the kitchen counter, glitter rubbing from my hands onto its black straps. I've started doing all my homework down in the kitchen now, since my desk and chair upstairs have been banned. I stand on tiptoes between the two barstools, which are emitting low-toned static, their version of a friendly reminder that they don't like to be sat on.

Samuelson has designed final exams to be one last-ditch effort at dooming our hard-earned GPAs. After months of lectures, homework, and quizzes, 25 percent of my semester grade in each course rides on these final tests. Four months of completing all my assignments, four months of acting interested in class, can all be ruined by one fateful three-hour exam session. Since my nightmare, I haven't been the same student I used to be. In early October, I ranked in the top ten in my class of more than three hundred students. I now spend my once-focused school days counting my steps, mentally repeating the contents of my lunch, staring at my toes to avoid cracks. With knotted hair and rotting breath, I don't participate in class. My embarrassment at my appearance keeps me closed within myself. My grades have suffered, obviously, but the strong foundation I set in the first two months of school have kept things more or less afloat. So far. I need to do well on exams or I risk not just hurting my GPA but ruining it. A semester of anything more than one or two Bs will dash any hope I had of an Ivy League education, the chance to leave this sleepy town and experience the world. I've done the math. I need to ace all my exams if I want a chance of getting above a 3.0 GPA this semester.

Exam week is a rigorous five-day marathon. Each day is segmented into two exam slots, and every student's seven classes are divvied up among the openings, rotating the exhausted student body systematically through the week. In a cruel twist of scheduling, I have my two hardest classes, chemistry and precalculus, on sequential days. Chemistry is tomorrow, precal on Friday. My shoulders sag under the weight of my future. It's going to be a long forty-eight hours.

I lean down and work to pull my chemistry binder and textbook out of my overcrowded backpack. The bag is stuffed so tightly that when I am finally able pull them out, my English book and two decaying sandwiches follow along and flop onto the floor. Flipping open the binder, I'm attacked by a heavy odor of rotting food. I gag violently and take a few steps back, eyes watering. The edges of all the notes clasped in the binder are tainted a watery brown. A mixture of old spilled Jell-O and the mystery juices that have seeped out of sandwiches, blueberries, and oranges crushed under textbooks. The smell is overwhelming. Even breathing through my mouth, I can feel it stinging the inside of my nostrils.

I pull out the final-exam study guide Ms. Matthews provided us in class last week. My stomach snarls at me, no longer begging for food but demanding it. I'm light-headed. But I need to study. Final exam tomorrow.

I flip through the multipage study guide, and as I turn to the last page, the damp, dirty corner of the paper slides across my forearm. Its cool ooze leaves a trail on my skin, thick like glue. My breath catches in my throat, and I'm gagging again as I stare at the phlegmy sludge on my wrist, trying hard to fight back the quick burst of nausea pushing up my throat. My stomach is turning violently, and I step backward, trying to aim my incoming vomit away from my schoolbooks.

After about a minute the feeling begins to pass, and I straighten up. I fling my arm hard, and the disgusting line of brown mucus flies off it. I haven't moved back to the counter yet—I'm still recovering with long, slow breaths—when I see my foot. Planted flat. On a crack in the kitchen floor.

The world stops. Everything is silent. And then—

CALCULATOR. NOTEBOOK PAPER. APPLES.

Oh no. No, no, no. Not here. Not *here*. Not *now*. My mind races into action, stumbling over itself as it tries to stop the hemorrhaging.

SHARPENING THE SAFE PENCIL DURING EXAMS. CHEMISTRY EXAM. There is a pause, and I can feel the kitchen being searched for another victim. There isn't much left. *PEANUTS. SALT AND PEPPER.* The presence is faltering. Sputtering as the options dwindle. I feel my eyes settle down onto the bright green running shorts I'm wearing under the huge sweatshirt. *THE COLOR GREEN.*

And with a release in pressure, just like usual, the tension quickly filters out of the air and I'm left in silence. A heavier silence than I've ever known. Without realizing it, I bring my hand up to my head and rub it hard against my forehead and eyes, letting out a long, deep sigh. I'm not able to cry. I just don't have the energy. But if I could, I know I would be sobbing.

I look up at the counter, the site of most of the massacre. Apples, peanuts, salt and pepper. They are filed away calmly in my crowded brain next to potatoes, oatmeal, bananas. All the other food items that, while missed, are manageable obstacles in my life. I know there are more victims waiting, big ones I will have to address and figure out how to move past. But I hesitate, holding on to the moment. Do I really want to know the truth?

Calculator. The idea pushes itself into my mind and I cuss harshly under my breath. Words I don't think I've ever said out loud. I'm on the eve of my two math-related finals, and I've lost my calculator. Freaking perfect. I was so proud of my plastic TI-83 calculator when we bought it at Staples over the summer. It's twice as big as my palm, and holding it made me feel immensely intellectual. Like I wanted to build rockets or solve giant equations on chalkboards. Or at least get an A in precalculus. I look up at the black calculator sitting smugly a foot away, and with a blast of rage, I shove my chemistry binder toward it so it flies off the counter, landing on the linoleum with a loud crack that echoes through the kitchen. Good, I think, it deserved that. I hope it's broken.

Notebook paper. My body groans against this one, which pops back into my head with the crash of the calculator. Notebook paper is an essential. Homework, essays. I need it. But, I think with an edge of optimism, I don't really use notebook paper during exams anyway. It's most important for homework assignments and taking notes in class. This one can wait until next semester. I shovel it over the fence in my mind. A problem for another day.

Safe pencil. My brain freezes. Safe pencil. The only writing utensil in the world can now apparently not be sharpened during exams. Over the past few weeks, I've written it down to a three-inch nub, barely big enough to grip in my hand. As I stare without seeing at the kitchen counter, I'm also reminded: chemistry exam.

Chemistry exam? My mind leaps in urgency. What does that mean? Like the whole test? The paper it's made of? I'm whizzing around the possibilities, each just as threatening as the one before. There is an emptiness in my chest. The feeling of my life melting down.

What do you mean, chemistry exam? I pose the question in my mind again, like I would have to my monster. But, I wonder, does God hear my thoughts? Does God listen to the confused, whimpered questions of a war-worn fifteen-year-old? I wait in silence, eyes closed, hoping for some sort of golden, glowing message to float down from the heavens. Tilting my head back in a gesture of openness, I lift my face to the ceiling, asking for an answer. A whisper. Something.

I stand in this position until my neck begins to complain. And by this time, at least a few minutes later, a growing gurgle of annoyance has developed in my stomach. Helllooooo? I offer into the silence, and it echoes like it would through a haunted house. I am completely alone. Abandoned.

This is my chemistry final! Worth 25 percent of my grade! What is going *on*? I am yelling at God, stomping, throwing a dramatic temper tantrum in my mind at his silence. These are my *grades*. This is my *future*. And you just mess around with it as you please? Like it's no big *deal*? The thoughts flow out of me before I can censor them. I don't have time to even hear what I'm saying before they've been delivered to the creator of the universe. My anger quickly transforms to fear as I realize what I've said and, more important, who I'm saying it to.

I immediately swing my head down to the counter and fill my vision with its vast white nothingness. Although it feels like there isn't much more in my life to lose, I thought the same thing ten minutes ago and sacrificed my calculator and notebook paper as a result. My mind calms a little looking at the white countertop. After a while, like a small child peeking out from behind its mother's leg, I tentatively raise my eyes to the ceiling. A quiet plea. Please help me, Lord. Tell me about the chemistry final.

I feel a sudden warmth in my heart like I've just offered up a heartfelt prayer. And within a few moments, he is here. Maybe it's not God himself, but it's something special and powerful. I can feel it in the air.

If you pass your chemistry final, your mom will die.

The statement isn't spoken. It just *is*. Unlike previous messages, it doesn't appear like an epiphany. Instead it's revealed as a long-held fact. Something that always has been and always will be true. A rule of Mother Nature.

And because you questioned me, you must stand on one foot until someone else gets home.

Or else.

I flinch at the suggestion, more from confusion than anything. I peer into the white countertop, eyes squinting. Stand on one foot . . . ?

What?

I look up at the clock on the microwave. It's only four p.m. Another two or three hours before I can expect one of my parents to get home from work. I slowly raise my left leg up like a flamingo, unsure of why exactly I'm doing it. It makes no sense, to be standing on one foot in my silent kitchen until my parents get home, but I have to admit that something about it feels right. The sound of two puzzle pieces clicking perfectly together. I wobble back and forth on my right foot, eventually finding my balance. God, it seems, is just as sensitive as my monster. He doesn't like to be challenged.

The minutes crawl by as I teeter from side to side. I'm going to fail my chemistry exam tomorrow. On purpose. To save my mother's life. I know it is both perfect and ludicrous. It is the truth but it's unbelievable. If I hadn't heard it from God himself, I think, I might try to fight it. Maybe barter a week's worth of food in exchange for not having to fail. But this is God. The be-all and end-all.

The sun dips below the horizon as I gaze out the kitchen windows, still perched on my right foot. I haven't moved since the warning. I'm not sure if I'm allowed to. There weren't very specific details provided from the beginning, and it doesn't seem like it's okay to ask. So I stand frozen, trying my best not to look at my open chemistry binder and the accompanying study guide spread on top of it. I wasn't told to not study for the test, but it just seems like I shouldn't. If I'm going to fail this exam, I want to do it the right way. The honest way.

One hour and thirty-seven minutes later, as I teeter on my screaming right ankle in the pitch-black kitchen, a garage door clangs to life below me. And I'm free. My knee pops as I lower my leg to the floor.

I gather myself for a few seconds, tiptoe over to the light switch on the wall, and flip it on, bathing the kitchen in light. I pick up my English binder from the floor and open it across the counter. Lowering my head toward its pages, I pretend to be studying intensely as my dad reaches the top of the stairs coming up from the garage.

"Honey, I'm home." He stomps into the kitchen doing his best *I Love Lucy* impression.

"Hi, Dad!" I glance at him over my shoulder and force a toothy smile. A grin that means a thousand different things, except the one he would assume. He and I used to have warm, lengthy conversations almost every night after my mom went to bed. As I try to hide my bare face from him, I realize we haven't really spoken in weeks.

There are only two good things about exam week. First, the tests don't start until ten a.m., so I get to sleep in. Second, I don't need any of my school materials for the exams, so I don't have to lug my giant pile around campus.

It's the second point that has me feeling a slight peep of relief this morning, despite what happened yesterday afternoon and despite what I know is ahead. Counting, tiptoeing down the concrete path toward the science building, I am bouncing on clouds. I sway my arms self-consciously at my sides. I've forgotten what to do with them when they're not holding the majority of my life's (safe) possessions. Do I just let them hang? I lift my hands to my jeans pockets, then remember I'm not wearing jeans but instead a light-blue pair of flannel pajamas. My hands fall back down to my sides awkwardly.

Squinting into the morning sun, that's when I see it. Green grass. Green bushes. Green fir trees. *Green. Green. Green.* Everywhere green. The air is suddenly clogged with a thick, invisible smoke. I take a breath in and almost choke. Holding on to the tiny amount of oxygen I have left in my lungs, I run toward the brick science building and launch myself through the glass doors.

I'm gasping, drinking in clean air, but the frenzied, tight-lipped stress of my classmates brings my focus to the exam ahead. Everyone around me is staring feverishly down at papers or notes. I count us all to class while trying to catch my breath.

Preston Lassiter reaches the door of Ms. Matthews's classroom at the same time I do, and we stop awkwardly, each trying to wave the other person through first. We step forward at the same time again, jerk to a stop when we see the other move, and step back. Preston is my main competition when it comes to nudging myself into the top five in the class. There are some kids I know I can't pass: Xian, Rodric, Mary Beth. But Preston. Preston with his bowl cut and cargo pants. Him I could catch. I can tell he gets a smug satisfaction from being "smarter" than me, so I make sure to remind him of the time I beat him in the seventh-grade spelling bee almost every time we talk. I get a sudden surge of adrenaline as I look at his untied sneakers, their frayed laces dragging against the floor. I'll show you, Preston. You're not smarter than me. Watch me ace this—

But no. Before the thought is even completed, my mind shuts it down and I'm slapped with reality. Preston and I aren't competitors anymore. I'm going to fail this exam intentionally. I'm going to get a C, or worse, in chemistry. And English, thanks to that *Les Mis* paper. I can see Preston's eyes working, trying to come up with a snide remark to shake my confidence before the test. Dropping my face to the floor,

I tiptoe forward into the classroom without acknowledging him, leaving him in the doorway with his mouth hanging slightly open.

I feel like I'm walking to my own execution as I approach my desk in the third row. No one is watching me, thankfully. They are too consumed with their notes and binders, muttering formulas and compounds under their breath. The wall to my left is usually decorated with a giant mural of the periodic table. But today Ms. Matthews has covered it in large sheets of white paper, making the room feel strangely naked.

I begin to sit down in my desk, but as my legs are moving toward the seat, I'm hit with the same electricity of the barstool in my kitchen. The same powerful anger and static billowing up from its surface. Involuntarily, I bend my body away from the seat and roll up into a standing position in some sort of awkward hip-hop dance move. The bell rings and I remain on my tiptoes, facing away from my desk with its cancer rays shooting like daggers into my back.

Ms. Matthews is at the front of the classroom in a thick red sweater. She thumbs through a mound of papers, counting out enough tests for each row, and begins handing them out to the seats in the front of the class. I'm the only other person standing in the room, so we make eye contact and my body clenches hard against her gaze. The expression on her face is some unknown mix of annoyance and distaste. Maybe an edge of nausea. "Allison. Have a seat, please." She lets out a long, loud sigh, like I'm the problem child, and clears her throat as if trying to keep herself from saying something rude. Ms. Matthews has never particularly liked me. There's something in the way she says my name that gives it away. But today it's much more than just dislike. Curious heads are popping up around me at her comment, only now noticing that I haven't yet sat down. She counts out a few more papers, takes a few more steps, and then looks back at me. Still wavering slightly on my tiptoes. She gives me the *What in the world is wrong with you?* look and moves her hand to her hip, daring me to speak.

I rip hard with my front teeth on a jagged hangnail on my thumb, and a sharp zing of pain shoots up my arm. "I can't."

She doesn't move. Her foot and hip pushed aggressively out to one side, her head tilted in a half threat, half question. "You can't?" She shakes her head slightly in confusion. "You can't what . . . sit?"

Her question hangs in the air over the classroom. Someone behind me snickers. The way she says it slaps me across the face. I inhale sharply. "I don't want to," I say, choking on my breath. I'm tripping over my words, suddenly nervous. "I mean"—I look around the room frantically for an escape—"I mean, can I sit at one of the back tables?" I jerk my thumb over my shoulder, pointing at the long black lab tables at the rear of the classroom. "My back hurts." I shrug with a grimace, almost shouting the words. I move my hand up to my lower back and bend over slightly like my dad. "My doctor said I shouldn't really be sitting in desks in the first place. He wrote me a note but it's in my book bag at home."

Brilliant lies like this always bring me a surge of confidence. I look her straight in the eye as I gently rub my back, impressed with myself. "It might be scoliosis."

Ms. Matthews's face is scrunched in toward the middle, clearly trying to figure out my intentions. With a tilted head, she squints at the lab tables, then scans the walls of the room and the messy lines of desks in front of her. She looks me directly in the eyes, lip pursed, arms resting on her thick stomach, for five full seconds. "Fine." She shakes her head and looks at the ceiling. "If you must."

I tiptoe down the aisle between desks, counting into the crowded but quiet classroom. I don't even care if they're staring. I'm just happy to have escaped.

The ten-foot-long lab tables come up to my hips and have thick, cold slabs of black marble on top of strong wooden legs. I reach to pull one of the tall stools toward me, but before my hand can touch the metal, I'm zapped. The searing electricity I've become so familiar with. I probably should have expected that, I think, as I look down at its gray frame. I take a tiptoed step a foot to my left to put some distance between us.

With a deep breath, I look down at the thin stack of white paper stapled together in the top left corner. *Honors Chemistry—Final Exam.* I flip over the cover page and finger through the sheets—ten pages, one hundred multiple choice questions. In bold, unflinching black font:

What are nucleic acids made of?
A. Sugars
B. Fatty acids
C. Nucleotides
D. Amino acids

I stare blankly down at the page. Most of these words are familiar, but only as a month-old memory. I know I've seen them before, highlighted them in my notes, but I have no idea what they mean. So this is what it feels like not to study. My heart drops as I realize this is the first time I've ever been in this situation. Completely unprepared for a test, staring at a guaranteed F. The edges of my eyes sear like I might cry, but of course I don't. Can't. My head falls slightly, and I let out a long, extended sigh. I glance down the rest of the sheet and flip through the next three or so pages. More of the same.

Straightening my back, I roll my neck slowly and adjust my nub of a pencil in my hand. It's three inches long and barely extends past my knuckles. Looking back at the test, I know I've just got to face it. Finish my business and get out of here. Cut my losses. I roll the pencil slightly between my fingers, and one hundred rows of bubbles, four bubbles across, stare back at me. I decide to make a zigzag pattern. A, B, C, D, C, B, A. A, B, C, D, C, B, A. The lead point on the pencil is still sharp and fills in each bubble with a dark finality. I try to push it out of my mind, but I know that the lead tip can't last forever. I just need it to survive through one hundred bubbles and a precalculus test.

My fingers cramping in protest of my tight, rigid grip, I shake my hand in the air, holding the pencil with my thumb and letting my fingers fly in all directions. I look down at the curvy design I've created on my answer sheet and my stomach sinks. This is suicide. For my chemistry grade, for my GPA, for my chances of getting in to Brown. Or Dartmouth.

Or anywhere that has hundred-year-old ivy growing on it. But I'm saving my mom's life! I yell to myself. Protecting her from cancer. It's worth it.

I think.

My hand is poised above the answer sheet, and for the first time I notice that the entire page is an odd shade of light green. And the borders around the individual bubbles and the lines at the bottom where I scribbled my name are a darker forest green. Green. Green. Green. Green, green, green. My brain is whipped into the center of a tornado, the room flying in a blur around me. I can't breathe. The air is caught in my throat. I feel myself lifting my arms in front of me in surrender and slowly backing away on my tiptoes. The only piece of the world in focus is the green answer sheet. And the memory of the green shorts I was wearing yesterday in the kitchen. And leaves and grass and bushes.

A quick gust of anger rises in my chest, and I look up to the ceiling, ready to curse my monster. He takes everything from me. And leaves me here to pick my way around the land mines. Not only do I have to fail my chemistry test, but the answer sheet itself is *green.* How am I supposed to function? What kind of life is this? I can't— But then I remember. It's not my monster. It's God. My eyes are glued to the ceiling, my body frozen like a statue of armor, as I press sharply on the brakes in my brain. Oh, right. It's God.

Th-th-thank you, God. I send the message to him in my thoughts. *Thank you for warning me about the color green.* I bow my head, recite the prayer formula, pound my chest twice, and point toward the sky.

I open my eyes and I'm looking up at my hand, still pointed emphatically at the ceiling. I can feel my heart swelling with warmth, and I know that I've been heard. That my messages have been accepted. The black marble tabletop is cold against my skin and a shiver runs through me. One of the fluorescent overhead lights is flickering on and off, covered in decades of dust. Its neighbor emits a constant eerie buzzing. The room feels so weird without the periodic-table mural. Kind of like a prison. Or an asylum.

I have already colored in about twenty-five bubbles. Their black marks are the only safe part of the cancer-green answer sheet that is glaring up at me from the tabletop. I feel its evil searing through my skin, waiting patiently until it has enough power to sprout into a tumor. I just need to get out of here. A heat is growing within me, but my body is shivering, from either fear or stress. This whole situation is a deathtrap. The longer I stay, the more likely I am to get myself into trouble . . . or terminal cancer. Screw this.

A wave of powerful determination boils up into my chest. Using my left thumbnail, not allowing any of my actual skin to touch the paper, I pin down the top edge of the answer sheet. A flicker of electricity immediately shoots up my finger, but I've just got to hope that cancer travels slower through nail than it would skin. In the back of my mind, in the small part of my brain still dedicated to rationality, the idea seems to make some sort of biological sense.

With one corner of the paper now stationary, I try to resume my zigzag bubbling. But without my right hand to touch the green surface and hold it in place, the paper only crinkles and moves under the pencil. My heart is pounding, anxious to get away from this test and back to the safety of staring at wide, blank countertops. Do something! I yell at myself, jerking up from my slouch. My head swivels on my shoulders, scanning the room for options. Without touching it, how can I hold this down enough to be able to fill in the bubbles? I need something heavy to put on the corner. A rock, or a paperweight . . . or a shoe. I'm looking down at my worn sneakers perched on tiptoes between the tiles. Yes.

Reaching down, I yank my tennis shoe off my foot, place it carefully on the corner of the answer sheet, and press my arm down on top of it. With my wrist bent down awkwardly from the laces, I can now finally bubble in the rest of the answer sheet safely. As I finish shading in the final circle, I think about my mission. Fail the test to save my mom. I look down at the zigzagged snake design covering my bubble sheet. This should do the trick.

I tiptoe unevenly across the room, bobbing up and down.

"Do you have a question?" Ms. Matthews glares up at me from the splayed newspaper in front of her, tiny reading glasses placed on the very tip of her nose.

"No, I'm done." I shrug slightly and place the test gently on the corner of her messy desk. At the sound of our voices, every single head in class rises up and looks at us. The room stays silent, but the air feels suddenly heavier.

I hear a few mumbles and someone whispers, "Oh my gosh, how is that even possible?"

"Done? It's only been twenty minutes." She gestures vaguely at the round clock hanging on the wall above her head. She squints at me and pushes her head forward. "It's a three-hour exam session." I feel her eyes drop and examine my body, looking at my thin pants and ragged T-shirt. The sneaker I used as a paperweight under my arm. My bare foot standing on tiptoe in the center of a tile. "Are you sure you're finished?"

"Yep." I respond before she's completed her sentence, cutting off most of the last word. I know I should smile, or grin, or something, anything, to distract her, to wipe the worry off her face, but it's not possible. I don't have it in me, and, I realize in the moment, I don't care what Ms. Matthews thinks anymore. So I nod at her once, turn on my tiptoes, and count my way out of the classroom with my sneaker held tightly underneath my arm, shoelaces dangling at my side.

CHAPTER 14

I'm lying curled in a fetal position on the carpet upstairs, my eyes jammed closed against the bright afternoon sun. I'm hiding from the world in darkness, and it's taking all of my energy. I haven't eaten today. There isn't much else I can do besides lie here, passing gently to and from sleep.

But more than hunger, it's the heavy weight in my chest that's drawing me into myself. Although I wasn't forbidden from passing my precal exam like I was chemistry, I wasn't allowed to study, which is basically the same thing. Exhausted and shell-shocked, I started crying in the middle of the final on Friday as I looked down at the completely blank five-page exam. A golden ticket to failure. With all my classmates staring, and under the pressure of Ms. Tisman's questions, I feigned food poisoning. After a few fake gags, I was given permission to come retake the test on Monday, tomorrow, the first day of Christmas break, with an entire letter grade deducted from my final score as penalty.

"Allison, honey! C'mon, this is the third time I've called you!" My mom's voice carries up the carpeted stairs to find me in the den. "It's almost halftime. You're missing the game!" I know she is talking to me, but I don't listen to it. Whatever she's saying doesn't matter.

But within a few seconds, I hear her muffled steps climbing up the stairs. She's coming to check on me. "You wouldn't believe what's just happened," she projects down the hall. "We *blocked* a field goal and—" Her voice cuts off as she turns the corner into the den. I feel her eyes freeze on me, taking in my emaciated body on the carpet. "Allison! What are you—" She rushes into the room and crouches down by my side, knees popping. "Are you okay? Why are you on the floor?" I ignore her, keeping my eyes closed and my head buried deep in the soft carpet fibers. I can't do this right now. *"Honey?"* She is screaming as if she has just seen me get hit by a car. A loud, frantic scream that oozes fear. "HONEY?" She grabs my right arm hard and shakes my body back and forth, jarring me out of my half coma.

"Whaaaat?" I yell at her, opening my eyes and squinting into the light. "Stop! Why are you shaking me?" My voice jerks under the violent pumps of her arms. She isn't crying, but she's on the verge. Of something. Her eyes are searching, manic, looking me up and down. She pats my arms, legs, head, as if checking to see I'm still intact. "Stop!" I jerk my body away from her, sit up a few inches, reclining against my elbow. I shoot her my best *What the f is wrong with you?* glare.

"Oh, you just looked . . ." She seems surprised to see me sitting up. "I thought you were . . ." A wave of relief sweeps over her face but her hand is still gripping my arm. "You just had me worried." She shakes her head slightly, mostly to herself. I look blankly up at her. I've never seen her like this. Frazzled and out of control. And scared. "Why are you on the floor? Why were you lying like that?" She's trying to sound serious, borderline angry, but I can hear the concern on the edges of her words.

"I was just taking a nap, you weirdo." I look at her quickly and then fall back to the carpet. Go away. Go away. Go away.

"You didn't look like you were taking a nap." She stares at me, waiting for a response, but I'm staring at the wall. "You need to get up. Come downstairs with us."

"No. Can't. Have to study." My voice is steady and robotic, eyes staring straight ahead.

"Study? Exams ended on Friday! There's no studying for at least two weeks." She fidgets with the edge of my pajamas. The same set I've worn for four days now because there is almost nothing else safe. And I'm too tired to change. She runs her hands over my clothes, flattening them out onto my bony skin. "Come on"—she gently nudges my shoulder, a touch of warmth filtering slowly back into her voice and face—"you don't want to miss the game. We could make the playoffs." I know she is projecting fake happiness on me, just like I do to her. It's really annoying.

"Exams aren't over yet, Mom. At least not for me." I clear my throat gently. "I guess I forgot to tell you. . . ." I lurch back up onto my forearm and look her in the face for the first time. I haven't forgotten to tell her. I was just hoping to take the test on Monday while she was at work and avoid this whole conversation. "I got really sick during the precal final on Friday and had to leave." A small noise pops from my mom's mouth, and I look down at my hand lying against the carpet. "But Ms. Tisman said I could just come retake it on Monday. Tomorrow." I let my gaze cross quickly over her face, avoiding her eyes, and nod twice with what I hope looks like conviction.

"Wait, what? You what?" She pushes her head forward toward me. The fake happiness is replaced with genuine concern. "You were sick? When? You didn't tell us?" The look she had in her eyes as she shook me on the carpet is back. The face that says: *Where is my daughter?*

"Well, I mean, no. It wasn't a big deal. It was food poisoning. I ate Taco Bell. Once I threw up a few times I felt better." I shrug slightly. "It's no problem. She said I could make it up." I'm trying to sound casual. There's a redness creeping up her skin from under the neck of her sweatshirt. She's looking at me like I've sprouted a third eye and it's winking at her.

"So, you didn't take your precalculus final on Friday?"

"No." I move my head once from side to side. "I was sick."

"And you're going to retake it tomorrow?"

"Yes."

"Without any penalty?"

"No. None." Just a whole letter grade.

"And you're just telling me this . . . now. On Sunday." She locks eyes with me. "After having food poisoning. On Friday." She is squinting at me, a dubious FBI agent questioning a suspect.

"Yes." The same short nod. I look at her like she's asking the obvious, trying to convince her with my eyes that this really isn't a big deal. It's just a math final. Her eyes move down across my face. She is searching for something. A clue, a hint, a sign to help her understand who I've become. Who I've turned into over the past ten weeks. I try my best to keep my face steady, but my lower lip creeps into my mouth. Will she buy it?

My mom reclines onto her side so she is lying face-to-face beside me on the carpet. It feels weird to see her in such a childlike position. The VP of Everything, lounging on the floor. She lets out a long, deep breath as if she has come to some sort of decision within herself. Something in her face has changed when she looks up at me. "Okay. Well, do you feel prepared?"

She's giving in! Without a fight! I've won! I clear my throat and shrug like I'm not concerned. "Yeah, I mean, I studied a lot last week. I probably just need to review some notes for a few hours." I point at the leaning tower of trash and books sitting beside my cancer desk. There is a bag of squished grapes propped against it on the floor.

"Good, that's good, honey." She reaches her arm up and smooths the hair around my face. "How about this." She pauses. "You take a break from studying right now. You deserve some relaxation." Her hand is still warmly cupping the side of my face, and I'm leaning into it against my will. I miss you, Mom. "So, come watch a little bit of the game with us, and then when it's over, you can come back up here and finish your work. I'll make you dinner and bring it up to you on a tray so you can eat and study." She tilts her head slightly and looks at me. "You've just been working so hard. Come take a break, okay?"

It's her hand on my face that draws me into her plan. Her skin is so soft, and it feels nice to be touched. My world of isolation is safe but also, I've just realized, incredibly lonely. Her warm skin has lulled me into a calm trance. And I nod at her. "Sure, I guess so."

She stands and, with her hands beneath my armpits, pulls me up as well. My head spins with the movement, and I stumble backward, then sideways, against my swirling brain. My mom's strong hand on my upper arm steadies me. We make brief eye contact, the wall behind her still swimming across my vision, and then I follow her out of the den and down the hallway.

The basement has no windows to the outside, and it's always about ten degrees cooler than the rest of the house. The fish tank glows and gurgles at me as I cross through the door.

"C'mon, pass interference!" My dad is screaming at the TV, his black mesh jersey wrinkling around his stomach. "Are you *blind?*" My mom clears her throat as she leads me inside.

"*Jeffrey* . . . ," she whisper-yells.

His head jerks sideways at us, and a genuine smile spreads across his face. "Well, well"—he tilts his head in fake surprise—"look who we have here." His favorite leather chair makes a few quiet creaks behind him, his body shape permanently imprinted into its cushions. "You're missing a real doozy. This referee, though, dang. Must be eighty-five years old, at least. Senile. Can't see a thing!" He pops a few pieces of trail mix into his mouth, chomping on them loudly as he looks at me across the room. "Well?" I'm still standing in the doorway, my arms wrapped around myself. This feels like a trap. Nothing good can come from so much exposure to my parents. From a whole half of a football game under their examination. "Are you gonna join us or just stand and watch from afar?" His smile is still there but fading. He is extending the bowl of trail mix to me, shaking it slightly so it moves around with a small noise in the bowl.

I open my mouth to respond but rethink it and give a small nod instead. I can feel both of them watching me as I count over to my usual spot on the couch. As soon as I look up, though, their eyes flick back to the TV screen. We're all trying our best to act like it's just a normal Sunday. Snacks, soda, the chilly basement. But there is a stiff tension in the air that says we're all very much aware of reality. I shiver under my thin T-shirt.

The old blue couches in our basement were a wedding gift from my grandparents to my parents. There's some sort of family story around every stain or patched hole—that time my mom spilled red wine on her thirtieth birthday, the burned patch from when my dad fell asleep with a cigar between his fingers. I'm looking down at the worn, soft cushions that have been a part of my life since before I was even born. And I see the truth. Or, really, I feel it. The waves of cancer, the layers of death emanating up from their surface. The high-pitched whine seeping out from the buttons and stitching. It doesn't talk to me. I hear no words. But they aren't necessary. I can sense the danger.

"Allison, honey, sit down. You're blockin' my view."

"Huh? Oh, sorry." I look over my shoulder at my dad, who is leaning to one side, craning his neck to see the screen around my body. "Um . . ." I shift a few steps to my left and stare blankly out at the room. I hear the TV blaring in the background, but it's almost drowned out by the screeching noise billowing up from the couch. I miss the soft, silent den floor. Football is for people who are happy. For people who are a part of this world. For people with things to live for.

The back of my brain is itchy. Not quite a twinge, but I can feel that there is something developing, something important. And again, without any specific message, almost like I have had this truth buried within me all along, I know what I need to do. I lift my right foot into the air and readjust my weight so I'm balancing on one leg. Wobbling, looking down at my stance, I don't know why I'm doing it but I know it's what God wants. I know it's right. Seeing myself on one foot is strangely comforting. Like I'm earning some sort of divine extra credit or karma. I'm going the extra mile to make sure I—

"Allison. Seriously, though. Sit down." My dad is staring at me from his leather seat, reclined slightly. "You're still in the way. It's distracting."

"Oh, sorry, I . . ." Unable to move any farther toward the wall, I walk across the room and stand on one wobbly foot by the opposite couch. Definitely out of my dad's TV line of vision.

He stares at me for five long seconds, at first smiling like I'm joking but then realizing this is something different. His face has changed, like he, too, now sees that winking third eye. "Why won't you sit down?"

"I just don't want to. My legs are sore. I'm . . ." I scan the room for ideas. Why won't I sit down, why won't I sit down? "I'm, yeah. I'm sore." I know it's weak, but I'm exhausted. Whatever.

"Sore from what? It's Christmas break. Cross-country is over. Track is over. You're not sore." He looks me directly in the eyes. "Sit down." A pause. "Now."

I'm staring down at the carpet, but I can feel his eyes on the top of my tangled head. I can hear his heart rate increasing just by his voice. I won't do it.

"Allison Marie"—he is taken aback when I don't move—"I said, *sit down.*"

"Jeffrey, just let her—" My mom reaches forward slightly but stops short when my dad shoots her a slicing glance.

"No. Enough of this!" He sits up in his chair and turns to face me. He's not quite yelling, but it's the most worked up I've seen him in a long time. Bringing his socked feet down from the ottoman, he rests his elbows on his knees and leans toward me. "Enough not eating, enough hiding upstairs, enough staying up until all hours of the night in that den doing *who knows what.* Enough counting." He scrunches his face with the word. "Just. Enough." He is shaking his head, his hand placed against his forehead. "We're going to sit here and watch the game like we always do. And enjoy ourselves." He looks at my mom first, then over at me. "So"—he gestures smoothly at my usual seat on the couch, like Vanna White—"sit."

I stare straight back at him, surprised. He never talks to me like this. I don't think we've ever had a fight. I know he didn't mean to hurt my feelings, but his tirade echoes through me like a punch to the stomach. He listed out my strange behaviors so quickly, like they were at the front of his mind. Like he's worried about me. Like he's afraid his daughter has become some sort of freak. I close my eyes against his gaze, hoping inspiration will come to me. A joke, a diversion. Something to make him smile and distract him while I sneak out the trapdoor. But all I can think about is his face as he spat out the word "counting," like it tasted sour. I feel myself retracting into my tattered, worn pajamas, trying to hide from him. And this basement and their burning stares.

We stay in these exact positions, me on one leg with closed eyes, my parents staring at me in disbelief, for what could be hours, days, weeks. Despite the basement chill, a heat is soon rising aggressively up from my chest. Why can't they leave me alone? *This* is why I don't watch football games anymore. *This*—I think about my wobbling ankle and my parents' openmouthed stares—is why it's easier to "hide upstairs." This is their fault. They brought me down here. They pulled me from my quiet safety into this deathtrap. With each point I make, my blood boils one degree hotter. I bite hard on my tongue. Enough.

I feel words squeezing up and out of my throat, but my voice is unfamiliar. Taut, strained. Exhausted. I can't let myself scream like I want to, let out all my frustration on them like they deserve. Clearly they're already on edge. I need to manage my reaction. Act normal. Don't scare the animals. I open my eyes and look at a place on the wall a few inches above my dad's thinning hair. "Well. That's enough football for me." I pivot awkwardly on my left foot planted on the carpet and, because it feels like the right thing to do, hop on one leg out of the basement. I lunge for the doorway, grab on to its side, and steady myself. I cough a few times, winded by the exertion, and then hop a few steps farther into the hallway. Finally putting my right foot down onto the bottom stair, I turn slightly over my shoulder and halfheartedly croak, "I hope we win," back into the room. I feel the comment land meaningfully on a thick silence.

"Do you see what you did?" My mom whisper-hisses at my dad as I leap up toward the kitchen, three stairs at a time.

As I turn the corner and resume my one-legged hop down the hallway, my blood is still boiling in anger. Don't they know what I've done for them? How many car accidents and violent murders I've stopped? I failed chemistry to heal my mom's cancer! I carry around pounds of rotting, stinking food to keep her safe. And yet they stare at me like I'm some sort of mutant child, like I've done something horribly wrong. I flop down onto the den floor and curl my body back into the fetal position, closing my eyes against the carpet. They have no clue the kind of tragedy I've prevented. I'm the only reason this family is still intact and not limping painfully to our deaths. The *only* reason. Assholes.

CHAPTER 15

I was supposed to meet Ms. Tisman at nine a.m. for my pre-cal exam and, glancing over at the clock, I see it's already nine fifteen. I clamp my eyes closed. There is a twinge drilling insistently into the back of my brain. Standing on one foot, I know what this feeling means, and I'm trying to fight it, frantically propping up a mental wall to stop its progress. But it's too powerful. I know that I will fail before I even begin, but I can't just let the thought storm in and tear down what little I have left. Even if it's coming from heaven. I grip my hand into a fist, fingernails cutting sharply into the soft skin of my palm. *These pajamas cause cancer,* it whispers. I shake my head vigorously back and forth as the thought feeds into my mind. No. No, they don't. I need these. I need these clothes. They're some of the only safe ones I have left. A terrible squeal is blaring against my eardrums from the shirt I'm wearing, and I lean my weight against my bureau for support. I need these clothes. They're fine. They've been safe for so long and they're still safe now. I have nothing else.

YOUR PAJAMAS CAUSE CANCER.

I flinch away from the screaming, from God's anger. No. They don't. I need them.

LISTEN OR YOU WILL DIE.

And with this, I freeze. My mind, my heart, my muscles. *CANCER.*

I know it's not going to stop. The screaming, the messages, the anger. I let out a long, slow sigh that completely empties my lungs and look down at the thin, holey T-shirt lying softly against my frail body. There's a static growing from it, and the muscles in my shoulders tighten into lumps. A rumbling is building downstairs, and I see myself with my head wrapped in gauze. Thick stains of blood seep through the bandages as I lie half-conscious in a hospital bed, attached to IVs, with my parents staring at me over beeping machines.

I'm exhausted. And starving. And I've heard all of this before. But I can't risk it. The tips of my fingers are like ice as they graze across the edge of my hip bone. With the sound of ripping fabric, I pull the limp red T-shirt off my torso and at the same time wiggle out of my now-oversized flannel pants. I throw the shirt to the other side of the room, flinging the pants with my toes so they land together in a pathetic pile. Naked, exposed to the full power of the ceiling fan, I jerk involuntarily against a wave of violent shivers. My body contracts inward, looking to itself for warmth.

I'm crouching with my arms wrapped tightly around my ribs. As my eyes skim the familiar walls, the home to a girl I barely remember, I realize that everything they land on has some sort of consequence. Stereo, curtains, stuffed animals, all the clothes in my closet and bureau. My bookshelf, the green chair, my crumpled-up cross-country uniform. My eyes dart one way: tumors. They move to the left: my mom's breast cancer. Here, death. There, sadness. I'm surrounded. This is prison. This room, this brain. It's hopeless. I cannot do it anymore.

I collapse onto the carpet, mostly from the weight of the fact that I have nowhere else to go. That I'm trapped. From the floor I watch the fan spinning aggressively above me. It squeaks as it protests against the bolts holding it to the ceiling. I roll my body into a ball and press myself hard into the carpet, hoping it can warm me up. Out of my periphery I see the edge of my black landline telephone peeping over the side of the top of the bureau. The phone I spent hundreds of hours on, chattering with Jenny and Sara. There's never been any specific warning against it, but I feel its anger billowing outward. It doesn't need a danger label. Its cancer rays speak for themselves. But while I look at it from the corner of my eye, I'm suddenly filled with a wave of blaring inspiration. A phone. I could call for help. I could tell someone. I could escape! And, before I know I've left the carpet, I'm lunging toward the phone and pressing *1* on speed-dial.

The ringing tone in my ear startles me. I did it. I actually did it. I feel God glaring at me from above and clamp my eyes against his anger. My danger list flips through my head and a panic rises in my chest. I can't believe I did it.

"Good morning, this is Maureen." My mom's voice filters through the black handset, which I'm holding in front of my face. I'm frozen, shaking. I guess I meant to call her, maybe? But it happened so fast, so unexpectedly, that I don't know what to say. Or what I'm allowed to say, I think, as I flit my eyes toward the ceiling. "Hello?" Her voice is still cheerful, but there is an edge of impatience. "Allison, honey? I can see it's you on the caller ID. Is everything okay?"

"Mom," I croak at her, barely squeezing words through

my lips, hoping the Lord won't be able to hear me if I mumble. The phone is whining into my ear, sending out the call for the army of bees sure to soon swarm over the horizon. The tears that started when she first answered the phone are now rolling down my cheeks.

"Allison? Sweetheart?" Her cheerfulness has been replaced with fear. The same voice she used in the den when she thought I was . . . whatever she thought I was. "Are you crying?"

A loud sob shakes through me as I unclench. Her presence on the other end of the phone is soothing. "There's nothing to wear." It's the best way I know how to put it.

"What do you mean, honey? Just put on something from your closet. It's cold out today, so make sure it's warm." She speaks slowly and carefully, like I'm a small child with a hearing impairment.

"*No!*" I scream. "I can't! They're all bad." Something is boiling up from my stomach. Cancer or maybe relief or maybe vomit. "They'll all kill me or hurt me. Or you." I pause for a moment, my thoughts swirling into a storm. Even as I scream, I know none of this makes sense. I know there's no way she will understand. "I won't wear any of them!" My entire body is shaking, convulsing, racked back and forth by violent shivers and sobs.

There is silence. I picture her at her desk, staring out over the top of her computer through the window. "Okay, honey. But today is your precal final, right? You need to get to school. It's already"—there's a pause as she looks down at her wrist—"oh, good Lord, it's already nine thirty." There's a rising urgency in her voice. "Allison, sweetheart. Put on your black track pants and just grab a sweatshirt. Ms. Tisman is being very nice letting you retake this exam. You don't want to miss it."

My stomach flips at her suggestions and I balk silently at the empty room. She's so freaking stupid. So clueless. "Mom, I *can't.*" It explodes out of me. A million thoughts packed into three words. And then, "I caaann't," in an extended wail that melts into uncontrolled tears.

For a few moments I forget I'm on the phone. But then I hear her let out a long sigh. "Okay, baby. It's going to be okay." She clears her throat. "I could tell you were . . . I noticed that . . ." She doesn't know how to talk about this any more than I do. "I think maybe it's time we go see Dr. Mark. Hmm? What do you think?" Dr. Mark is the physician I have seen since childhood. The man with the fruit-flavored cough syrup and smiling eyes.

I almost can't hear her over the high-pitched whine of the phone against my cheek. It's starting to heat against my skin, its static surely digging into and poisoning the bone marrow on the left side of my face.

"C'mon sweetie," she coos over the noise. "I'll call and make you an appointment for tomorrow." Cancer, cancer, cancer. I can hear her adjusting in her computer chair. I haven't moved and there is a large wet patch of tears growing on the carpet. "I'll also call the school and let them know you won't be making your math test." She pauses, and I know she is scribbling a note to herself on the pad by the phone. "For now, go take a warm shower, have some nice soup, and rest. I'll try to get home early." I grunt and nod. "I love you, Allison." Her voice is warm. "See you soon."

With a small click, she hangs up and I inhale sharply, the phone falling out of my open hand as I roll into a ball on the carpet. I'm suddenly surrounded by flying debris: thoughts, messages, warnings, alarms. A swarm of bees, a screeching whine. Is God going to be angry at me? I slam my eyes shut against the torrent, against the consequences of my phone call. I scrunch my shoulders up to cover my ears. The side of my face still burns where the phone touched my skin. If I weren't curled on top of my hands, I'm sure I would reach up to find cancer blisters popping to life. There is a strange, heavy silence in the empty house. One that tells me I've not only rocked the boat but capsized it. There's nothing else to do but hide in darkness behind closed eyes. Both from the world and from myself.

Six hours later, I'm jarred awake by the rumbling of a garage door. Still scrunched in the same place on the carpet, my body is a rigid shell that has been slowly frozen throughout the day. I haven't moved to eat or use the restroom. I haven't opened my eyes. I haven't gotten a blanket. I spent the entire day wafting through an almost sleep, only moving to readjust myself in a tight ball. It just seemed like the safest thing to do. But the sound of the garage door clanging open below me flips some sort of switch and I'm immediately sitting up, heart pounding. My head spins from the sudden movement, or maybe lack of food, and my eyes dart frantically around the room, a rabbit that's sensed a predator.

I scramble up from the carpet, my bones creaking and

209

popping with the movement. In two gazelle leaps, I'm beside my bed and throw myself into the sheets as I hear my mom's heels on the hardwood floor of the hallway. "Allison!" Her voice carries up the stairs and her footsteps quickly follow it. "Honey, I'm home," she calls. It's the same *I Love Lucy* impression my dad does on a regular basis. Even after a day on the floor, I manage to roll my eyes. My mom's head pops around the corner, her fake smile plastered sturdily on her face. "How was your day? How are you feeling?" She moves into my room and sits on the edge of my bed, reaching up to touch the side of my face. "Did you get to— Oh, honey! You're freezing!" She yanks the comforter up around my shoulders. "My stars, you're shivering! Why are you so cold?" She brushes her hand soothingly across my cheek, and her fingers get tangled in my nest of hair. "Don't worry, baby. We are going to the doctor tomorrow. I got an appointment at nine." She pats my calf through the comforter. "We'll get this all figured out." She gives a few convincing nods and looks down at me. I peer back at her over the edge of the blankets. "I also wrote an e-mail to Ms. Tisman, explaining the situation. She—"

"What situation?" They're the first words I've spoken in six hours, and they come out as a raspy cough.

"Well"—she hesitates—"I told her that you've been sick for the past few weeks. Months, really. And it made it difficult for you to study and to focus in class." She isn't making eye contact with me. "I said we would get a note from Dr. Mark tomorrow, just for her peace of mind. She was very polite about it. She said she hopes you feel better and that you can take the test in January. It will show up as an incomplete on your report card for now." I picture Ms. Tisman reading my mom's e-mail with crossed arms and pursed lips, and despite the layers of bedsheets, a shiver runs through me. "Don't worry, baby. Mom's here. I'll take care of you. Everything is going to be fine." Her hand is resting heavily on my thigh, and I feel tears growing behind my eyes. I don't know whether to be thankful for her help or scared for my soul. Fearful of disobeying the only one who matters. My mom and I make eye contact. She looks tired. Ragged, even. There are two deep creases across her forehead and dark, puffy circles under her eyes. I pull my gaze away from her and roll over onto my side, pretending to be ready for sleep. My mom sits beside me, hand on my leg, for a full thirty seconds. She pats my head, gently whispers, "It's going to be okay," and pads quietly away down the hall.

I want to believe her. I want to know everything will be okay. But the hollow feeling in my chest warns me I've just ruined everything. I've chosen this world, my happiness, my comfort, over a direct relationship with God. And there's no way that's going to end well.

CHAPTER 16

The doctor's office is warm. Too warm. It makes sense, given the tiny icicles I can see hanging from the roof through the window, but I'm starting to sweat. A thin layer of perspiration keeps appearing on my upper lip, no matter how many times I wipe it off. My mom is sitting beside me, her hand just a few centimeters from mine on the armrest. She has a thick, well-worn magazine splayed open on her lap, but she's staring blankly across the room at nothing. Her thick-heeled left shoe is jiggling incessantly against both of our shins. I'm wearing crumpled clothes that I discovered in the laundry hamper this morning. As far as I can tell, it's the last safe outfit in my possession. CNN is on mute on the television on the wall. A woman with perfect hair in a perfect suit mimes at us about the cold front pushing in from the Atlantic Ocean.

Is this a good thing? Is being here allowed? Can I tell Dr. Mark what's been happening? *Should* I tell him what's been happening? I glance to my left at my mom, who is clearly in her own world. From the beginning of . . . this . . . I've known these messages are sacred. But since driver's ed, when I realized my thoughts are truly divine, they've taken on a new weight. If God has decided I am his vessel, the sole trustee of life-changing secrets, is it really my place to share? If he had wanted the world to know, he would have told us. Or put it in the Bible. Or something. Right? Just because this battle is hard, does that make it okay for me to spill the beans on the true causes of cancer and tragedy and death? I don't think it's my secret to tell. My stomach gurgles at the questions, loosening up the heavy pit of bile that sits constantly ready to sneak up my throat.

The wooden door on the other side of the waiting room swings open, and an overweight nurse in pink scrubs looks down at her clipboard. "I'm looking for a Miss . . . Allison?" We make eye contact and she gives me a smile of recognition. She's greeted me almost every time I've come to the doctor for the past however many years I've been seeing Dr. Mark. I can't smile back at her. These next few steps carry the weight of the past few months.

"Come on, sweetie." My mom folds her magazine closed, and I hear it smack down onto the small coffee table. I can feel her standing in front of me, but I'm looking down at my half-eaten nails and cuticles. Do I go? I'm asking myself for advice, frowning slightly at the torn skin of my fingers. I can't *not* go, I whisper silently back—I have almost no safe clothes, no toothbrush, no pencil. I can't keep clawing my way through life, starving in tattered pajamas. But . . . but . . . *still.* I'm just going to tell Dr. Mark that God's been talking to me, telling me the secret codes of cancer? I'm going to casually explain that I failed my chemistry final to save my mom's life? It's the truth, obviously. But even as I try to think of a gentler way to put it, I know he can't handle it. There's no way he will understand.

My mom clears her throat and I look up to see her hand extended toward me, resting a few inches in front of my face. She wiggles her fingers at me. "Allison. The nurse is waiting." Our eyes meet and I can see I don't have an option.

My knees pop as she pulls me up out of the chair, and briefly I understand what it must be like to walk toward the gallows for your own execution.

When I get to the door, the nurse's smile has morphed into a furrow of brows and crow's feet, but she pats me gently on the back as I pass by her anyway. Her soft hand on my shoulder, she guides me toward the digital scale in a small cove with an eye chart. I step onto the clear glass platform and it gives a few beeps. Three enormous zeros appear blinking on the screen. Blink, blink, blink. A pause. *95.*

Ninety-five . . . pounds? What! Last time I was here over the summer for my annual physical, I was more like 115. I haven't weighed less than a hundred pounds since middle school. Since I was about eleven. The nurse leans over my shoulder and I feel her freeze for a moment, as if ensuring she saw the number correctly. She lets out a small "hmm" and scribbles my weight into my chart, slapping it closed when she's done. "Okay, then. Follow me, please." She leads me down the familiar hallways, painted a gentle blue, which I assume is meant to be calming. There's that antiseptic smell in the air, harsh and sharp. The smell of getting swabbed before a shot in the arm. She points us into a small beige room that is twenty-three steps from the scale.

Eyeing the large examination table, I realize that all the furniture in the office has been silent. I've felt no static, no anger. Without even thinking about it, I sat down in the waiting room on the upholstered chair next to my mom.

And now I'm positioning myself on the elevated table to wait for Dr. Mark. Maybe it's because I haven't spent much time here. Everything at home and school has a consequence and a danger because they've had months to be discovered. The constant tension in my shoulder muscles relaxes one notch. I've forgotten what it's like to only hear words from people.

I watch the nurse walk out of the room, and the door clicks closed. I'm looking at a laminated, illustrated poster of the cardiovascular system pinned to the wall. The room is suddenly and completely quiet. I shove my hands underneath my thighs against the thin paper covering the exam table, and it crinkles loudly into the silence. My mom is to my left, sitting in a normal chair against the wall. I really don't want her to talk to me, but this tense silence isn't much better. What is she thinking over there? Sitting with her hands in her lap against her black slacks, still wiggling her foot multiple times per second. What did she tell the receptionist when she called to make the appointment? ("Yes, hi, my daughter has stopped brushing her hair and has lost twenty pounds—can we see the doctor sometime this week?") I can tell she's upset—a mysterious mixture that's part worry, part stress. I think about her conversations with my dad behind their bedroom door. I've been so wrapped up in myself, in my own battle, that I haven't really looked at this from their perspective. All I know is that half the things I do are for them and their safety. And they haven't once said thank you.

There are two small knocks on the door as it swings inward slowly. "Well, hey there, y'all." Dr. Mark moves into the room and settles onto a rolling stool, opening my medical file on the small table beside the sink. He spins toward me with a gleaming smile, and I notice that his face doesn't change when he sees my knotted hair and pimples. "I would say I'm glad to see ya, but I know you're not feeling your best and I'm sorry about that." I'm sure he uses this same opening line for every patient, but it sounds so genuine. He's got big, thick, hairy hands that are resting patiently on his thighs. After looking at me for a few moments, he blinks and says, "So, what brings you in today? It sounds like you may be having a tough time. . . ." His voice trails off slightly, and I know it's my cue. But what do I say? Glancing up at his friendly blue eyes, I'm reminded of the time I sprained my ankle on my brand-new scooter in our driveway. It was a few years ago—I was about ten—and Dr. Mark came into the office on a Saturday to bandage my knee and wrap my ankle, still in his dirty uniform from the softball game he had left early. And here we are now. The doctor who has always dispensed grape-flavored cough syrup and written prescriptions for my strep throat is prodding at my deepest secrets. His eyes are friendly and I've known him for most of my life, but I just can't do it. I'm not sure what the consequences would be if I told him, but there's no way it would be good. Looking at his framed medical school diploma with its loopy calligraphy, I know that this, whatever this is, isn't something that will be fixed with a course of antibiotics. And, I wonder to myself, is it something I want to "fix" in the first place?

Seeing my hesitation, he shifts his eyes over to my mom, who clears her throat. "Allison, you don't want to try to tell

Dr. Mark what's been happening?" Why am I here? Why did I agree to this? She means well, her voice is gentle, but that familiar anger is rising like lava in my chest. Why did she make me come? I will take no responsibility if she gets breast cancer as a result of this trip. I cross my arms and stomp my foot in my head. This was all her idea. "Allison?" I shoot a mean look at her and give one definitive head shake no.

"Okay, well, I guess I'll start." She shifts in her seat, straightening her back. "It's been about two months or so . . . I'm not sure exactly when it all started." I can feel her looking at me, but I'm staring down at my thighs, shoulders rolled forward. "We noticed she had lost her appetite, wasn't eating as much. Her grades have dropped, and there's been a marked change in her behavior." Dr. Mark is making notes in tiny chicken-scratch letters I can't quite read from my perch.

"How so?"

"Well, for example, she seems to have issues with choosing clothes to wear"—neither of them look at my tattered pajamas, but I can feel them nodding internally—"as well as counting out loud and tiptoeing." It's like she's had this spiel prepared in advance in her head, filed away in her mind as the "list of things wrong with my daughter." As she talks, though, I realize she can only see a fraction of the situation. My counting and tiptoeing and clothes are just the exposed tip of the iceberg. They are merely the symptoms of a dark and complicated truth that she knows nothing about. I'm the only one inside my head. She seems to have run out of steam, and again I feel her eyes on me. "Allison, your input would be helpful here."

I roll my eyes. Shut up, Mom. Angry tears are building somewhere between my stomach and chest. Is this what she and my dad whisper about? They've gotten so concerned, so worked up, over lost weight and low grades? What started as embarrassment as she listed out my problems quickly turns as I realize just how little she knows. She thinks she's laying all my cards out on the table in front of Dr. Mark, but I have two more thick, full decks in my back pocket. A cool shiver creeps up my neck. I'm still on my own. And I'm not sure that's a good thing.

They're both staring at me. I have to say something. After a small clearing of my throat, and without looking up, I manage, "Yeah, um, that's about right." My voice is raspy, mucus caught in my mouth. I grip my hands tightly together with my fingers interlaced.

Dr. Mark scoots a bit closer to me on the stool. "Okay, okay."

He is unwrapping the stethoscope from around his neck, the overhead light glinting off the silver. "Allison, I'm just going to check you over, make sure everything seems to be working right. Then, we'll do a few tests together. And I'll probably take a small sample of blood just to make sure we cover all of our bases. How does that sound?" He stands up slightly so our faces are aligned, and I nod at him, my lips closed tight. "Okay, I'm going to start with listening to your heart." Dr. Mark presses the cold stethoscope against my skin and moves it around, requesting deep breaths at strategic moments. I tense briefly as the metal glides across my back, wondering if he notices I'm not wearing a bra or underwear. He then shines a light in my eyes, up my nose, and down my throat. He mashes on my lymph nodes and then my intestines. His fingers are chilly but soft, and I feel myself relaxing as he clinically moves his way around my different body parts.

"Well, everything looks good," he says as he lowers my calf back down after hitting my kneecap with a small rubber hammer. "You seem to be in fine working condition." Even though I'm not looking, I can feel the big smile in his voice. "Okay, now what we're going to do is test some of your motor skills. If you wouldn't mind raising your arms for me." We run through a series of movements—alternating touching my nose, then his hand, then back to my nose, and then flipping my hands over repeatedly. You're way off here, doc, I think as he tells me to balance on one leg while covering one eye and then the other. God's messages about my health and my family's safety have nothing to do with whatever *this* tests. And it definitely has nothing to do with talking furniture and angry clothes and bartering away all my food.

I'm still balancing, arms extended out to my sides, when there is a small knock behind me on the door. The nurse in the pink scrubs is back, and she's pushing a cart filled with needles and gauze and the dreaded bottle of rubbing alcohol. She takes a few vials of my blood, and with another gentle pat on my shoulder, she leaves the same way she came, behind the squeaky cart.

"So, I'd like to ask you a few questions, if you don't mind?" He is looking at me intently, but I'm pretending to be focused on the tight new bandage on the inside bend of my arm. With a short, sharp breath in, I glance up at him with half nod. I feel a small warmth inside. He's really taking this seriously.

"So, tell me about school. Your mom says your grades have dropped a little bit this semester. Why do you think that is?"

I let out a long sigh but try not to let Dr. Mark hear. "Yeah, I mean, I don't know. School is hard. Precalculus is hard. It's just a lot of work." He nods at me without smiling, his mouth pursed and pushed to the side like he's thinking.

"Okay, I understand that, definitely. And friends? How's that going? Do you all get along?"

I shake my head up and down at him a bit too quickly and enthusiastically. My mom has no idea that her once-bubbly daughter has become the ultimate pariah, a total social outcast. While it's no more shocking than my other antics, I suppose, for some reason it feels much more embarrassing. I'd rather she not know that I've single-handedly scared away the people I used to call my best friends. "Friends are great. Definitely." I nod at him longer than I should. "Lots of friends."

"Okay." He looks at me and then puts a few small marks on his lined paper. "That's good to hear. And what about your appetite? Have you noticed a change?" He flips back to the top page of my chart, running his finger under the newly marked 95.

"No, not really. I mean, maybe a little, but"—I give a small shrug—"I feel fine." My mom rustles in her chair. It's taking all her strength not to interject.

"Well, you *have* lost a significant amount of weight, so that's something we're really going to want to look out for on the blood tests. It can sometimes signal an issue with your thyroid or lymphatic system." Another scribble on his notepad. "Just a few more questions now, and for these, I'd like to ask your mom to step out." It takes a few moments for his words to register in my mind, and when they do, I jerk my head up at my mom with surprise. From her expression, she seems much less alarmed by his suggestion than I am, and she quickly stands and gathers her things like he asks. Dr. Mark rolls across the floor and opens the door. "It will only be a few minutes. I'll send Allison out to get you." She is raising her eyebrows as she passes and he responds with a kind but firm smile.

I don't think I've ever been alone with a doctor before. It's kind of exhilarating, but what could he not ask in front of my mom? He lets out a long, slow breath while he looks at me, half evaluating my hair and skin and clothes, half seemingly thinking to himself. "So, Allison. How are things at home? Do you get along with your parents?"

My head shifts back a few inches. My parents? My mom is constantly bothering me, questioning me, checking on me and, yes, it's incredibly annoying but I'm also bending over backward to save their lives multiple times a day. They're infuriating, but they're everything. "Things are fine. Good. We get along." I shrug at him again, still a little confused by the question. It feels weird to be in here by myself.

"Okay, and what about your moods? Do you feel sad sometimes? Maybe angry?"

I consider this one for a few moments, chewing gently on the inside of my bottom lip. Is it even worth denying? I'm sure he can read the truth written in the hollows around my collarbone and my dark-rimmed eyes. "I guess so." I'm kneading my hands in circles. "I feel sad when . . ." I run the nail of my pointer finger over an inflamed sore I've created on my thumb, not sure where to go with the sentence. "Yeah. I feel sad."

"Okay, all right." A small note. "Have you ever had dark thoughts? Have you ever contemplated suicide?"

My eyes shoot open at this, almost choking on a guffaw. *What?* Just the word itself is scary. *Suicide.* It makes my shoulders tense up. This whole thing, my whole life, is the opposite of suicide. My main goal every day is to stay alive, to keep living despite the danger surrounding me. I know he's just fishing, looking for something to help him diagnose me, but I'm almost offended at the question. He clearly doesn't get it. "N-no." I stutter slightly on the word. "No, never."

He seems relieved at my response and flips my file closed. "If you wouldn't mind, go ahead and bring your mom back in." He stands up and begins washing his hands at the sink in the corner. I slide off the table and wave my mom in from the hallway. She almost jumps toward the door.

Dr. Mark takes his time wiping his hands, adjusting his white coat, sitting back on the stool. My mother is tense beside me, her presence bringing a tightness to the room that wasn't here before. To her, this is the moment of truth. The wise doctor is going to bestow his medical knowledge on her daughter and I will be cured. My hair will magically untangle, my teeth will brush themselves, and I'll be back to reaching for seconds at the dinner table. I'm interested to hear what he will say too, but it's going to be wrong. Asking about my parents and my appetite? Dr. Mark is a nice guy and a good doctor, but for the past thirty minutes he's just been stabbing in the dark. No questions about God or cracks or cancer. There's no way he can be even remotely close to the truth.

It flashes into my mind that maybe he's actually found some sort of tumor, a sign of the disease that I spend my entire life fighting away. A sudden panic rises to my throat but deflates just as quickly when Dr. Mark looks up and smiles. He may be a doctor, and he may be running all sorts of tests, but somehow I know that whatever's going on inside me cannot be diagnosed.

"Well, we'll know more about exactly what's going on here when we get the results of your blood test in about two or three days. In the meantime, you should make it a priority to get lots of rest and hydrate." He looks back and forth between us. My mom is nodding at him seriously, like he is explaining how he will cure me of polio. "And, while we're waiting for your blood work, there's someone else I think you should see, someone who can help you." He dips his fingers into the deep pocket in his white coat and fishes out two business cards, handing one to me and one to my mom:

DR. JENNIFER ADAMS, MD, PHD

FOCUS IN CHILDHOOD

AND ADOLESCENT PSYCHIATRY

The small white card feels suddenly heavy in my hand. A *psychiatrist?* I reflexively look up at Dr. Mark, my mouth open, hurt oozing from my eyes. Haven't we been talking about something medical here? Weren't all these tests to measure my thyroid levels or my motor skills or my imbalances? Isn't the blood test supposed to tell us why I've lost weight? I know the answers to the past few months aren't related to any of these things but . . . but . . . a *psychiatrist?* Dr. Mark—I thought you knew me! I'm a straight-A student. I'm on the cross-country team. I—

I stop myself, almost choking on my next thoughts. I *was* a straight-A student. I *was* on the cross-country team. I'm not either of those things anymore. But I'm also not crazy. I'm *chosen.*

"I've coordinated with her office. She has an opening today at two p.m. that the nurse"—he gestures toward the door—"will reserve for you when you go to check out. Jennifer is a personal friend of mine. We went to undergrad together at UVA. Top of our class. She goes to my church. She's a great physician and a great person. I think she will be a good resource for you, Allison."

I'm peering at him through squinted eyes. He's speaking more to my mother than to me. My mom is holding the card reverently in her hand like it's a piece of communion bread, and a small thought creeps forward in my mind as Dr. Mark continues on with Dr. Adams's resume. Why did he have these business cards in his pocket at the ready? He didn't leave the room during the appointment, so he had to have brought them in here with him before we even talked. . . . And he already knew that she had an open appointment this afternoon.

I glance at my mom, then at Dr. Mark, and they're looking at each other like they've forgotten I'm here. My mom is smiling slightly. "Thank you," she says with so much emphasis and emotion you would think he just saved my life. "This really, really means a lot." And that's when it dawns on me. They planned this. I don't know how he knows or when he would have found out, but Dr. Mark clearly knew the entire situation before he even opened my medical file. My freaking mom. I can't even go to a doctor's appointment without her poking her nose around. I think about how quickly and eagerly she responded when he requested she leave so he could ask me questions. These little weasels. This whole thing is a ploy! Dr. Mark came into this appointment knowing that this business card would be the end result. Why did he even bother with all those tests in the first place?

I'm looking at them both in disbelief, but they're so involved in their conversation, neither of them seems to notice my expression as we move into the hallway. My mom hands the receptionist a form, and without acknowledging us, she picks up the phone and jabs the buttons with her nails. "Hi, yes. I'm calling about a Miss"—she looks down at the form—"Allison." She is squinting at the paper. "Yes, Yes, that's her. The one we spoke about earlier." I feel my mom tense beside me at this hole in her cover story, but I act like I didn't hear. That is not a conversation I want to have. "Yes, two p.m. Okay, thanks!" The receptionist hangs the phone up with a clatter and sheepishly looks up at me with a kind of half smile tainted with pity. "You're all set, dear. Dr. Adams looks forward to seeing you soon." She is talking to me like I just lost an elderly grandmother, speaking gently like I might be unstable. "You be strong now, darlin'."

I sneer at her painted lips and enormous hair. What the heck? Be strong? My face crinkles up at her and I shove my head forward in mock confusion. I'm not headed off to the front lines here, lady, I'm just . . . it's just that . . . my family doctor thinks I'm crazy. And apparently my mother does too. They staged this whole thing because they are both convinced there is something wrong with me. Something wrong with my mind.

Zipping up her wallet, my mom nudges me gently in my arm and we push through the heavy wooden door out into the sloshy winter mess.

CHAPTER 17

Dr. Adams's office is in an aged town house a few miles from downtown. There is a thick golden placard engraved with her name positioned above the door knocker on an imposing red-painted door. Shivering against the angry sleet falling relentlessly from the sky, I push open the heavy door and scamper into the waiting room. Warm air rushes forward, pulling me toward its comfort, and we are welcomed into what looks to be the Ritz-Carlton of doctor's offices. Plush couches stretch across an enormous Persian rug. They reach out from the walls, patiently waiting to hug me into their overstuffed cushions. The lamps are an aged copper, and the walls are covered with sprawling paintings of gundogs frozen at the ready, looking out into the tangled forest as their masters aim long, golden rifles.

"Hi, there. May I help you?" A beautiful brunette is smiling at us both from behind a desk in the corner. My mom moves up to the reception window, and I turn back to the opulent waiting room.

Again, as in Dr. Mark's office, the furniture is politely, if not mysteriously, silent and I let myself flop into one of the couches, relaxing slightly as I watch my mom talk with the receptionist. While she fills out forms and hands over her insurance card, I bury myself under a mound of throw pillows, trying to pile them on top of me as a makeshift blanket. I notice that my fingers that were just a few moments ago a sickly shade of blue are regaining some color in the warmth of the office. I shove them down under my thighs to help the process.

There's some sort of tinkling Christmas music playing in the background, and with my eyes I trace a strand of garland that weaves across the back of the couches until coming to an end on top of a large bookshelf filled with what look to be pamphlets. It's like one of those displays at a touristy hotel that's stuffed with brochures for local amusement parks or historical walking tours. Looking at it a bit closer, however, I see it is nothing as lighthearted as that. Instead, each individual stack of papers is labeled with a bold-type illness: schizophrenia, bipolar disorder, multiple personality disorder. It's a listing of the kinds of diseases that you know exist but no one ever really talks about. The kind of diseases that happen in movies and to celebrities but not to real people and not in this little town.

Without realizing I've stood up, I find myself shuffling toward the display stand and fingering through the different piles. For some reason I'm drawn to them and begin lifting one and then another out of their holders. I feel my mom's eyes watching me from in front of the reception desk, so I work my way methodically through the collection, making sure not to spend too much time on any one disease. I don't want her getting any ideas. I know she means well—she's just being a mom—but goodness gracious, the woman can meddle.

Looking through the pamphlets, I'm shaking my head slightly, only becoming more sure that I don't belong here.

Dr. Mark and his dumb questions. My mom and her stupid comments about my hair and grades. I don't know why I can understand furniture and clothes or why God has chosen me to know that pencils and notebook paper and cracks are dangerous. But it definitely has nothing to do with *this*. The thin, open pamphlet in my hand is describing "periods of rapid intense food consumption followed by habitual purging, also known as vomiting." I flinch internally at the mental picture and flip the pamphlet over to the cover—bulimia nervosa. Not me. I slide the white paper back into its pile and pick up the next one: bipolar disorder. The inside of the front cover describes people moving back and forth between periods of incredible happiness and energy followed by intense depression. Nope. Really not me. I drop the brochure back down behind its partners.

What a joke. What a waste of time. I hope my mom will be annoyed that she took an entire day off work with no result. That's what she deserves for getting involved.

The next brochure in my path is typed in the same standard Times New Roman as the other pamphlets. There is a thin orange border running around the edges of the paper and a small picture of hands being washed in the center of the cover. Obsessive-compulsive disorder.

I've definitely heard of this one, I think as I flip it open. Freaking out over germs, arranging things in straight lines. Everyone knows OCD. I picture the mess of unwearable clothes strewn across my bedroom floor and the plaque growing on my teeth after weeks of not brushing. It's almost funny to think of myself with this one. I'm the opposite of clean and orderly. I skip over the first few paragraphs to the symptoms section and find a column of bullets.

Those with obsessive-compulsive disorder may suffer from:

- **Persistent, unwanted thoughts or urges**
- **Incessant or repetitive actions**
- **Invented rules and rituals to control anxiety**

My heart stops and I feel my eyes freeze on the words. *Persistent. Unwanted. Incessant. Repetitive.* The next paragraph explains:

Obsessive-compulsive disorder involves obsessions, which are uncontrollable thoughts and fears, that lead the patient to perform compulsions, or repetitive actions. Sufferers find brief relief from the anxiety that accompanies the obsessive thoughts by performing compulsions. The person may or may not realize their thoughts are irrational.

Holy.

Crap.

My eyes shoot to the other side of the room at my mom gathering her purse up from the reception desk. I lurch toward the display and shove the pamphlet back into its place, my hand knocking loudly against the wooden case as she turns toward me. Holy. Crap. Holy. Crap.

"Everything okay?" She walks past and lets her hand rub gently across my back. "Come sit with me over here. Look at these beautiful couches."

My heart is pounding in my ears like a precursor to rapid-fire labeling, but instead it's the beginning of a hot storm cloud forming in my gut. No thoughts pass through my mind. I am completely still. Holy. Crap.

"Allison, honey." My mom is reaching toward me, her soft, warm hand on my arm. Her voice has that worried tone, and I'm ripped from my freeze, pulled back to the waiting room out of pity. "What's that look on your face?"

"Hmm?" My eyes focus on her, and I lift my cheeks in an effort at a smile. "What look?"

"You just looked . . . confused. Perplexed. Like you're thinking about something."

"Uh, no." I look at the ceiling like I'm trying to remember. "No, not really. Just, um . . . I really like these couches." I take a few steps and with a little jump flop myself into the deep cushions. My mom joins me, puts her hand on my leg, and smiles at the side of my face. I ignore her, covering myself with another throw-pillow blanket and trying not to stare at the wrinkled stack of pamphlets against the wall. The words are inked across my mind in the same large Times New Roman that stretched across the white paper. I start to let them form in my mouth, but something immediately ushers them away, shooing them out of the light. Inside me I know not to say it. I don't know why—just don't.

"Allison?" The heavy oak door swings open and a round, middle-aged woman in a sweater set is looking directly at me. Her thick brown hair is cut into a clean bob. "Are you ready?" Hands clasped in front of her, she is smiling at me with her eyes.

I . . . I . . . don't know? Am I? For the past few months I've oscillated between sheepishly hoping someone would throw me a life raft and ardently attempting to hide my thoughts and symptoms from the world. God is talking to me, he has chosen me, but if I'm honest with myself, it's ruining my life. And my relationships. And my future.

But it's still *God,* I scream inside, flinching. Without meaning to, I look at my mom, who nods at me, patting my knee. I know I can't tell Dr. Adams, or anyone, the real truth. But there doesn't seem to be a way for me to get out of this. As I stand up, a heaviness floods into my stomach. With this step, I am officially seeing a psychiatrist. It doesn't matter so much that I know there's nothing wrong with me—it's what everyone else will think. I am now a *psychiatric patient.*

I don't look to my right as I pass the stand of pamphlets, and, thankfully, none of them try to talk to me. Dr. Adams extends her hand toward me. "Hello there, Allison. I'm so happy you've come here to see me today. It's a pleasure to meet you." For a few moments, I squint my eyes at her, my head cocked to the side, before realizing it's my turn. With a short hesitation, I extend my clammy hand to her, and she shakes it enthusiastically. "Let me show you into my office."

I plod behind her, my flannel pants swishing against the warm air. I feel God watching my every step. Her office is at the end of a short hallway, and it's smaller than I expected, almost cozy. There is a replica of the couches from the waiting room against the window, and she gestures me toward it with another smile. I lean back into the cushions and watch her as she settles into her high-backed chair about five feet away. After adjusting her clipboard and cardigan, she looks up at me, and for the first time I really see her. Big, blue eyes shine across the carpet. Her plump, rosy cheeks leak happiness and optimism. There's something calm about her. She smiles at me gently, as if waiting for me to finish my appraisal of her.

"How are you today?" We make eye contact.

"Fine," I peep, barely opening my mouth wide enough to let the sound escape.

She nods at me, giving me the opportunity to return the nicety, but I don't. I don't know you. I don't know why I'm here. I don't need to—but the thoughts catch on the memory of the pamphlet in the waiting room. Times New Roman flashes against the back of my eyes.

"Well, that's good to hear." She doesn't move and continues to look at me across the carpet. At least ten seconds pass. To break the tension, I shake my head once up and down and do the cheek lift that I use in place of smiles. "You don't need to be uncomfortable, Allison. Today we're just getting to know each other. We're just going to talk. I promise. Nothing serious." I nod at her, my lips pursed tightly together. I wasn't going to tell you anything anyway.

"So," she begins, "I've heard you run cross-country?"

With this, we begin a meandering question-and-answer session. I run cross-country and track and play soccer in the spring. I'm an only child. Yes, I do well in school. Spanish is

233

my favorite subject. Math is my hardest. Yes, I like my friends. Yes, I have a good relationship with my parents.

As she promised, the forty-five minutes pass with no hard conversations, no probing questions. We stay at the surface. Her smiling, me nodding. At the end of the appointment, as a small alarm chimes from the clock on her wall, she flips her notepad closed and places her hands on it with finality. She is looking at me again. That patient, calming stare. I'm not exactly sure what it means.

"I want to thank you, Allison. For today." I feel my eyebrows rise and bring my gaze up to her face. "We've just met, and I know that it's a strange experience for you to spend this time with me, talking about your life. But I genuinely appreciate that you participated in this conversation." She is holding eye contact with me. "Thank you for trusting me."

I don't know what to do with this statement. Or my hands, or my face. My eyes shift around the room awkwardly, and there's something growing in my stomach. It's acid or bile or anger. But . . . no. It's . . . warmth. Comfort. Relief?

I open my mouth but, realizing after a few moments that I have nothing to say, close it again with a small squeak. I nod at her once.

Her smile is bigger than ever as she stands and guides me out of her office and down the hallway. "I think I'd like to see you again tomorrow, if that's okay with you?" I'm nodding at her, grunting slightly as I push against the door in the hallway. Something in my heart feels lighter, and as I move into the waiting room, it seems like maybe the sun is shining a little brighter. The angry sleet is now a pretty, gentle snow.

"Mom, time to—"

But my mom isn't the only one in the waiting room anymore, and I find my eyes looking at the top of a slick of brown hair. The shaggy mane is falling forward slightly. He's leaning down, tying a pair of extremely clean Air Jordans. Sensing my presence, the head looks up, revealing a navy blue polo shirt and khaki pants. And the world stops.

His eyes shoot open and I see the muscles in his jaw tense. I'm staring at Joe Thompson. A junior in my precal class. On this year's homecoming court. A basketball player. And football player. He cuts his eyes from me, to his mom, to Dr. Adams, and back to me. His mouth is open. There might be tears in his eyes.

"Well, hello there, Joseph." Dr. Adams's voice bursts across the tension. "Nice to see you this afternoon! You're a bit early. Just let me finish up here, okay?" Her smile is glowing at him but there is an edge of anxiety in it. I don't think patients are supposed to cross paths.

I glance back once at Dr. Adams, and, pushing my head down and staring into the floor, I speed-walk across the waiting room and out into the winter. My mom stays behind, filling out a form at the checkout desk. She unlocks the car through the window and I fling myself into the passenger seat.

Joe Thompson. I see his face again. He was terrified. "The Joe Man" was at the psychiatrist. At my psychiatrist. So I'm not the only one. I think of the stack of pamphlets against the wall. Which one is he? Bipolar disorder, depression. Maybe even the one with the orange border and black-and-white clip art.

Maybe he doesn't wear pajamas to school or cry during exams, but if he's here—I look through the frost-covered windshield at the town house—he must also have something mysterious bubbling inside him. Even though we've never actually spoken, I've known him most of my life. We went to the same middle school. He was a boys' counselor at the summer camp I went to last year. Popular, athletic. He's so *normal.* Or at least he looks like he is.

I've been thinking about Joe all day. Not just Joe, but Dr. Adams and her smile and those couches. And the pamphlet with the orange border. I'm still counting around my house and starving and praying, but my thoughts are missing some of their sharpness. Like a giant eraser has gently smudged the edges of the dark hole inside me. I'm still the chosen one, the carrier of secret messages from above, but maybe I'm also—

No. I snap the thought shut before I even know it's coming, shaking my head hard to throw it off its path. It's not allowed. I don't even need to be told specifically by my protector—it's obvious. Turning these sacred ideas and warnings into anything other than what they are feels like cheating on the Lord. A dangerous step in the wrong direction.

But even as I turn away from the mental image of the pamphlet and Joe, a piece of it is still there. I can't say it or think about it, but I feel its presence lingering just out of sight.

The next day, I rub my freezing, exposed arms with my palms after launching myself into the warmth of Dr. Adams's waiting room. My mom greets the receptionist and moves toward her desk. As if being pulled by a magnet, I'm walking straight toward the stacks of pamphlets, almost surprised by my own actions. I hear my mom taking out her wallet, pulling out a card, signing a form. Eyes locked on the clip art of washing hands, I know I only have a few more seconds before she turns around. My heart is pounding, and I feel God watching me from heaven, shocked that I'm betraying him. He shakes his head in disappointment, regretting that he ever trusted me. The wallet zips and she is adjusting it in her purse, keys rattling gently against coins and pens. Now or never.

In one flailing movement, I lunge toward the display, grab the pamphlet, and stuff it down into the waistband of my pants. I'm adjusting the bottom edge of my shirt as my mom turns toward me.

She gently grabs my arm and brings me with her toward the couch. I sit down beside her, the thin paper crinkling softly under my shirt.

"Allison, dear!" Dr. Adams appears in the doorway in what looks to be the exact same sweater set she was wearing yesterday. She smiles at me like we're old friends and waves me over. "So good to see you again! Such beautiful weather we're having today, right?" I stand up to walk toward her, and there is a sudden tickle on my skin. My pajama pants are too loose, and I feel the secret pamphlet I stashed in my waistband slipping down my thigh. I smack my hands hard against my leg with a small gasp, and both my mom and Dr. Adams jump slightly.

Now they're staring.

"Yeah! Definitely! Weather!" I nod hard in agreement, first at my mom, then at Dr. Adams. I see them make eye contact with each other over my shoulder. Ugh, crap. Ducking my head down and waddling slightly to hold the pamphlet in my pants, I walk quickly through the door and down the hallway toward her office. I'm almost settled on the couch by the time she catches up and closes the door behind her.

She is looking at me, eyes a little wider than usual, but her smile still seems genuine. "Well, yes. Okay, then. Like I said, so very nice to see you today, Allison." Her head tilts slightly forward for emphasis. "How have you been since I saw you yesterday?"

She actually sounds interested. She actually sounds happy to see me. I crunch my lips to the side and she waits patiently for me to respond. I like her. And I don't really know why, but I trust her.

I think about Joe. Even though he sees Dr. Adams, even though he's also a psychiatric patient, he still has friends and wears normal clothes and takes precal finals without crying. I could have that too. Maybe. Possibly. I could talk to Jenny and Sara. I could wear blue jeans and tennis shoes and a polo shirt. My heart swells in my chest. I could be *me* again.

Isn't it worth it? Isn't my life, my future, worth it?

Dear God, please forgive me.

Shifting to my left on the couch, I reach my arm down into my flannel pants. As I pull out the slightly crinkled, warm pamphlet, I look down at the words across the cover. OBSESSIVE-COMPULSIVE DISORDER. When I glance up at

Dr. Adams, she is still waiting patiently, watching me from across the carpet.

I clear my throat and roll my head once on my shoulders. A deep breath. Do it.

Dr. Adams and I make eye contact for a few moments and I extend the pamphlet toward her, my arm shaking slightly. "I think I have this."

CHAPTER 18

She tilts her head softly to the side, scoots up in her chair a bit, and takes the wrinkled pamphlet from my hand. "Hmm," she says to herself, readjusting in her seat. Her eyes look up at me, and they are somehow softer than usual, like I've just told her a heartbreaking story. She is trying to hug me with her expression. "Thank you for sharing this with me, Allison. I'm very proud of you."

My heartbeat is pounding through my body, just as strong down in my fingers and toes as in my chest. I did it. I can't believe I did it. I give her a small nod, only because she is staring at me.

"Could you tell me a little bit more about why you picked this pamphlet up?" She moves forward in her chair, leaning toward me. "What in here sounds like you?"

My entire body is tingly. In a tiny voice, barely opening my lips, I say, "Bad thoughts."

She nods at me with her whole body. "Yes, good. Very good." Smiling across the carpet, her eyes are encouraging me to go on, but what is there to say? Apples. Pencils. Cracks. Calculators. Notebook paper. Cancer. Hairbrushes. Television. Cell phones.

"So, when you say bad thoughts, do you mean scary? Do you mean angry? Sad?"

"Scary," I peep in a cloud of rancid breath. "And sad."

"Scary, sad thoughts. Very good." She nods at me, barely

looking down at her paper as she makes a small note. Pausing a few seconds, she is waiting for me to elaborate. But there are no words for this. No real explanation that anyone would understand. And I'm betraying the Lord. I'm picking at the hangnail on my thumb, and a fat drop of blood grows out from under the skin. "Tell me a little more about these scary thoughts, hmm?" She shifts in her chair. "What are they about?"

The word feels dangerous even as it forms in my mouth. It comes out like a puff of tobacco smoke. "Cancer."

Her eyebrows crease briefly, almost immeasurably, before bouncing back into an interested smile. "Yes, yes. Okay. Cancer, hmm. Who does this cancer affect?"

"My . . ." I can't believe I'm doing this. I concentrate on shoving the anxiety into a corner of my mind. My left temporal lobe is pounding at the site of the tumor. "My . . . mom . . . and dad. And me." She nods at me and moves her hand in the air, wordlessly asking me to elaborate. Deep breath. "I'll . . . we'll . . . get cancer. From doing certain things or being near certain things." I hesitate here, and she opens her mouth slightly to speak, but I've got more. "Or they'll get hurt or die because of something I do."

She is looking me straight in the face now, nodding and writing. "Good. Hmm. Okay." She lets out a powerful sigh. "Thank you for telling me this. I know it wasn't easy." My mouth feels suddenly dry and tight. I never thought I would speak these words. But they came out so easily, almost like they've been waiting to be shared all along.

I think Dr. Adams is talking to me, I can hear her voice somewhere in the background, but I'm too absorbed within myself to listen. So are my thoughts not from God? Have the past few months really been some bizarre mental illness, instead of secret messages of survival? Has all of this been completely wrong?

Of course they're from God, I hiss at myself, angry and offended. I cower slightly, half expecting a lightning bolt to strike me dead. This is blasphemy. God has been trying to save me and my family for months now, and with a few sentences on a piece of paper and eager head nods from a stranger, I'm just going to throw it all away?

But the pamphlet! And Dr. Adams. And *persistent, unwanted thoughts* and *incessant or repetitive actions*. The tip-toeing, the standing on one foot, the counting. Even as I deny it to myself in an effort to please the heavens, a warmth inside me tells me that there's something here.

"Now, besides illness, cancer, are there other repercussions to your actions? Or do you feel like that's your main concern?"

"Yes." That's a big question.

"Yes, what?"

"Yes, I worry about other things." I know I'm being difficult, peeping out these short responses, but God is listening. My eyes are busying themselves, looking at everything in the office besides her face. Is this really the best idea? It's like I'm walking to the end of the diving board but I'm not sure if the pool below is filled with water or if, after a graceful swan dive, I'm going to crunch into a pile on its dry concrete floor. I'll only know the truth once I've jumped, and then it's too late.

Do I jump?

Should I jump?

Dr. Adams is nodding at me. I can tell by the calm half smile on her face that she has practice in coaxing information out of timid patients. "Okay, let's try this. I'll list out some common fears or rituals associated with OCD, and you just nod if I hit on one that seems familiar. How about that?"

I nod once at her. Good idea.

"Hmm, okay, let's see." She flips to a clean page on her lined legal pad. "Do you ever worry that you will be contaminated by germs? Like if you don't wash your hands or body you may get sick or get others sick?"

I move my head left, then right. Nope. My tongue runs over my fuzzy, plaque-covered teeth.

"What about a concern that something you do will negatively affect others? Outside of cancer, I mean. For example, someone might get in a car accident or be injured as a direct result of your actions?"

Without realizing it, I'm shaking my head vigorously at her. Yes, yes, yes. That's me! Every day. Every minute.

"Okay, good! Good. Can you tell me a little more about that?"

I clear my throat a little. Something close to excitement is rising in my stomach. This could actually be . . . real. "Well, like, sometimes I worry that my parents will get in car wrecks or be murdered. And I try to not do certain things to prevent it from happening." Basically, I'm single-handedly saving my parents' lives multiple times a day. I gently give myself a mental pat on the back.

Dr. Adams makes another small "hmm" noise and scribbles on her legal pad. "How about unlucky numbers or colors or words? Have you experienced anything like that?"

The word "green" appears in my mind, taking up my entire brain. It buzzes like a neon sign against the darkness. I don't know if I respond. I'm staring intently at the glowing word and imagining my chemistry answer sheet, and the trees and grass outside. Taking a giant breath in, I hold it in my lungs like a balloon. Just to be safe. Looking up, I see her scribbling and I know she's gotten the message.

"You are really doing great, Allison. I have to tell you that. I'm very proud of you." We make eye contact but she doesn't skip a beat. "What about concern about offending a religious figure? Do you worry about angering Jesus or God?"

My muscles jerk tightly and I'm clenching myself against her words and the strange wave of fear or excitement or anxiety breezing through me. I mean, yes. One thousand times yes. That's the whole point of . . . that's why I'm doing all of this. . . .

Holy crap.

By the time I'm back from my thoughts and look up at Dr. Adams, she is scribbling. It must be written on my face.

She gives two hard nods and closes her folder with finality and a sigh. "Well, Allison, I think I'm going to have to agree with your self-diagnosis." The pamphlet is folded on her side table, and I feel it smirking at me. "You seem to have hit the nail on the head, my dear." She beams at me across the carpet like it's a good thing. And even though I'm tempted to agree with her, even though there is an unfamiliar sense of lightness in my chest, I'm hesitant to embrace this whole thing with as much enthusiasm as she does. I still can't be sure the pool is filled with water.

"And, you know, it's actually quite typical for symptoms to start presenting themselves right around your age, at the start of puberty." Even though she is a medical doctor, I blush self-consciously at the awkward word. *Puberty*. It makes me cringe.

After a few more questions, a small bell chimes from the clock on the wall, telling us our time is up, and Dr. Adams's smile reaches its beaming climax. "Allison, thank you again for today's session. Thank you for trusting me. Thank you for talking with me. You've really done something amazing. It's only going to get better from here." She holds eye contact for a few seconds longer than I'm comfortable with. "Now, before we head back to the waiting room, I do need to talk with you about something." I look up at her, unsure what's coming. That kind of intro doesn't typically lead to anything positive. "Now, this is completely up to you. I'm your doctor and this is your information. But I would like to talk to your parents about what you told me today."

My head snaps up, almost offended at the suggestion. My *parents*? Uh, isn't the whole purpose of us talking in this private room to keep things just that—private? To prevent my parents from finding out, to prevent *anyone* from finding out? I'm opening and closing my mouth like a gasping fish. And again, it's like she expected this.

"Look, look"—she waves her hands in the air, trying to dismiss my concern—"I'll keep it very vague, very high-level. I won't tell them anything specific, no actual fears or thoughts you're having, but they're your parents, Allison. And whether you realize it or not, they're very concerned about you. I think it would be the right thing to do to keep them in the loop. At least a little bit. Hmm?" She leans toward me and actually puts her warm, squishy hand on my kneecap. I can feel her happiness through my thin flannel pants. "I think they would really appreciate it"—she leans back in her seat—"but of course I won't do it without your permission." The room is silent for a few seconds. I'm pulling at the hangnail on my bloody thumb. "What do you say?"

I know she's right. I hear my mom's screaming voice when she found me curled up on the den floor. I think about her sitting on the edge of my bed and the way she whispered that everything would be okay, her soft hand running against my hair. "Yeah, sure. I guess."

That night, I'm pushing kernels of corn individually around my plate, hiding them one by one under my dinner roll. Hunger sears through my body—my hands are shaking slightly—but somehow the sharp pangs sting a little less than usual. I'm still starving, still eking my way through the day on a few gobbled bites of food, but since my first appointment with Dr. Adams, it's like a match has been lit in what was previously a lonesome, pitch-black room. I can't eat, can't wear my clothes, can't brush my teeth or use towels or soap, but a weight has been lifted.

These thoughts are blessings from God, but they are also inexplicably tied to that pamphlet. Dr. Adams, with her medical degree and years of experience, has agreed with me. It seems like there could be a chance. Of something. I'm just not exactly sure what.

"So, sweetheart"—my mom's voice is pleasant, like for the first time in months she doesn't notice me swirling my food around my plate—"we spoke with Dr. Adams this afternoon." I don't take my eyes off my corn. Like the "becoming a woman" talk and the birds-and-the-bees talk, I don't want to be an active participant in this conversation. No eye contact. "She told us a little bit about the pamphlet you found in her office and the talk you two had about obsessive-compulsive disorder." I flinch at her last words and accidentally drop my fork, and it clatters loudly against my plate onto the table. There are a few seconds of silence while we all recover. "Um, so, right. She told us about your talk and she suggested that we"—I feel her look at my dad—"talk with you about what you think is the best kind of treatment." There is another bout of silence. I don't look up, so I'm not sure if she is waiting for me to respond or hesitating before she continues.

"She explained that OCD is most effectively treated with a combination of medication and therapy. We would start with a low dose of a drug called an SSRI, like Paxil or Lexapro, and you and she would work together to find the balance that works for you. It all—"

"Absolutely not." I break my promise to myself, and I'm looking up, first at my mom and then at my dad. "No way am I taking medicine." I see my brain being bombarded by tiny particles of pills, and instead of doing whatever it is Dr. Adams thinks that they will do, they sprout into millions of miniscule tumors. It's karma for betraying God or bad luck or another secret of the universe. OCD medicine causes brain cancer. I know it. It's obvious.

"Well, Dr. Adams really seemed to think this was the right path forward. She said that when you combine therapy and medication, as opposed to just therapy, you tend to see much quicker—"

"I don't care," I say through clenched teeth. "I don't want medicine." My head is throbbing. Maybe even talking about medicine can cause brain cancer. Stranger things have happened.

My parents exchange a long look, and my dad gives a half shrug. My mom is staring at me, mouth slightly open, but I can't read her expression. I can tell it's taking all of her self-control to keep her thoughts to herself. My dad reaches his hand over and places it on her arm. She looks toward him and relaxes slightly. With a sigh, she says, "Okay, then, sweetie. Whatever you want."

"Well, Allison," Dr. Adams says the next day, clasping her hands on top of the papers on her thighs and adjusting her glasses on her nose, "I'm a psychiatrist, and since you aren't yet interested in taking medication, I don't know how much help I can really offer you." She recommends a local psychologist who has spent her entire career treating cases "just like mine" and, recognizing my hesitation, spends the rest of our time together singing my new doctor's praises. This appointment, like the one a few days before with Dr. Mark, ends with a small white business card:

DR. VIRGINIA NELSON, PHD

SPECIALIZING IN CHILDHOOD AND

ADOLESCENT OCD AND ANXIETY

CHAPTER 19

So far I'm not impressed. Even the drive here was ugly. We stayed on the highway until exiting on a ramp surrounded by strip malls and empty factory buildings. There were no quaint parks filled with playgrounds and strollers like on the way to Dr. Adams's. Standing in front of a row of boring, non-descript brick town houses, I can already tell this is a mistake. Dr. Nelson may have experience and credentials, but something here doesn't feel right. She doesn't even have flowers beside the front steps. Just a sad-looking scrubby bush.

I pull at the front door, and it gives with a small sucking sound. My dad is already in the waiting room, sitting awkwardly in a chair that seems somehow too small for him. He looks up and shoots me a small, hesitant wave and smile. He's uncomfortable. This is the first doctor's appointment he has been to with me and my mom, and it's obvious he doesn't know how he is supposed to behave. His eyes are asking me how he can help—act like nothing is wrong, tell a joke, wrap me in a hug? I give him a tiny shrug. I'm not any better at this than you are, Dad.

I look at the large bay window facing out to the parking lot and scan my eyes across the waiting room. It's a sea of beige. Beige carpet, beige walls, beige upholstery on the seats. All the artwork is of stately-looking brown horses prancing through fields, jumping over fences. There's a large bookshelf against the wall, but in front of the books are about a dozen painted horse figurines. There's a vase holding fake flowers to my left, with a herd of horses running across the porcelain. *What the heck?* She's a crazy horse lady. I look up at the empty reception desk. There's a small, vacant chair with a sweater draped over the back. *And she's her own secretary?*

What kind of half-rate therapist did Dr. Adams send me to? No plush couches, no festive Christmas decorations. I glance up at the aged watercolor of a horse posing in front of a barn. No gold-framed oil paintings. I've gone from the Ritz to a motel.

My mom is patting the chair beside her, asking me to come sit down, trying not to notice that I'm standing on one leg. As I move toward her, there is a rustling down the hallway, and soon a thin, lanky, middle-aged woman appears in the doorway beside the reception desk. Her straight brown hair is graying slightly, and it's cropped short above her ears. She's wearing a plain light-pink cotton T-shirt over loose khakis. On her feet are a pair of Teva sandals that look remarkably like the ones my dad insists on wearing whenever he's not at work. And, also like my dad, she pairs them with thick wool socks.

I guess I shouldn't be surprised. Plain brick town house, monochromatic waiting room. If beige were a person, it would be this lady. I'm biting the inside of my lip, frowning. The tiny light that flickered to life inside me after my visits with Dr. Adams is dimming rapidly.

"Hello, there. I'm Dr. Virginia Nelson. If you wouldn't mind following me back to my office"—she extends her arm behind her—"I'd like to spend a few minutes talking to you as a family." With this, she turns in her sandals and walks back down the hallway. Still standing on one foot, I look to my parents across the waiting room. They're looking between me, each other, and the now empty doorway.

"Okay, then," my dad says with another shrug as he pushes himself up out of the creaking chair. "Let's do this thing." I crunch my face at him. Nice try, but no.

We move together down the beige hallway into an equally beige office. Dr. Nelson is getting situated in a high-backed brown chair in the corner, and she gestures my parents into two seats across from her. The first thing I notice are one, two, *three* more horse paintings hanging on the wall. But unlike the bare waiting room, the painted walls around the frames are plastered in hand-drawn pictures. The one closest to me was clearly made by a child, probably around eight or nine. It has a small stick-figure boy in the middle thrusting a giant sword into the air. A word bubble near his mouth declares, *Take that, OCD!!* I move my eyes up to the one above it, also done by a kid but maybe more middle-school-aged. At the top in scrawled letters it reads, *Aiden will face his fear of . . .* and below is a bulleted list with small illustrations: bumblebees, snakes, airplanes, dogs, sidewalk cracks.

Sidewalk cracks.

"Allison, would you like to sit?" Dr. Nelson points toward the other side of the room. "You can scoot that chair from the corner over here with us." I follow her finger toward a kid-sized chair tucked under a large wooden table covered in markers, crayons, paper, stickers. The chair doesn't say anything specific to me, but I can feel its static. It doesn't seem happy.

"Nope, I'm fine. I like to stand." My voice comes out peppy and lighthearted like I hoped. I push my right cheek up at her and raise my leg so I'm swaying slightly on the other. She looks down at my stance. I'm watching her face closely, but her expression doesn't change. As if patients always stand on one foot during their first meeting. My dad is shaking his head slightly.

"Well, I'm glad we were able to fit you all in so quickly. I had a last-minute cancellation, so I'd say you have pretty good timing." She smiles at me for the first time, but I only stare back at her. You aren't Dr. Adams. She clears her throat and looks back at my parents. "I spent some time this morning discussing Allison's condition with Dr. Adams." Opening a thin manila folder, she pulls out a stack of papers covered in writing. Is there really that much to know about me?

"Based on some of her comments, it seems like Allison is presenting with sudden-onset obsessive-compulsive disorder. But before we get too deep into what that means and some options for moving forward, I'd like to first get your input"—she's looking at my parents—"and hear a bit more about what you've seen since"—she glances down at her paper—"October." With this, Dr. Nelson puts her notes down and eyes my parents expectantly.

"Oh, um, sure." My dad. So awkward. "Well, I guess I'll start. So, uh, this all really began a few months ago. At the start, there wasn't really anything we could put our finger on. She just wasn't herself. Always hiding upstairs, acting almost . . . manic?" He freezes here and jumps forward in his seat. "I mean, not like *manic* manic. Sorry, I know that's a whole different thing, but just, uh, you know, she was much more talkative, kind of rabidly energetic. Like she was trying to convince us that everything was fine, or distract us from whatever strange new thing she was doing." Dr. Nelson is nodding and writing on a white sheet of paper that I can now see is labeled in bold, black letters: INTAKE FORM.

"And from there it all went downhill so fast. She was tiptoeing. She stopped eating. I would find her up in the middle of the night in the den reading the Bible. There's the counting. Oh, and the standing. She's always standing." All three of them glance at me but then immediately try to hide it. "And you know, it was like every week, maybe every day, it got a little bit worse. It was kind of like watching our daughter . . . disappear. . . ." My dad's voice trails off, and he is looking down at his hands while I stare intently at the carpet. I didn't realize it but I've been picking at the skin on my index finger. The cuticle is completely raw. A line of blood dribbles down to my knuckle and I wipe it on my flannel.

After a few moments, my mom picks up where he stopped. "Well, and also, Jeffrey, you're forgetting a few things. Mostly around her appearance." She gestures toward me but doesn't look over. "She hasn't really been bathing. Or brushing her hair or doing her makeup. It's all very unlike her. She's stopped getting dressed for the day, and there are only a few items of clothes she is willing to wear. She won't put on a jacket, even when it's freezing outside." My mom is moving her arms broadly as she speaks, like she is trying to make sure Dr. Nelson really hears everything she is saying. "And her schoolwork. Her grades have dropped significantly. She used to be a straight-A student—literally. But now . . ." Her voice, too, trails off, and she stares out the window for a few seconds. "I'm just not sure what happened. And, like he said"—she tilts her head toward my dad—"it was so fast."

Dr. Nelson continues to nod as she finishes writing out her last sentence. "Okay, good. And, Allison?" Three heads turn to look at me. "Do you have anything you want to add to this?"

My heart is pounding in my head. I'm too embarrassed to speak. Of course they noticed my counting and standing and terrible grades. How could they miss the tangled hair and dinner plates full of food and tiptoeing? While I know they're still really only scraping the surface of the darker, deeper problem, my stomach tightens in on itself. It was the way they *said* it. Hello, I'm *right here!* I can *hear* you, you know, as you talk about me like your once-perfect child who has now fallen from her pedestal. Like I'm some adolescent freak of nature that you're scared of, that you whisper about when I'm not around. And after *everything* I've done for you? All the terminal cancers and car wrecks I've prevented? My teeth clench together. This feels like an intervention, like the ones I've seen on television. Concerned family members and therapists gather around, telling the person how they're ruining their own life. But I'm not a drug addict or an alcoholic or a criminal. I'm just trying to protect us. I don't want to die.

"Allison?" It's my mom. "Do you want to share anything with Dr. Nelson?"

I glare up at her with a look that I hope tells her how much I hate her in this moment. How ridiculous this is. Yes, all the things they said are true. But they don't get it. They will never understand. In their eyes, I'm now just a failed version of my former self, the girl who could have been so many things, but instead she's . . . *this*. Emotion welling in my eyes, I trace the edge of my torn T-shirt with bleeding fingers. I open my mouth and look to the ceiling to try to keep the tears from rolling down my cheeks.

There is a silence and I know they're all watching me. Dr. Nelson breaks the tension. "Okay, well, what I'd like to do now is talk to you individually. Mom and Dad, we'll start with you, and then after about ten minutes, we'll switch and I'll talk with Miss Allison. Does that work for everyone?" My parents nod, and I keep my eyes focused on my ragged fingers. Dr. Nelson stands up, moves in front of me, and opens the office door. I shuffle past her with my eyes down and she whispers, "It will just be a few minutes, dear. It's going to be okay." Without thinking, I raise my eyes up to her face and we hold eye contact. She doesn't say anything, doesn't even smile, but the churning waters in my stomach smooth under her gaze. There is something calming about her. Raising her voice back to normal so my mom and dad can hear, she adds, "Help yourself to some bottled water in the fridge. I'll send your parents to get you when we're done."

The door closes gently behind me and I'm in the dark, carpeted hallway. I stop in my tracks and listen to her walking back toward her brown and boring chair. "Okay, so, take me back to October, to the beginning. And try to walk me through the progression of her symptoms." I hesitate in place. I'm ravenous to know what else my parents might say about me, what else they might know. Do they know about God? Talking furniture? Safe step allotments?

My dad's voice cuts across the air. "It got out of hand before we even realized that something serious was going on. She . . ."

My entire body clenches at his words. Without realizing it, I find myself shuffling silently down the hallway toward the waiting room. I don't think this is information I actually want to hear. Kind of like Jenny and Maddie and Rebecca gossiping about my eating habits, sometimes it's easier not to know the details.

Staring at the row of three chairs against the wall in the waiting room, I realize that they're quiet. No static, no anger. A little surprised, I plop myself down on the closest one and it gives a few noisy creaks. Maybe this place will be silent like Dr. Adams's and Dr. Mark's after all. That would be nice. Three of my fingers are oozing a mixture of pus and blood, so I press them hard against the fabric of my thin pants. The towering bookshelf is to my left. Moving my head slightly to see around the horse figurines, I spot six shelves jammed full of titles like *The Boy Who Couldn't Stop Washing* and *Breaking Free from OCD* with a smaller, italicized subtitle: *A Workbook for Young People.*

My eyes scan the shelves. Book after book after book, all aimed to help people who seem to think exactly like me.

Maybe Dr. Nelson does know what she's talking about. Her office is underwhelming, so incredibly beige, but she seems professional. Plus, Dr. Adams trusts her. And I trust Dr. Adams. The tiny light that almost disappeared because of the bland décor and horse paintings is suddenly beaming inside me. This could be my chance. A strange gurgle rises in my stomach. At first I think it's bile, or a cramp of angry hunger, but . . . it's hope. Maybe even happiness? I squint my eyes and look around the room, almost suspicious of the feeling. I felt an edge of it at Dr. Adams's, but now powerful waves are sweeping over my head, and I willingly let myself be pulled under.

And, really, what's the alternative? Refuse to talk to Dr. Nelson, continue to keep all these thoughts and fears inside me? Looking down at my ragged clothes and gnawed-off nails, I know that isn't even an option anymore. If I step back from the pressure of pleasing God for just a second, I know that my life has melted into nothing. I've ruined my grades, my reputation, my relationships with my parents and friends. I can't go any further. I don't want to know what comes after rock bottom.

And this whole doctor-psychiatrist-psychologist process has reached the point of no return, I think as I scan my eyes around the waiting room. I hear the soft mumblings of my parents down the hall. They wouldn't let me get away with not cooperating. Not anymore, not now that they've grasped what's really going on. Maybe I could weasel out of this specific appointment by pulling another precalculus food poisoning, but I would be back here eventually. And if not here, then at the very least back at Dr. Adams's.

As much as I want to believe that the Lord is sending me secret messages, as much as it feels powerfully true inside me, this is all too much to be a coincidence. *Pervasive, unwanted thoughts* and *incessant, repetitive actions*—images of angry textbooks and clothes flit across my mind. Months of moldy sandwiches. My stubby, unsharpened pencil. Sara's face as I leaped, counted, and tiptoed to class. Peaches, pennies, potatoes. The computer. My cell phone. Calculators. The seemingly never-ending danger list runs itself in a loop through my mind.

And suddenly, sitting alone in the silent waiting room, blood oozing from my fingers, I know I'm ready to talk.

I'm ready to face this.

CHAPTER 20

My eyes jerk away from the bookshelf when I hear the office door open down the hall. My parents appear in the doorway to the waiting room. The stress is vivid on their faces, pulling their wrinkles deeper into their skin, but as soon as they see me, they both break into forced tandem smiles. "Hi there, big girl! Your turn!" My poor dad, he's really trying.

Dr. Nelson is standing patiently behind them, her hands clasped casually in front of her. As my parents settle into the seats beside me, I know it's my cue to stand up, but I can't move. It's not that I don't want to, but something much more powerful than gravity is holding me in place. I've decided to talk to her, I've decided to give this a try . . . but. But. But . . .

"Ready?" She's smiling gently at me from about ten feet away.

No.

Five seconds pass. "Allison, honey." My mom nudges me with her arm. "Come on, sweetie. Go on back with Dr. Nelson. We'll be waiting right here." She acts like I'm scared of Dr. Nelson, of being in the quiet office with a stranger. And once again I bristle at how wrong she is. It's not the doctor or the separation that's worrying me. It's tumors and mutating cells and lumps in breasts. Cold graves, beeping hospital beds, God's wrath. She nudges me again. "Go on."

I roll my eyes in irritation and halfway through the loop accidentally meet eyes with Dr. Nelson. Her eyebrows are

260

raised and there's a slight smile curving up at the corner of her mouth. She gives a tiny nod, gesturing me to follow her, and turns down the hallway. I shoot both of my parents an annoyed glance, just so they're clear how I feel.

Dr. Nelson is at her chair in the corner, picking up the manila folder on the cushion before sitting down. The room is somehow less dingy than it was just a few minutes ago. Still overwhelmingly horsey and brown, but it's like the curtains have been opened and the sun has come out from behind the clouds. Maybe it's because my parents aren't here anymore. Or maybe it's because of my decision to finally talk to someone. Or maybe, probably, it's just the last edge of light before the incoming thunderstorm.

Sitting patiently, legs crossed, Dr. Nelson is looking at me, waiting for me to make the first move. I'm holding my breath, listening for messages or rapid-fire labeling or a swarm of bees. Some sort of sign to warn me that what I'm about to do is a terrible mistake. I can feel the small wooden chair at the art table behind me buzzing frustration as it did before, but the rest of the furniture in the room sits calmly. To my left, resting on top of a large decorative rug, is a high-backed chair positioned across from Dr. Nelson that I know I'm supposed to sit in. I can feel it looking at me. And, unlike any other piece of furniture before it, it's smiling. Beckoning me into its stiff, brown, upholstered arms.

A friendly chair? I feel my face scrunching up in confusion. Well, this is a . . . surprise. I lift my left leg up so I'm standing on one foot while I survey the wooden base, the aged fabric. It looks like something from a nursing-home yard sale. But, then again, that does seem to be the décor theme.

"You don't have to sit if you don't want to. I also like to stand sometimes," Dr. Nelson says nonchalantly. "Helps me think." She taps twice with her finger on her temple.

My muscles tighten, preparing for a wave of annoyance at her for interfering, but when I look up at her, something about the way she is sitting, or maybe the way she is looking at me, slows the emotion. She isn't trying to meddle, not the way my mom does. She's being genuine. I think.

"Huh? No, I was just . . ." My hands clench into fists, my nails pricking sharply into my palms. "I mean . . ." My mouth is open but there are no words to come out. Eyes zipping around the room, I find myself moving toward the chair and sitting gingerly on the edge of its thin cushion. With a small nod, Dr. Nelson settles a little farther back in her seat across from me and smooths her hands along the wrinkles on top of her khakis.

"Welcome back," she says with a singsong voice and a well-timed head bounce. "So"—she sets her hands down on top of the papers in her lap—"how are you today? How's your Christmas break going?"

Even though she looks like the personification of beige, her voice is strong and confident. It's on the opposite end of the spectrum from Dr. Adams's syrupy sweet, grandmotherly tone. It's got my attention. It's got energy.

"Um, fine." I look down at my worn shirt and pajama pants and think about stopping there. Make her work for her information. But, for some reason, the usual tactics don't feel right anymore. If you're going to do it, I whisper inside myself, just do it. "I mean, it's nice to be off school and all. But I still have another exam to take when school starts, so I can't really relax." I inch back in the chair. "And it's cold out. And I don't like to be cold."

"Ugh! Me either! About every year at this time I ask myself why I don't live in Florida." She's shaking her head, seemingly very into the conversation. "My husband says he likes the winter because he doesn't need a refrigerator to keep his beer cold." A small snort pops out of my nose. The beginning of a smile rises in me, catching me by surprise. It doesn't make it very far up my chest, but I haven't even come close to really smiling in . . . forever?

I can't help but reply. "Once last winter my dad left a whole pack of Pepsi in his car overnight when he was parked outside and they *all* froze and exploded in the trunk."

Dr. Nelson gasps loudly. *"No."* She slaps her leg. "Oh, that's terrible! I've heard of cans exploding in a freezer but not in an actual car. Oh, my stars!" She lets out another loud laugh that fills the room.

"Yeah, he was sooo mad. It was great." I let out small puff of relief as I think about my dad scrubbing his trunk in rubber gloves. I don't remember the last time I interacted with someone like this. It's a real conversation. She is talking to me like I'm a real person.

"Isn't it the best when things like that happen? To *other* people, I mean. Once when my son was young, my daughter let him give her 'tattoos.' He was about five and she was seven or so. He wrote his name all over her body, and only

later at bath time did we realize he had been using permanent marker!" She yells this last word, lurching forward.
"Oh myyy, she was so upset. Little thing had to go to school
for at least two more days with her brother's name scrawled
all over her arms and legs." Shaking her head, she looks up
to the ceiling, beaming at the memory. "One of those things
that's not funny but still funny, you know?"

And as I look at her, there it is. My eyes creasing, my
mouth pulling up at the edges. A smile. As soon as I feel it,
I jerk back in surprise and it melts away. But it was there.
The first one in months. I crease my eyebrows at her again.
What's going on? I don't even know you but I just . . . smiled?

Maybe I can do this. Maybe I can do this with her.

There's a long, quiet pause. It's not awkward, surprisingly,
but it comes to an end with a small and meaningful throat
clear across the carpet. I know what's coming. Time to be
serious. "So I've talked to Dr. Adams. I've talked to your
parents. But I'm still missing the most essential part to this
whole puzzle." She tilts her head to the side. "The only part
that really matters."

That's my cue. I can feel her staring at the top of my
head, waiting for an opportunity to make eye contact. But,
looking down at my fingers, I don't move.

She adjusts in her seat and continues on despite my
silence. "Your parents noticed some of the more obvious
changes in your behavior. Dr. Adams told me about what
you called 'bad thoughts.'" Again she pauses here, hoping
naively that I might join in the conversation with her. "She
said that, specifically, you mentioned your fear that maybe

264

something you did would cause one of your parents to get hurt or sick." Five-second pause. "Could you tell me a little bit more about that?"

What does that even mean? Tell you a little more about that. Everything I do, every action throughout the day, is invisibly linked to some sort of negative outcome for me or my parents. And it's my job to do my best to save us. It's simple.

"Allison." My head still tilted down, I shift my eyes to her, looking at her beneath my eyebrows. I'm sitting perfectly still on the edge of the seat and notice the clock ticking against the silence.

"Okay, okay. Another way to do this." She waves her hands in circles in front of her, literally clearing the air. "Tell me something specific. Tell me about a time when you felt like something you did was going to hurt your parents."

Something specific. I see myself standing on one foot in the dark kitchen, my eyes staring pointedly away from my chemistry notes. I'm at a lab table bubbling in my answer sheet with zigzags. With a slight chill, the words build in my head and take shape in my mouth. They feel thick and dry like cotton balls. Come on, I needle myself. Do it.

I take a deep breath in and exhale out loudly, letting my words ride the wave forward. "I failed my chemistry exam so my mom wouldn't die."

I'm looking straight at Dr. Nelson and see her eyes widen slightly, eyebrows raising. But it's not surprise, it's more . . . interest. "So, when—"

"And I don't wear my clothes because something bad

will happen to me or my parents," I interrupt her. "It started with the pink sweater but then I realized it was all of them." Suddenly I have the overwhelming need to talk. To tell. The words are bursting out of me like I've popped the cork on my tightly bottled champagne. "I keep all the food from the lunches my mom makes me because throwing it away would make her get cancer. Or some other scary disease. My school binders will make me fail my classes if I keep them in my locker, so I carry them around." I shift slightly in the seat and my back pops. "Sidewalk cracks cause cancer. But I count my steps, so that helps. Even though it's pretty exhausting. And annoying."

I pause to think, and breathe, and Dr. Nelson lifts her hand gently toward me. "Okay, wow. Okay. So it sounds like your obsessions aren't just focused on your parents, but also on yourself, and maybe your schoolwork?"

I nod at her enthusiastically. "Yeah, for my parents, it's like car accidents or murders. And also cancer. For me, it's usually brain cancer but also just cancer in general. That's the main thing. It's almost always about cancer. Lots of cancer."

"And your schoolwork?"

"My binders are the only thing that threatens my schoolwork. But . . ." I hesitate, about to move into foreign, unexplored territory. I don't even really know how to start. "But . . . a lot of the things that have to do with school or homework are things that will also give me or my parents cancer."

"Okay, what do you mean? What *specific* things about school do you worry about?"

"Oh gosh. Um. Well, so I told you about my binders." As my mind moves on to the next words, I hear the swarm of bees in the distance, and the tumor near my temple starts to pound. "I don't like pencils. They cause cancer. There is only one that doesn't but sometimes I'm not allowed to sharpen it. Like during exams. And it's also really tiny. My calculator, erasers, pens." The words feel like acid in my mouth. "I can only use a certain amount of notebook paper for each assignment and it's usually not enough." My voice trails off as the bees fly in angry, invisible loops around the office. I close my right eye against the pain in my head, my shoulder instinctively rising up toward my ear. My mouth fills with saliva, trying to cleanse it of the words.

"Okay, good. Very good, thank you." She again raises her hand up toward me, this time a little more urgently. She looks alarmed as I lift my head from my shoulder and open my eyes, the bees receding back to their hive.

"Wow." She lets out a strong exhale, her pen still streaming across the paper on her lap. "Thank you for telling me all of this." She makes eye contact. "Thank you for trusting me." I recognize this line from Dr. Adams. They must teach it to everyone in psychology school.

"So how many hours a day do you think these kind of thoughts affect you?" A casual shrug—she scrunches her face and waves her hand in the air. "Just an estimate."

"Uh . . ." I look up at the ceiling. "Twenty-four. Or, I guess, sixteen. If you don't count sleeping."

"Twenty-four hours a day?" Her voice is incredulous, slightly higher than a few seconds ago. "So . . . always?"

I nod sheepishly at her. Yeah. Always.

Constantly.

"My next question was going to be if you feel like they interfere with your daily well-being. If you find yourself being taken away from your real life because of these obsessions and compulsions. But I think you just answered that for me."

I give her one hard up-and-down nod. Do they interfere with my life? They *are* life.

She makes a small note on her paper. "Okay, well, given all this, I think we better get started!" Looking up at me quickly, she wiggles her eyebrows twice and reaches into the small filing cabinet beside her chair. After rustling through a few folders, she smiles triumphantly as she leans forward to hand me a piece of white paper.

"I'm about to give you a little homework. But you're on Christmas break so you won't mind." She winks at me and keeps talking. "Before our next appointment, I want you to try to fill in this chart." I look down at the sheet of paper in my lap. On the front is a large grid. Across the top there are four columns labeled TRIGGER, OBSESSION, COMPULSION, TEMPERATURE.

"'Trigger' means the thing that gets you anxious, so, using what you told me earlier, sidewalk cracks. 'Obsession' would be what it makes you worry about, so, like you said, brain cancer. In the compulsion section, write what you do when you encounter that trigger." Her pointer finger is pressing down as if to mark her spot. "What do you do when you come upon a sidewalk crack?"

"I hop over it. And count my steps just in case I make a mistake."

"Good! So that's what you would put there. And, lastly, 'temperature' refers to the intensity of your anxiety when you have to deal with one of these triggers. If, for example, it's the worst fear you've ever felt, it's a ten. If it's just scary but not terrible, maybe it's more like a five." She places her hands on her lap and pauses for a few moments. "Try to write down everything you can think of, even if you're not sure it's right. Things that affect you, things that affect your parents, your schoolwork. Everything." Looking up at me, she asks, "Does this all make sense?"

I nod, flipping the sheet of paper over and seeing that it's blank. There are only about twenty rows on the chart. I've never gone through and counted out my danger list, but I know it's way more than this. "Yeah, yeah, it makes sense. But"—I hold up the paper so she can see there is nothing on the back—"I'm going to need more paper. *A lot* more paper."

CHAPTER 21

It's like I've been drowning, struggling for air, and now I can finally relax on the edge of a life raft. I can finally catch my breath. I only talked to Dr. Nelson for twenty minutes at the most, but it seems to have changed everything. I still think God might be behind all of this, somehow. But the terrible guilt and fear I once felt for confessing his secrets have evaporated, replaced by a beaming ray of light.

Even though I just met Dr. Nelson, I've already told her the thoughts that I've been guarding so closely for months. It's the psychological equivalent of going way further than kissing on the first date. But it was the right thing to do. I know it by the way I feel. The mercilessly tight belt that's been squeezing on my muscles and my brain has loosened a notch, maybe two.

I'm sitting down gently on the carpet, legs bending under me. My heart leaps with excitement, my brain already filling, brimming, with dangerous buzzwords to fill in the charts. *Soap, apples, rubber bands.* Oh, Dr. Nelson, wait until you see this. A strong surge of optimism blows through me as I imagine her, wrinkled khakis and Tevas, looking at me from across the brown room during our next appointment. She'll smile at me as I hand her these scribbled sheets, one of her rare but genuine smiles that crease in deep at her cheeks. *Thank you for sharing this with me,* she will say. *I'm very proud of you.* A small warmth glows in my chest.

I lean forward, laying the papers against the carpet, and crouch in front of them to begin my list. For myself and for Dr. Nelson. I'm rolling the tiny safe pencil nub in my fingers. It's finally sharpened, now that exams are over, but barely big enough to grip in my hand. The empty paper on the floor gazes up at me, and I stare back down at its black lines. Where to start?

My mind travels backward to that early-morning nightmare in October, the gray dawn when it all began. The yellow painted wood of the pencil is pushing hard into my pointer finger, turning the skin surrounding it a ghostly white. In the first blank, I tentatively write *brain cancer* and, after examining it for a few moments, add a question mark. At our appointment, Dr. Nelson said it would be considered an obsession, but I know it's much more than that. It's everything. It's the nucleus of the next few months. Under "temperature," I write *10*. Exclamation point.

And then the list continues. Mentally retracing the ragged twists of my mind, I fill in row after row in the order each obsession appeared. When the first page is full, I push it up on the carpet a few inches so I'm facing the next blank sheet.

By the bottom of page three, flinging my hand in the air to loosen a cramp, I've reached exam week, where the wounds are still swollen and raw. Studying for precal, passing chemistry. The color green. Calculators. Standing on one foot.

Chronologically, I've run into the present, but I've still got so many unacknowledged words floating around my mind. Continuing on the backs of the papers and in the side margins, I list the miscellaneous, homeless triggers. They're ones that weren't part of a major battle like the first afternoon in the kitchen or the night of the *Les Mis* paper. It feels like there are thousands of them. Tiny, seemingly unimportant volunteers that when grouped together as one form a strong, formidable battalion. Rubber bands, tissues, most pairs of shoes. Going to Melanie's party. Grass (because it's green). Trees (because leaves are green). The gift cards I got for Christmas. Lettuce (mostly because it's lettuce but also because it's green). Carrabba's Italian Grill. Our family cat, Scratch. Asking questions in class. Chewing gum. Toilet paper.

About an hour after crouching down to the carpet, I've depleted my store of obsessions. I'm exhausted, mentally and physically. So this is happening, I think with a light sigh. It's all here. Months of angry monsters, pounding steps around the corner, swarms of bees. Messages from God. It's all here in these sheets of paper. It doesn't feel right. It all looks so simple. My whole life boiled down into just three pages.

I pick up the small pile. Even though almost every inch of the papers is covered in tight scribble, I know that no amount of writing could really capture what this is. But if there's anyone who can come close to understanding, I think it's Dr. Nelson.

Our next session is two days later, on Wednesday. I allow myself to relax a little in the comfort of her waiting room. Looking around, I see that it's still just as beige, but something in its blandness is also its appeal. Surrounded by the office's simplicity, I don't feel embarrassed to be wearing tattered pajamas. I'm okay with my blaring acne and greasy, dreadlocked hair. I don't need to worry about appearances. I'm with Dr. Nelson and her wool socks and horse paintings. There's no need to be self-conscious.

I have my danger list stuffed into the waistband of my pants, OCD pamphlet-style. My mom knows something's up because I'm mysteriously crinkling with each breath, but she pretends she doesn't notice. Even though she knows the truth now, even though she knows her daughter has OCD, there is something inside me that is still fiercely protective over my condition and its secrets. The idea of her knowing I even filled out these sheets of paper, or that I have three pages' worth of fears in the first place, is terrifying. I get that she's my mom and needs to be kept in the loop, but I have a powerful need to keep this to myself.

Dr. Nelson appears in the doorway. I don't know if I crack a smile, but a blip of happiness jumps inside me when I see her. Without looking at my mom, I push up out of the chair and walk toward her. "Hi!" I say in a remarkably chipper tone.

As we settle into our seats in her warm office, she rubs her hands together. "All right, all right, all right. Let me see that homework, eh? I'm very interested to learn what's going on inside that head of yours." She has her arm extended toward me, wiggling her fingers over the carpet. I pull the folded sheets out of my waistband, and I realize how warm they are, and how strange this might look. Keeping my papers hidden in my pants like a spy. But Dr. Nelson continues to beckon for them and takes them out of my hand as if I brought them in a leather-bound briefcase. A dense cloud rises in my chest, and I have an almost overwhelming urge to thank her. Thank you for not raising your eyebrows. Thank you for letting that strange moment pass without a comment. Thank you for being you. Thank you for helping me.

She is looking down at the lists, the lid of her pen in her mouth, nodding. I watch her eyes scan through each line. "Mmm, okay," she mumbles to herself. "Yes, yes, I remember that one." Her words become garbled under her lips, but I see her eyes open wide, then her head tilt, as she reacts and thinks.

"Well. Okay, then." She taps the papers on the top of her thigh to align them in her hands. "Very good work, Allison. And I have to say, quite an impressive list," she says with a small laugh as she sits back in her chair. "I'm going to go as far as saying this is the most obsessions I have ever seen in one patient—at your age, at least."

A beam of light shines from my face. The most . . . ever? Me? Oh, Dr. Nelson, you shouldn't have! What an honor! I know that the more obsessions I have, the more battles I have to fight in the future, but I still feel special, despite the implications. Maybe she'll always remember me. Maybe I'll always be her "toughest" patient. If I can't excel in school anymore, at least I can excel at OCD.

"Now that we've captured most of your concerns here"— she places her splayed fingertips on the sheets—"we can go through them and try to decide where we want to start. So, looking through here, it seems like there are some general themes. Like, for example, there seem to be a lot of food items. Uh"—she runs her eyes down the page—"apples, potatoes. Gum, granola bars. Bartering food? What's that?"

"Oh, um, that's when I trade food to protect myself after stepping on a crack or when I need more steps when I run out."

"Huh, right." She gives a slow nod. "That sounds like its own thing, not really related to food, at least not in this way. Let me make a note," she mumbles as she scribbles in between the rows. "Okay, so we've got food. Then, it looks like school-related things: calculator, studying, notebook paper." I'm nodding so hard at her that she blurs out of focus. "Right. I agree. That's very important. Maybe the most important, but let's keep going. Uhhhh"—she lets her voice drag out as she keeps moving down the list—"all right, how about hygiene? Or, okay, wait, not just that. Let's call it . . . Bed, Bath, and Beyond. Hairbrush, hair dryer, soap, clothes. Makeup. Toothbrush." She lifts her eyebrows at me, clearly tickled by her own cleverness. I can't help but give her a small smile in return. It's not funny, but it's funny.

"And, of course, not everything is going to fit into one of these main categories. For example, you have here standing up. Then there's talking and/or angry furniture." She reads the words matter-of-factly.

"Well, those two are related." I hold my index and middle finger apart in the air and then bring them together. "They're kind of the same thing."

"Which ones?"

"Standing up and talking furniture."

"Oh, interesting. How so?"

"Well, sometimes the furniture, mostly chairs and couches, don't like being sat on. They shoot out this angry static and it's high-pitched and hurts my ears and makes my head pound. I can just tell they're dangerous and that something bad will happen to me if I sit on them. Or even if you stand too close, because the cancer waves can spread pretty far. At least a few inches."

"Hmm, okay." She draws a curved line between their rows on the paper and makes a small note.

"So I usually just stand because it's safer. And then sometimes—well, always—I need to stand on one foot. It just feels better. So that's what that one is. I think it's on the second page."

Dr. Nelson flips through the sheets. "Yep, I see it. Making a note." Again her pen wags quickly in the air. "Okay, well, anyway, you get what I was saying. There will be these big general categories, but also many completely separate fears and issues that we can handle individually as needed." She pauses here, resting her hands on her lap. "Do you have any questions?"

Uh, nope. I shake my head at her, wide-eyed.

"Okay. Now that we've reviewed your lists, it's your turn to tell me where you want to start. Of the things we talked about, of all the things you wrote down for homework, which one bothers you the most? Or, in other words, if you could choose to get rid of one of these categories or fears first, which one would it be?"

276

It's like bringing a starving person to a buffet. Amazed by the huge menu of options, I just stare at them in awe. But, soon, one concern rises above all others. "My schoolwork," I say to Dr. Nelson. Over the past few months, I have set fire to what was once my foolproof five-year plan. The fast track to a northeastern college with centuries-old stone buildings and US presidents as alumni. But I could still rescue my life. If I could start next semester with a clear head, and a pencil, calculator, and notebook paper, I could redeem my GPA and turn this loose cannon around. There is still a chance, but only if we act now.

"I think that's a good choice, Allison. I really do. Both for your stress level and your own sense of confidence. Getting that back on track will help immensely in many ways. Good, and then what? We'll start chipping away at school-related items, but let's also decide on your next priority."

"Oh, definitely Bed, Bath, and Beyond." I grin slightly against my will. School is the most important. School is life. School is college. School is future. But the harsh truth is you don't lose your friends for failing chemistry. No one stares at you for bad grades. Everyone stares at you when you wear flannel cat pajamas in the cafeteria.

CHAPTER 22

There is traffic, and the early-afternoon sun glares off the rearview window of the red Pontiac in front of us. "Come on!" my mother yells angrily at the line of cars, her knuckles white against the steering wheel. "What's happening! We're going to be late!" I have never known my mother to raise her voice, except over the past few months. We are on our way to my third appointment with Dr. Nelson, and although I feel the claws on my brain loosening, even though there is now a silver lining around my clouds, I have yet to make any signs of outward improvement. I'm still counting, tiptoeing. All of the above.

My mother frantically jabs at the radio presets before mashing it off with her thumb. I can feel her stress emanating over the center console. She would never say it out loud, but I know it's been almost impossible for her to leave work so often to ferry me to these appointments. She moves meetings, takes phone calls at night, pecks away on her laptop until the early-morning hours. She doesn't complain, would never complain, but the stress oozes out through her skin.

We pull up to the brick town house and ease to a stop and I hop from the car. The buzzing uncertainty I felt prior to my previous therapist appointments is gone today. I've strangely been looking forward to seeing Dr. Nelson. Virginia. She isn't Sara or Jenny, but in her own and maybe more powerful way, she's my friend. I almost skip from the car to her nondescript front door. The bland, beige waiting room that was so unappealing a few days ago now greets me with a rush of warm air and the familiar lemon air freshener.

"Well, hello there, Allison!" Dr. Nelson sends me a gleaming smile from behind her desk. A blue, lumpy cardigan hangs from her thin shoulders. It's endearingly obvious she knit it herself. My heart swells with fondness, and I feel a sudden sense of gratitude. Just entering her office has forced the dark clouds hanging above my shoulders to part. A few rays of sun are able to peek through into my chronically overcast life.

"Hi, Dr. Nelson!" A switch has flipped inside me and I'm suddenly in conversation mode. Ready to chat and smile and laugh. "Oh my gosh, guess what! I heard the funniest thing on the radio on the way here. I have to tell you all about it. So there was this guy . . ." I trot past her desk toward her office without an invitation, my oversized flannel pants flapping in the air as I talk to her over my shoulder. Moving down the hallway, I pass the small kitchen with an array of snacks and a refrigerator filled with bottled water. I pause to examine the buffet of treats. Snack-size candy bars, miniature bags of peanuts. Although today was fairly successful (I was able to eat a piece of toast at breakfast as well as a bag of carrots at lunch), my stomach still snarls greedily for more. I scan the possibilities until my eyes are snagged on a basket of pretzels and my mind clinches tight. Pretzels, pretzels, pretzels. Cancer, cancer, cancer.

Walking up the hallway behind me, Dr. Nelson interrupts. "And?" Pulled from the blaring alarms, I turn to look at her. Pretzels. Cancer. Pretzels. Cancer.

"And what?"

Her forehead scrunches slightly. "And what happened to the guy? From the radio. You just kind of stopped mid-sentence."

"Oh, right." I know I need to keep talking, to tell her the rest of the story, but the pretzels. They're staring.

I feel my right foot slowly rising into the air so I'm perched on one leg. There is a dangerous cloud spreading up and outward from the kitchen. I hold my breath without thinking about it, just to be safe. Dr. Nelson's warm presence fades, and it's only me and the pretzels in the room. Death. Death. Death.

Suddenly there is a soft hand on my upper back. "Let's sit down in my office, shall we?" Her voice is calm and level, but I can tell she has sensed something. She's trying to goad me out of my trance. "Come along now." Both her hands on my shoulders—it's not quite a push but more of a forceful suggestion. *This way.*

Her voice pulls my eyes from the cancerous snack, and, holding my breath, I reluctantly follow her down the hallway. Turning to close the door to her office, I see my mom, hunched over, typing on her laptop.

I slide my eyes toward the small clock on the wall above Dr. Nelson's head and smile to myself. Her sitting in her high-backed brown chair, me perched stiffly on the cushion

280

across from her, we've spent the first twenty minutes of the appointment swapping gossip like old friends over dinner. With stories of Samuelson, cross-country practice, and Sam, it almost feels like the long phone conversations I used to have with Sara and Jenny, and I'm glowing with happiness. I know that she's my doctor, and older than my mom, but it feels so good to talk to someone again.

I see Dr. Nelson looking at the clock as well, and, realizing the time, she clears her throat. "Well, well, enough chit-chat for today, I think." She smiles at me. "Time to get to work, wouldn't you say?" Flipping open the manila folder on her lap, she thumbs through a small pile of paper and continues to talk. "For our last appointment, you put together that rather impressive list of all of your obsessions. Three pages of them. We will use these lists over the next few weeks to choose different obsessions to target and overcome." She glances at me. I nod at her silently. "You'll also remember that we went through the list and talked a little bit about your priorities. You said your first goal was to be able to do your schoolwork again. Getting your grades up seems to be the most important initial step." Again, a nod. Eye contact. "Well, today we are going to pick what specific obsession you want to work on first." She closes her folder and hands me a photocopy of the three-page list of obsessions. "If we look through here, I think there are a few of these that make more sense than others to start with. We are looking for something small, simple."

My eyes skim over the black-and-white sheets of paper, and an ache appears deep in my head. Despite the pumping heater, I shiver slightly underneath my tattered running shirt. The handwriting scrawled across the paper is messy and frantic, nothing like the loopy, bubbly style I perfected during the first few weeks of school. Gently rubbing the edges of the paper, I examine the list. Each individual obsession, each line of text on the page, is a serious threat to the life of someone I love. And the pages are filled, covered, with them. There is nothing small or simple here. Just reading the words "peaches" and "calculator" sets off the panic alarms. A low buzzing threatens to overcome my thoughts, a million bees swarming into action, ready to protect their hive of obsessions. My eyes focus on the curves of the letters, the swish of the *s* and the cross of the *t.* They spell death.

With my extended silence, she continues. "Okay, well, here, let's try this. I'll list out some of the obsessions from the list that affect your schoolwork, and we can narrow it down from there. . . ." Her voice trails off. I can feel her eyes on me but I cannot tear my stare from the sheets of paper, which have now grown heavy as boulders on my lap. What have I done? What have I done? "Allison, hey, up here." She snaps once. I drag my gaze up to her face. My mouth is open, my eyes wide. "We're going to go through this together. We're only picking one."

My heart is pounding in my throat. It shakes my entire body. What have I done?

"Okay, starting from the top. Limitations on paper. It says you are only allowed to use a certain number of sheets of notebook paper to finish your homework or do a school assignment, and it's usually not enough. That could be a useful one. Also, let's see, your computer. That could be good? It would be very helpful for your schoolwork." She tilts her head to the side in consideration and raises her eyes to me hopefully.

"Absolutely not! *Not* the computer!" I yell the words before I even know I've thought them. "Are you crazy? I can't just *use* the computer." I am surprised at the surging annoyance I feel toward her, a powerful sense of disappointment. In my mind I see the keyboard, the mouse, the monitor all sitting silently, covered with a thin layer of dust, on my desk. They practically glow with cancer. "That's not an option." I scowl at her. I guess she doesn't actually understand my beast after all. She doesn't know what she is suggesting.

"Okay, that's fine, that's fine. We will leave that one for later." She casts her eyes downward and pretends not to notice my hurt expression.

"Yeah," I retort, "*much* later." She makes a small scribbled note beside the entry for *computer* on the list.

"Other options: counting your steps. It's not necessarily schoolwork, but it would make the school day much easier for you. One less thing to focus on. Hmm . . ." She pauses as she scans the list, a crease between her brows. "Oh, here, what about pencils and pens?" She lifts her head quickly and we lock eyes.

I wait for the emergency alarm in my head to call the troops to battle, but, to my surprise, the corridors of my mind are silent. The objection that has formed in my mouth sits quietly, patiently. I wait for a few seconds, swaying slightly as I try to sit perfectly still, but there are no warning messages.

"Huh," I say out loud, as much to myself and my brain as to Dr. Nelson. "Yeah, I mean, I guess that could work." I'm stunned by my own eerie silence, and the words come out slowly, as if trying not to wake the sleeping monster. "All of the other things like my computer and notebook paper are important, but they do me no good if I can't write. I need pencils."

Dr. Nelson nods enthusiastically and claps her hands together. Now we can begin. "Wonderful, just wonderful." She flips to a clean page on her legal pad and scribbles as she smiles at me. "There is one main type of therapy that is used to treat those with OCD. It's called Exposure Response Prevention, or ERP." With a few creaking noises, she lifts herself from her chair and shuffles over to the easel, which holds up an enormous pad of white paper. "Its name is pretty self-explanatory. With Exposure Response Prevention, we *expose* you to the source of your anxiety or fear—in this case pencils—and *prevent* you from *responding* with your normal compulsions." As she talks, she writes *ERP* on the easel and underlines each letter for emphasis. "Typically, we find this to be most effective in combination with pharmaceuticals, but"—I shake my head vigorously and move to interrupt—"yes, I know, but as you have expressed before, that is not something you are interested in at the moment." My shoulders relax. "ERP will still be effective without medication, it will just be a bit more challenging and perhaps take a while longer." I look at her with a blank face. She is trying to goad me into the same conversation I had with Dr. Adams, but I refuse to bite. Medicine is not an option. A brain on medicine is a brain on the path to cancer. "I completely respect your feelings on the topic, and I am not here to push you into anything. Just know medication is something we can revisit at any time, if you change your mind." I give her the eye roll that gets me in so much trouble with my mom. Without a response, she returns to her easel.

"Anyway, let's get started. If this were a normal situation, if we weren't doing ERP, and I took out a pencil right now, what would happen? How would you feel? What would you do?"

"If you took out a pencil right now? Oh, wow, that's scary." Looking off into the corner, I think back to sitting in a quiet classroom, the tiny noise of scribbling pencils surrounding me, and the tumor sprouting to angry life in my gray matter. "I would get a splitting headache immediately— that is always the first alarm. It feels like my brain is being both squeezed in a clamp and torn apart at the same time. I would hold my breath and stand on one foot, just because it makes me feel better. I guess, then, I would be told what I needed to do in order to undo the danger of the pencil. It's hard to predict what it will be from one time to the next. But I would have to give up something useful or important. I would also maybe pray and do my hand gesture. A few times. I would probably increase the number of Bible pages I read that night too. Just to be safe." I've told her that I have compulsions involving religion, but I haven't admitted that part of me still feels like these thoughts might be delivered from the heavens. That despite being diagnosed with a mental illness, I'm not completely sure that that's the full truth. But I know there's no way I could say that aloud.

Dr. Nelson looks at me in silence, but I cannot read her expression. "Okay . . ." She extends the word as she lets out a breath. "Well, with ERP we take baby steps. To start, I will hold a pencil and ask you to stare at it. You can blink, of course, but do your best to stay focused on the pencil." She turns back to her easel, uncaps a blue marker, and draws a diagonal line down the page. "You must try your best not to pray, not to hold your breath, not to do anything that you usually might do to ease your anxiety.

"You're going to feel very uncomfortable, especially at the beginning." She gestures at the top of the slanted line. "But, as time passes, your level of anxiety will slowly decrease"—she traces her finger down the line—"until you eventually feel yourself calming down." She writes *Pencils, Allison, Part 1* across the top of the sheet of paper. "It may take a few minutes, particularly these first few times, but it only gets easier with practice. If you need a break, if it's too much, just tell me and we can stop immediately."

I feel like I am being prepared to undergo some sort of major surgery. If I need a break? Is it going to be that bad?

"How does all of this sound? Do you think it's a good plan?"

"Yeah, sure," I respond, knowing its my only real option. I shift in my seat and pick at my bandaged fingers. Last night, against my will, my mom spent about an hour over the bathroom sink "doctoring" my hands. I have always had the horrible habit of picking at my cuticles and fingernails, in both good times and bad. Lately, however, this distasteful habit has turned into a violent crime. I have methodically torn, gnawed, and picked my fingers into bleeding nubs. With a look of nausea, my mother slowly covered each oozing wound in antibacterial gel and wrapped them in gauze. Eight of my ten fingers are immobilized under thick, mummified casts. I'm just glad she hasn't seen my toes.

"Here is what's going to happen: In a few moments, I am going to take out a pencil." She continues despite the small noise that slips from my mouth. "As soon as we begin, I will ask for you to rate your anxiety on a scale from one to ten, ten being extreme panic while one is perfect calm." She turns and labels the top of the diagonal line with a *10* and its bottom point with a *1*. "Every thirty seconds or so, I will ask for your anxiety rating, and we will track your progress on this line. Once you reach a rating of three or four, we will take a break, talk it over, and try again." She rummages deep within one of her desk drawers and looks up at me. "Ready?"

CHAPTER 23

The overhead fluorescent light beams off the edge of the sharpened lead. The pencil's six long inches stretch their yellow across my vision, culminating in a nefarious, unused pink eraser. It is brand-new, shiny, sharpened to a point. I can almost smell the cancerous lead. There is a thin cloud of disease spiraling out of its tip like the smoke from a cigarette. My ears fill with the sound of pencils scribbling. Thousands, millions of pencils being dragged across paper. I feel my head land against my hand as I lean for support against the beige arm of the chair. I see the pencil in Dr. Nelson's grip being used to fill out my death certificate. *Time of death: 3:45 p.m., cause: terminal brain cancer.* The pencil draws a picture of my mother's sleek white sedan crushed into a tree, my dad's lifeless body on the kitchen floor, a wail of sadness lofting above a tombstone. I am lost in the scribbling, the images, the . . .

"Okay, what's your rating?" I hear Dr. Nelson, I register that she is speaking, but there is no room in my mind for her. "Allison," she says a bit louder, "Allison, come on. On a scale of one to ten, how are you feeling?"

I groan loudly. "A nine at least. Definitely a nine." Leaning against the chair, I press my face hard into my hand. I mash my eyes inward, applying pressure until bright colors span across the blackness. My brain is screaming, the scratch of a thousand deadly pencils blocking out all other noises.

A searing pain in my head signals a new tumor, my final destiny.

"Okay, you're doing great, but I need you to open your eyes and look at me." I raise my head from my hand but stay hidden behind tightly closed lids. My head leans to the left with the weight of my developing cancer. "Close but not quite. Look up here, Allison. Open your eyes."

The room appears through a tiny slit made smaller by a line of eyelashes. A flash of yellow against a background of beige. Dr. Nelson clears her throat, and I force myself to unclench my face.

"It's been thirty seconds. You are doing so well. Where are you now?"

"Uhhh . . ." I can't think—the scratching, the writing, the buzzing. "Um, I guess an eight. I mean"—my eyes are open, my shoulders have dropped slightly—"I don't know. A seven?" The clock sounds out the seconds against the silence of the room. I feel my lungs inflate fully for the first time, and the muscles in my neck relax with the exhale.

"Okay, good, good, you are through the hardest part. Just keep looking at it. Very good." Dr. Nelson makes a small mark a little way down the line on the easel. The dark border around my vision slowly fades, and I'm now holding my head up without the support of my hand. My heart is still pounding, but as I draw my eyes across the length of the pencil, the knots in my shoulders and abdomen loosen. My windpipe relaxes, the air no longer catching in my throat.

"Okay. We are at one minute now. How are you?"

I can feel the anxiety dripping off me, but what started

as a downpour has turned now to a steady trickle. "I'm a five," I mutter.

"Okay, keep it up!" Dr. Nelson dances slightly in front of her easel as she makes a mark halfway down the diagonal line. "You're doing great!" With an extended groan, I focus my eyes on the pencil wobbling in her hand. Staring at its yellow paint, I realize it is no longer emanating the evil and death that it was just a minute before. As if someone has turned down its danger volume, it seems to have lost most of its power. I know deep within me that pencils can kill me, but right now, as I stare at it across the carpet, it feels remarkably harmless.

"What's your rating? We're at two minutes."

"I think a three or a four. . . ." My voice trails off, still pondering the pencil's drastic transition.

"Great. Well done, you made it! How was that?"

"I'm not sure?" I look at my bandaged fingers, surprised by the experience. Dr. Nelson was right. "It was terrible at the beginning, but after about a minute I definitely noticed a difference. I started to feel less scared and less stressed just on my own, even though you were still holding the pencil and nothing had changed."

"Yes, exactly. Over time, as we keep exposing you to pencils in situations like this, you will see that your reactions begin to improve. Instead of beginning at a nine, in a few days a pencil will only get you to a six, then maybe just a four." She redraws the individual marks she drew on the line, noting at what time I reported each one. "If you continue to expose yourself to your triggers, eventually they lose their power. The more you resist them, the weaker they become." She continues as she rips the top sheet off the easel and draws another diagonal line on the clean sheet below. "Fighting OCD is like boxing. Each time you go against a thought, it's a punch to its strength. Each time you listen to your OCD, its biceps get bigger and it becomes a more powerful opponent. It's a war of attrition—you just have to keep fighting."

I nod at her with an enthusiasm I have not felt for months. Angels sing in the background. A rainbow appears across a mountainscape. I was just in the same room as a pencil, stared it down in its beady little eyes, and lived to tell the story. Just an hour before, I wouldn't have thought it possible.

"So, you ready for another round?"

I extend my head toward her, forgetting my glimmer of happiness. "What! Again? We just got done!"

She chuckles at me. "This is a marathon, Allison. Maybe even an Ironman. We will do this over and over and over again until you no longer feel anxious when you see a pencil. Then, instead of me holding the pencil, we will have it sitting on your leg. Once you're okay with that, you will hold it and eventually write with it."

"You want me . . . to hold a pencil?"

"Well, yes, that is the overall goal, right? For you to be able to write, do your homework, get back to the student and person you used to be. Unless I'm mistaken?"

Sheepishly, I nod in agreement.

"I'll tell you what. Let's call it a day on ERP. We will revisit

it again next appointment, so just come ready for that."
Dr. Nelson sits down in her chair across from me. "Does
this all make sense, Allison? Do you feel like you understand how we will fight your OCD?"

"Yeah, I get it. I guess after pencils, we do this with something else?" My voice is hesitant as I realize the implications
of this process.

"Right, exactly. After pencils, we will move on to the
clothes in your closet, the shower, brushing your hair, whatever you decide you want to focus on. I think you will find,
too, that we won't need to do ERP on every single obsession
on your list." She gestures at the papers I have folded and
crumpled onto themselves over the past few minutes. "Typically, as you begin to loosen the hold of some of your obsessions, others kind of die off on their own. Collateral damage
from ERP. One day, you will wake up and realize you are no
longer bothered by grass, for example."

I raise my eyebrow. "I'll believe *that* when I see it." Grass
is terrifying. It's so green.

She smiles at me. "Just you wait a few months, Allison,
darling, I think you will surprise yourself." I can't help but
return her smile. "So, we are done for today, but I have a bit
of homework for you. Nothing serious, but it will make a big
difference for our next session." I perk up at her mention of
homework. A way to prove myself, a way to make Dr. Nelson
proud. "Between now and Tuesday, I want you to stare at
every pencil you encounter. Around the house, at your desk
at home. When you go back to school, you'll want to seek
them out. Get as much exposure as possible. Don't just look

at it, really experience it. It will be uncomfortable, I'll admit that, just like it was today. But, like I said, this is a war of attrition. Hard work is what will move us along. Your hard work." She looks me directly in the eyes. "What do you think?"

"Um, yeah, I can do that. Stare at pencils, got it." I fidget with the tie on my pajama pants. Despite my effort to sound flippant, my insides are roiling. I feel a wave of nausea as I see myself in class surrounded by pencils, as I picture making eye contact with a yellow-painted No. 2 cancer stick.

We move quietly back down the hallway toward my mother, who is typing fervently on her laptop. "Hey, Momzilla," I call as I enter the light of the waiting room. "Time's up!" She makes a small noise and continues to peck rapidly until she finishes what she's doing. I fiddle with a collection of stickers and tattoos in a small basket on Dr. Nelson's desk.

"Hi, my turtledove." A kiss lands on the side of my head as my mom approaches. "How was it?" She leans down to Dr. Nelson's desk and quickly scribbles out a check. I ignore her question and act intently interested in selecting a sticker.

"See ya Tuesday, Dr. Nelson!" I throw over my shoulder as I lean into the heavy door leading to the parking lot. I grip my arms and clench my jaw in preparation for the arctic wind to devour my thin, pathetic T-shirt.

"See you soon, Allison. Don't forget your homework!" I beam at her through the open door and give her two thumbs up. "Don't you have a jacket, sweetie?"

"Jacket? No, no jacket. Do not like jackets. It's not that cold, anyway."

"Okay, well, we're going to need to add that to the list, clearly." Dr. Nelson looks openmouthed at my mom, who can only shrug. She is holding two different jackets for me to choose from, one fleece and one wool, if by some miracle I decide I want one. At this point, she has accepted that she cannot force me to wear a coat (or eat my dinner, or use my computer). Unlike Dr. Nelson, she knows what happens when she pushes me too far.

"Did I hear Dr. Nelson say homework?" my mom asks as we slide into her car from the freezing air. "What kind of homework?"

"Yeah, it's nothing," I say, turning to look out the window with my back toward her. "Just a thing between me and Dr. Nelson."

I watch the dead, sparse trees whiz by on our way down the highway. Despite the gray skies and threatening clouds, I feel a creeping edge of warmth that lifts the corner of my mouth into a hesitant smile.

CHAPTER 24

I feel better. I feel . . . I feel like this might be okay. Almost. These thoughts I'm having aren't true. I mean, they are true. Very true. But not in a real-life kind of way. Something heavy inside me has shifted, and it's like I can see again. It's still a bleak winter's day, but I might have found my way out of the blizzard.

I think about Dr. Nelson constantly. Her thick socks and warm smile and brown chairs. The way she laughs, her boyish bony shoulders, the weird horse paintings that, I now see, aren't *that* bad after all. I carry her around with me. Her face and smile sit on my shoulder, weighing down with a gentle pressure as I hop over cracks.

I'm going to see her tomorrow. And it will all be okay then. Then I'll have an hour to relax. An hour to be free. I want her to be proud of me. I want to have brilliant stories to tell her about how I stood toe-to-toe with my fears and punched them hard in the face. I want to! But pencils are so pencily and I've spent the past twenty-four hours decidedly avoiding the den, the only room in the house where I'm likely to encounter them. It's almost dinnertime. My parents will be home soon. I need to do my Dr. Nelson homework. Now.

My feet slide hard against each individual carpeted stair as I trudge toward the den. And homework. And cancer. And a smile from Dr. Nelson. And tumors.

Walking into the room, I cling to the left wall to keep my body as far away as possible from the glowing desk, chair, and computer in the opposite corner. They're surrounded by a radioactive cloud, like Chernobyl. I move toward the bookcase that is home to my pen and pencil holder and reflexively pin my eyes shut. Two steps later, I bang my left knee hard into a leather recliner and jerk forward. I hit the floor with a loud thump that echoes through the house and shakes the windows.

I give a little grunt. It didn't actually hurt, I just feel sorry for myself. Rising up from the floor, I forget my mission. Until I remember. Pencils. With my eyes intentionally pointed at the ceiling, I can sense a heat on my face. I know there is a pencil sitting in the wire holder on the bookshelf directly in front of me. But I can't bring myself to look.

I hear Dr. Nelson. We're in her office, and she's holding the pencil horizontally in front of her, the easel and giant notepad beside her. *Look up here. Open your eyes.* The beige carpet. The drawings on the wall. *Look up here.*

And there is the pencil. Standing tall like a soldier beside a neon-pink highlighter in front of me. We make eye contact and I immediately know he's evil. More so than any other pencil I've ever encountered. His yellow paint sears into my eyes. I feel it passing through my irises and straight into my brain, where it ends with a damp sizzle. My head is in the clamp again. The one that somehow squishes it together while ripping it apart. *You're doing so well—where are you now?* Shut *up*, Dr. Nelson. You're the reason I'm here. Burning my brain with cancer. The pencil is showing no sign of fatigue.

I'm leaning forward, most of my weight on my palms against the carpet. Pencil, pencil, pencil. *You're doing so well—where are you now?* I want to scream at her. Not words this time but something more carnal, like an animal. A growl. I'm a ten! Okay? A ten! It wasn't like this in her office. It was bad but not this. Not frantic. Not out of control. I'm a ten. This is ten. Ten, ten, ten. Pencil, pencil, pencil. I feel my eyes ungluing and moving down the length of the wood to where it reads TICONDEROGA. In green letters. *Green. Green. Green.* For a moment I'm paralyzed, but then the feeling slowly morphs. My eyes dart back up to the tip. You sneaky rat. I glare at him. Was that a threat? Those green letters? I trace the wavy line where yellow body meets wooden tip. My intestines gurgle out loud as they twist around themselves. *You're doing so well—where are you now?* I'm an eight. And with this thought I feel my heart pump with adrenaline. I'm doing it. I'm doing ERP! And I'm at an eight. Keep staring. Only a minute longer. I hate you, pencil. And I won't let you win.

That's when I know I'm a seven. I even find my eyes hovering, if just for a moment, over the evil lettering. I ain't scared a-you, Mr. Pencil. Mr. Surprise Green Letters. My head hurts. But it's not the lumpy tumor pain. It's like I've been squinting too long into the distance, trying to read a billboard down the highway. The muscles in my cheeks, my brows, the ones behind my eyeballs, are screaming. I intentionally try to relax my face, forcing my cheeks down and rotating my jaw. And with this, and a long exhale, my shoulders and neck relax too. Seven, six, five. I don't know how long it's been, but my eyes are dry. When I blink, they burn against my eyelids. The pencil hasn't moved, at least not that I've noticed, but it's different now. Slouching, maybe. Defeated. Five, four. It's just a pencil. Now that I look at it. I mean, I wouldn't touch it or hold it—or, heaven forbid, use it—but looking at it, leaning toward it on the carpet, I can tell. Four, three, two. It's just a pencil.

Just a pencil.

Since when is that a sentence? When did that become possible?

I look around the den in near disbelief. That wasn't easy. Not even close. At the beginning it was terrible. Really horrible. But I did it. And lived. I examine my arms and legs, looking for signs of damage. Everything seems . . . okay? Better than okay. Everything seems perfectly fine.

Oh my gosh. I feel Dr. Nelson's calm presence on my shoulder again. I can't wait to tell her about this tomorrow!

Less than twenty-four hours later, sunshine is bursting out of my chest as we settle into our respective chairs. I can feel the light pulsing out of me, and I'm sure she can see it too. I've been thinking about this all day. I did ERP. I aced my homework.

"So, how are you today?" Hand-knit sweater, this time gray. "You look . . . good." She tries to hide the rise in her voice on this last word. But I can't blame her for her surprise. I feel . . . good. Maybe. Against all odds. Could that be true? Am I allowed to feel good?

We talk casually for ten minutes before I notice her start to glance at the clock. Her hands are crossed politely over her kneecaps, head tilted to the side, and I know she's telling me to wrap up my story. I let my last words trail off because as I'm talking Dr. Nelson bends down into her filing cabinet and takes out a fistful of pencils bundled together in a rubber band. Brand-new, sharpened No. 2 pencils. The pencils of standardized tests. The pencils of death.

But I stop suddenly at this thought. It comes automatically, flowing forward out of habit. Pencils, cancer. Pencils, cancer. Except today it falls flat. Like my favorite song being played off-key. It doesn't feel like it used to. Something's different.

"Hey!" I jerk upward as a rubber band flies by my face and smacks into the back of the chair. Dr. Nelson is holding her pose, one hand outstretched, one eye closed.

"Aw, man! So close!" She slaps the side of her leg, then arranges the pencils, laying them individually on top of her thighs. They make small wooden noises against one another. If the cancer rays in their tips were turned on—which they aren't, for some reason—they would be slicing me in half through the middle.

The clamp is tightening on my head, slowly but continuously. In such quantity, the pencils have a Darth Vader-like power and I feel them gripping tightly around my neck from across the room. My muscles cramp into knots and my shoulders rise up toward my ears.

"Don't worry about the pencils, Allison." She snaps twice and my eyes are pulled up to her. "Don't pay attention to them. They're just sitting here, minding their own business." Looking me straight in the eye, as if keeping me on course, she asks, "So! Tell me about your homework. How was trying to interact more with pencils? How did it go?"

Oh! I'm torn from my headache and suddenly remember. The pencil. The battle.

"The homework!" My brakes squeal across the carpet and I've done a 180. A smug smile spreads across my face. The homework! "Okay, so, I did it. In the den last night."

"Good! And? How did you feel?"

"Oh my *gosh*, at *first*. . ." I yell these words at her, leaning my chest forward, talking with my body. I take a quick breath in. "At first, it was terrible. Sooo bad." I hold out the "ooo" just to be sure she understands. "Soooooo bad," I repeat for emphasis. "Like, worse than it was the first time, even. I felt so, just, consumed. I guess. I don't know." My voice trails off as I remember myself back on the carpet across from the bookshelf.

"And did it pass? Were you able to keep going?"

Ha! I snap back into the moment. "Yes!" I look at Dr. Nelson, and her eyes are open wide at me like I'm telling the most interesting and suspenseful story she's ever heard. "Yes! It took a while, you know, a few minutes or so, but soon I really started to feel less . . . I don't know what. Just less." I shrug at her, and she nods like she gets it. "And once it kind of got to a seven or so, it got better much faster. It's that first part that's really bad." I move my hand in the air in a straight line and then jerk it diagonally downward to show the path.

She's smiling and I'm smiling and we nod at each other in silence for a few seconds. "Very good, very good. That's great to hear! So it may have started out worse than when we did it together, but you see that it still decreases over time. It loses its power when you resist it."

I'm still smiling at her. "Yep."

"So, are you ready to get started again?

"Started again with—"

But before I finish my question she's lifted one of the pencils up off her lap (weird, I think briefly, that I forgot those were there) and is holding it by its eraser so it's pointed toward the ceiling. My heart leaps like someone has jumped out at me from hiding.

"What's your rating?"

"An eight!" I say loudly, talking over my muscles. But then I unclench slightly and really look up at it. Yellow paint, sharpened tip. Just like the one from yesterday. "Mm, well. Actually. A seven. No, an eight. No . . . a seven." The pencil feels angry, but like it's been wrapped in a few layers of bubble wrap. Somehow muffled. "Yeah, a seven." I tilt my head and look at it quietly for about five seconds. "Now almost a six."

"Wow, very good. It's been forty seconds. Stick with it."

The clock ticks a handful of times into the silence. "Five."

"Four."

"Three."

I look up at Dr. Nelson and she wiggles her eyebrows at me twice. "Well, check. You. *Out!*" She almost squeals as she jumps out of her seat and leans forward for a high five. Laughing out loud, I smack her hand with equal enthusiasm.

"Oh my goodness. Way to go! I mean it, Allison. Amazing progress."

I bloom with pride. Dr. Nelson is happy. Pencils are just pencils. This is happening.

We do two more rounds of ERP. They both start at sixes, quickly plummet, and end with a raucous high five across the carpet. My cheeks hurt from smiling.

"We have one more order of business before I can let you go for the day." She lifts her hands a few inches and looks down at her paper. "School starts back on Wednesday." She pauses here, knowing what's coming, and I let out a long groan.

"Schoooool. Nooooo." I dramatically flop over onto the arm of the chair. "Don't make me."

"Yes, yes. Well, you will understand if I don't feel *too* bad for you, because I haven't had a Christmas break in, ohhh"—she looks down at the watch on her wrist—"twenty, no, twenty-five years." She lets out a long, melodramatic sigh. "One of the downfalls of getting old."

"That doesn't mean you have to wish it on me!" I pretend to balk at her.

Tilting her head, she purses her lips at me, trying to hide her amusement. "I really want to get you off on the right foot this semester. And I think we can do it. No, I *know* we can do it. But we need to have a plan. So start thinking about what else you want to target. What makes the most sense for your schoolwork, for your happiness? You've done so well on pencils, we'll be running through this list in no time."

I flinch. "Lists, you mean."

"Hmm?"

"Lists. It's *lists*. Plural." I appreciate her optimism, but let's not get carried away here. This isn't a scribbled to-do list of Sunday afternoon chores. We'll run though it in no time? Don't be so casual. I shrink away from her in my seat.

"Yes. Yes, lists, you're right. We've got some big boulders ahead, that's for sure." She straightens a few papers against her thigh before sliding them into her folder, aware that she's struck a nerve. She looks up at me. "And that's why we've got to work that much harder."

I feel a surge of warmth and nod at her. Much better.

"Also, speaking of school, I've spoken with your guidance counselor, Ms. Dickerson, and the vice principal, and I've advised them that it would be in your best interest to hold off on retaking your precal exam until later in the semester. I think that at this point it would be a major disruption for you, a major cause of stress that you don't need. And that, frankly, it would delay our progress."

My eyes shoot open with the mention of the precal exam. I completely forgot that I'm supposed to retake it. That I hadn't studied and had no pencil and cried in front of everyone. Craaaaap, I moan to myself. And now I have to go back to school and sit in that same classroom with those same people. How did I forget?

If Dr. Nelson notices my misery, she pretends that she doesn't and continues. "We've also discussed alternative options for you this semester in regards to your schoolwork. Now that you have been officially diagnosed, Section 504 of the Rehabilitation Act provides for certain measures that can be taken to help"—she pauses for the right phrase— "ease the load on you." She makes a gentle hand gesture, swaying her arm to the side.

"For example . . ." She flips over loudly to a full page of notes. I think I see my name written across the top, and there's a doodle in the corner. She traces her finger through the writing, mumbling under her breath, looking for the information. "Ah, okay, here. So, we discussed extended testing times. Instead of having to complete a quiz or an exam in the usual class period, you will be allowed extra time. I think that will help with your stress level during the test. You will feel less rushed, less likely to get anxious. More time to deal with any OCD issues if they crop up." She looks up at me and I have no idea what my face is doing. She quickly returns to her notes. "We also discussed alternative testing sites. For example, you might feel more comfortable taking your tests in an empty classroom, in the library. Even at home."

My stomach gurgles with hunger into the silence. I guess this is good news? Less pressure, less stress. Can't hurt. But I picture everyone watching me as I walk with my stapled test out of the classroom while they remain seated in cramped rows. They're going to think I have a learning disability. Or that I'm emotionally unstable. They'll think I've gone crazy and get special treatment because of that legendary time they've all heard of when I burst into tears in the middle of a precal exam. Regardless of what they think, though, they're going to *know* that something is wrong with me. That I'm different.

"What are your thoughts on all of this?"

I wish I could sigh without her hearing. Thank you, I guess? Yes, this will probably make a difference, in some way. But it's not going to help my reputation.

"Yeah, uh. Sounds good."

It's clear she was expecting a little more enthusiasm, but she only hesitates for a moment before clapping her hands together. "Okay!" she yells happily, mostly to snap me out of my funk, I think. "Back to the fun stuff, right? Have we talked about homework yet?"

I give her a half head shake. I'm trying to feel glum. I want to wallow in my self-pity for a while. School is coming back. And I'm still a freak. But I can feel Dr. Nelson's enthusiastic eyes waiting for my attention from across the carpet. As much as I want to, I can't resist.

"No, but we just did three rounds of ERP," I grunt.

"Yes, but that doesn't have any impact on your *homework*. Do you really think I would let you get off that easy?" She acts appalled, her hand to her chest. "We need to keep pushing hard on pencils. I think you saw today that it's already starting to get easier, hmm?" She cracks a wide smile at me. My faux foul mood evaporates and I grin back at her. And my heart glows. "Let's keep working on that. Every pencil you see, look at it." She gestures enthusiastically with two fingers from her eyes outward. "Experience the anxiety. It's going to come, so just let it. And then wait. Know that there's an end. That if you just keep staring, keep looking, in just a little while, in just a few *seconds*, there's relief." She's leaning forward and I'm leaning forward. It's a pep talk. And I'm into it. "You just gotta stick with it. Like boxing, remember. Outlast it." We nod at each other.

I sit up, surging with energy. I'm gonna do it. I'm going to seek out pencils and I'm going to stare. Them. Down.

305

The alarm on the wall chimes gently and Dr. Nelson claps her hands together. "That's our cue!" She stands up quickly and walks toward the door, my file tucked under her arm. With her hand on the doorknob, she pauses and turns around to face me. "Hey." I look up from my bandaged fingers at her. "Really great job today. Really great." There's a silence, and for a second it feels like we might hug, and I don't think either of us knows what to do. "One more time?" She's holding her hand up in the air, and I look at her, pause, then smack it with a surge of happiness.

"Well, look at you!" My mom pops up out of her chair as I come into the waiting room.

"What?" Lifting my arms out to the side, I glance down quickly at my shirt and legs. "What?"

"You're just smiling, that's all!" She, too, is smiling but it's mixed with confusion or surprise. Like she's half preparing for me to yell at her. "It's been . . ." Catching herself, knowing it wasn't going to come out right, she adjusts. "It's a very nice thing to see." She gives an awkward little head nod, almost a bow, and I squint at her.

"Yeah. Thanks." It comes out drier than I meant it to. But how am I supposed to respond to that? She's hunched over, digging in her purse, looking for her checkbook, and I feel a strange wave of guilt. She's just happy to see her daughter smile for the first time in months. Cut the woman a break. I pick tentatively at the stickers in the wicker basket on Dr. Nelson's desk. There's a Dory and a Nemo, a SpongeBob and a Squidward. Giant word bubbles exploding with all-capital phrases like YOU DID IT!! and WAY TO GO! I pick up a red-and-blue firework exclaiming YOU'RE THE BEST! and stick it on my mom's left hand as she writes out the check.

She is mumbling out loud to herself—"Doctor . . . Virginia . . . Nelson . . . January"—but stops when she feels my fingers on her skin. She looks at the sticker for a few moments and then up at me. I bump her gently with my hip and our eyes meet. I haven't really thought past this part of the plan. I don't have anything to say. But as we look at each other, she quietly bumps me back, and I dart my eyes up to the ceiling to hold in the sudden tears. Mom. I missed you.

CHAPTER 25

It still smells the same. That unique mixture of old building and cleaning supplies. Walking toward first period, it feels like it's been both one day and one year since I've been here. Passing the colorful bulletin boards and rows of lockers, I'm flooded with reminders of Sara and cross-country practice and openmouthed stares, but so much has happened over Christmas break (Dr. Adams! Dr. Nelson!) that they're also somehow distant. Almost like a terrible nightmare.

It was Dr. Nelson's idea that I should leave my pile of books at home, at least for now. "I think you're already carrying enough, as it is," she said with one of her meaningful looks. "For the first few days, let's ease you back in, okay?" A discussion followed:

"But what about my papers?"

"What about your papers?"

"I need them."

"Why?"

"Well. Because." I thought about the brown juice-covered stacks of notes with tattered edges. "And my binders! And all of my class notes." And my mom's sandwiches, and the paper towels, and the pieces of worthless junk I'd accumulated since learning trash cans caused cancer. But I didn't mention these out loud. They sounded ridiculous enough in my head.

"It's a new semester. You won't need your notes from last

semester. And, if we're being honest here, you won't need your binders because—and I'm not trying to be rude—you aren't able to write. Yet."

My mouth hung open. I thought about being offended (*I'm not trying to be rude, but you're still a freak*) but she had a point. There was no use for notebook paper and school materials if I couldn't use them.

We decided that I would take one binder with me to use as a decoy in all my classes. I could still store any important handouts from class in my book bag, she assured me. (And loose trash and my lunch, I reminded myself.)

I don't know what expression I should have on my face as I turn in to first period. Does anyone notice I don't have my pile? Do they still remember the things I did before Christmas? I'm tiptoeing and counting and I've got dread-locks and screaming acne. But my hands are hanging freely by my side and I don't smell like rotting lunch meat. Despite the warm stares of my classmates on my pajamas, I feel like I'm floating. No pile. No second bag stained with old food. This is awesome.

With Dr. Nelson's voice on my shoulder, I scan Ms. Michaels's art class for ERP targets and find the room mirac-ulously free of pencils. She is introducing a new project, and as she talks, she distributes trays of small oil-pastel crayons to all the tables. She sets the metal tin down in front of me, and to my surprise, I look up at her and smile. An actual smile. It's the mix of not having a pile, the comforting presence of Dr. Nelson in my head, and Ms. Michaels's familiar, paint-stained apron. I see her face adjust as she tries to hide her own surprise, and then she flashes a smile back at me, patting me on the shoulder quickly as she walks by. I love art class.

When I look down at the tray of oil pastels, my body flinches and my brain lurches into action. *Bad, bad, bad.* Goose bumps spread across my arms and my muscles tense, in case I need to jump up and escape. But then, just as quickly as the warning leaped to life, it fades. False alarm. Just an oil pastel. It's like my brain revs up out of habit: Oh, there's a writing utensil, time to freak out. But as I look at it, I know it's just a tiny crayon wrapped in black paper. A week ago I would have heard swarming bees and raging alarms. I shrug slightly to myself. That was before I met Dr. Nelson.

But English class is different. I can tell by the air that the room is filled with pencils. I hear their tiny sharp points screeching against unapproved notebook paper. Ms. Griffin is jumping around in front of the chalkboard in a valiant effort to hold our attention, her hair slowly growing in size as she begins to sweat. I've got my sole binder flipped open, and I'm leaning forward, almost hunched over my desk. My eyes are focused downward, staring at an old page of notes, and my neck is beginning to ache. I know what I should be doing. I let out a long breath. Okay, fine.

Before searching out a pencil, I pray three times, making sure to hit my chest extra hard with my hand signal and blast my arm into the air, pointing at the ceiling.

"Yes, Allison?" Ms. Griffin's voice pulls me from my closed eyes and *amens*.

Still hunched over, curled into myself like a turtle, I raise my head to her. "Huh?"

"Do you have a question?"

"What?" Twenty-five teenage heads swivel toward me. I make the mistake of looking out into the crowd and see Sara's wild hair and my breath catches in my chest. I almost choke on it. "Uh . . . no."

"Your hand's up?"

I look up at my hand pointed toward the tiled ceiling. "Oh, sorry. Uh. Just, uh, stretching." Yanking it downward, I slump even farther into my desk, trying to make myself as small as possible. "Sorry."

I melt into my seat, heat boiling in my cheeks. Awesome. Great. Well done, me. I keep my eyes closed until I'm sure that no one could still be looking in my direction.

It takes another ten minutes before I'm recovered, and by now I'm angry. This is stupid. Making a fool of myself is stupid. Listening to these thoughts, letting them ruin my life and my grades and my friendships, is stupid. I need to stop this. And the only way to do it, it seems, is to keep working. Keep seeking out things I'm scared of, keep staring them down. Even though I know it's a risk, I pray three more times and pump my hand in the air. I'm going to need it for this.

I roll my neck slowly. You can do it. Just like in Dr. Nelson's office. Just like in Dr. Nelson's office. With my head hovering inches above my notebook in an effort to appear like I'm paying attention to Ms. Griffin's lesson, I slide my eyes as far as they will go to the right. Looking through chunks of tangles, I see a hand with blue nails gripping tightly on a pencil. Megan Perkins. Her hand and pencil are streaming across the paper, unaware of my gaze. It's a six. And then quickly a five. Chipped nail polish, a turquoise ring. Four. I'm breathing freely, no buzzing, no tension. Three. Two.

A whoosh of joy blows through me, and I shift forward in my seat, my arms against my desk, and lift myself up slightly so I can see over Lauren Madison's shoulder. She's got a mechanical pencil, and even though I'm staring at it, there's nothing. No spike in my number, not even an itch. To my left is Dan Bennett. He's on the wrestling team and insists that chewing sunflower seeds in class helps him burn calories before Wednesday weigh-ins. Through his slurping and crunching, his pencil lies slack in his hand, his notebook paper blank. Five! Five. Five. Five. Aaand now it's a four. The wood around the metal eraser has deep teeth marks. Still a four. He moves forward, blocking my view, to spit out a glob of seeds into a plastic bottle. Ugh. When he sits back I see his pencil again. Three, two.

By the time I'm walking to sixth-period chemistry, my head is buzzing, but not with fear or cancer. With energy. And happiness and pride. Tiptoeing through the frigid air, I forget that I'm shivering in worn pajamas and that I still haven't taken my precal final and that my danger list is three pages long. The only thing on my mind, the thing filling me to the brim with glowing light, is the fact that I can now look at pencils without holding my breath, without even any real discomfort. It's a miracle.

And it's with the sun gazing down on me, tiptoeing and counting down the sidewalk, that I know I've crossed a bridge. I don't know when exactly I made the transition, whether it was the last appointment with Dr. Nelson, when I was finally able to see real progress, or just today in English, making eye contact with multiple pencils and still living to tell the story. Gradually, or maybe all at once like a lightning strike, I'm here. The thoughts are from God, obviously. He's still watching over me. But they're also something much more local. Much more controllable. Divine but also a product of my own mind. Or something like that.

I walk straight to one of the lab tables in the back of the chemistry room, avoiding eye contact with the desk that was so angry at me during exams. Ms. Matthews is scribbling on the chalkboard as I perch my feet carefully in two tiles. I plop my binder on top of the cool surface, and as I open it, I notice a long pencil lying coyly about two feet away from me on the table. It's almost too much of a coincidence. It's like the world is testing me. *You're so smug, but can you handle this?*

I scoff out loud. Can I handle this? I stare at the pencil and barely hit a four. I look away at the wall for a few seconds, letting my memory clear, and then dart my eyes back to it on the table. I get a small spike that quickly disappears, like the tiny waves that spread from a rock plopped in the water. This is kind of lame, I tell myself. I don't think this is helping.

And then I feel the edge of an idea and it's accompanied with the new feeling of buzzing adrenaline and happiness. Watch this, I say to myself, and also to the universe, as if I'm about to do some sort of amazing trick. With a straightened back, and after two quick prayers, I lean toward the pencil, stretch out my pointer finger, and poke it gently. It sizzles like a droplet of water on a hot pan. Poke. Poke. I wait for it to quit moving and come to a stop. Poke. And then I press down on it like a piano key. Press. Pressss. It's burning my fingertip, but my heart is pounding and a flood of joy drives me forward. Press. I hold it for two seconds. There's a sharp pain in my brain, but it almost feels good. Like the ache in your muscles when you've done ten too many squats. Press. Five seconds. My nail is turning white, and the ridge of the pencil leaves a small indentation on my skin.

This is amazing! Press. Press. Hold. Press. Press. Hold. And then suddenly, before I can stop myself, before I can calm the wave of ambition that rams me forward, I've swept my arm across the table and I've got it in my hand. The pencil. Is. In. My. Hand. It's in my hand. It's in my hand. The thought is running circles in my mind, and I'm trying to catch up. What do I do? Pencil in my hand. Help. Help. *Help.*

This is a nine. We are at a *nine.* Man your battle stations. *Incominnnggggg!*

My arm is thrust out away from me to the side, and waves of cancer are pulsing up it toward my torso. I feel its germs spreading to my blood cells, convincing them to turn into leukemia. My mind is in a trash compactor, and my eyes are being forced forward in their sockets, about to pop out and roll onto the table. Nine. Nine. It's a signal, a code, a secret message: I have nine months to live. I won't make it to junior year. I won't make it to a driver's license. The cancer is moving from my blood to my bones now. Bone-marrow transplant, radiation, morphine. My knuckles are white, screaming in pain against my rabid grip on the pencil. I look at its tip sticking out of my diseased skin, and it's just like the ones Megan and Dan were using in English. It's the same No. 2 Ticonderoga that Dr. Nelson spread across her lap in her office last week. Now I'm an eight and my head is lying sideways on my shoulder. The tumor is too heavy to lift. Pencil in my hand. Pencil touching my skin. Pencil in my hand. Pencil touching my skin. I don't want to die! Crap, why did I do this? Why did I *do* this!

You're doing so well—where are you now? I groan out loud, one eye closed against the pain in my head. The calmness of her voice guides me toward the surface. An eight. Maybe. Or a seven. *Keep going.* I'm able to straighten up now, no longer needing support for what seems to be a shrinking tumor. Bringing my fist with the pencil down to rest on the lab table, I'm able to get a closer look. It's dull, and I can tell it was last sharpened on a cheap manual pencil sharpener. The kind mounted on the walls above the trash cans (*trash cans!*) in every classroom. Those green letters (*green!*), the yellow paint. I've seen this pencil a thousand times. And I sink to a five. It's wood, and lead, and nothing much else. It has no special power. It doesn't cause cancer. It's a pencil. And I'm a three.

The storm suddenly over, the menacing clouds parting, a ray of sun shines from the ceiling directly down onto me like a spotlight. I throw the pencil to the floor and then swing my arms up into the air in celebration. A pop star after a dramatic mic drop. Take that, pencil. Take that, brain. I lift my head to the ceiling, my arms all the way out to the side now, basking in my success. I think of Dr. Nelson and

I feel her beside me, my eyes closed as we both take in the moment. We did it.

When I bring my head up, the three kids in the back row have all turned around to look at me. Probably because I threw a pencil across the room. I'm radiating happiness and I give them a small wave, beaming.

It's the next day. Dr. Nelson lifts up one of the pencils she has had resting on her lap and spins it between her fingers. "So, tell me about your homework."

I've been waiting for this. I extend my arm toward her, palm up, like I'm asking for money and wiggle my fingers.

"This?" she asks, confused, gesturing to the pencil in her hand. I only continue to wiggle my fingers in response, a smirk spreading across my cheeks. After a few seconds, she leans forward slowly, placing the pencil in my palm.

A knife slices through my brain when it touches my skin and I almost drop it. My head falls to the side, resting on my shoulder, and I close my right eye, scrunching my face up. It burns, it burns, it burns. Part of my brain is sizzling into nothing, wrinkling up like a raisin. But after about ten seconds it begins to dissipate, and I'm sitting up straight, and soon I'm able to look across the carpet and make eye contact with Dr. Nelson. Her eyebrows are raised halfway up her forehead and her mouth is hanging open dramatically.

"Oh. My. Goodness," she whispers. "Well, isn't that something."

CHAPTER 26

I'm counting my steps intensely. Walking alone, staring at the cracks ahead, my eyes zooming around the pavement for obstacles. I forcefully count each step aloud. The more careful I am, the more I'll have left to eat at lunch. But also, and probably more important right now, it's comforting. I'm battling pencils, with a massive danger list waiting in the wings. It's nice to count and tiptoe and wrap myself up in my own world, just for a few minutes. As much as I want to be the old me, current me has its benefits. I just need a break. Then I'll get back to work.

"Whoa! Watch where you're going!" I find my face crunched into something damp and warm. When I look up, I realize it's an armpit. Mica Smith's armpit.

Mica and I grew up together. He lives down the street, and we were friends before it mattered that he was a boy and I was a girl. For about two years we spent our summers doing tricks off the diving board and splitting microwave pizzas from the neighborhood pool snack bar. But then we hit middle school and he grew a foot, his voice changed, and he started hanging out with his older brother's upperclassmen friends. That was the end of that friendship.

I pry my face from his body, equally disoriented and embarrassed. He smells like Sam.

"Oh." He lowers his voice when he sees it's me. "Hey, Allison. Sorry, didn't mean to yell. I didn't know it was . . ." He stops midsentence as his eyes scan over me, then launches in a different direction. "*Whoa!* Rough night? You look like me with a bad hangover."

"Huh?" I'm still thinking about Sam, but the questioning look on Mica's face drags me back to the hallway. "Yeah, oh." I glance down at myself, my hand automatically rising up to smooth my ragged hair. "I was just up late. Studying. All-nighter. That's why I'm dressed like this." I swing my pointer finger from my head to my toe, shaking my head. "Just didn't have time to get ready this morning."

He raises one eyebrow at me. "You must be in some intense classes. Studying that hard in the first week of the semester." Although he's a member of the popular crowd, Mica and I have almost the same course load. He's a closet smart kid. "Maybe I need to up my game?"

I feel a thick lump in my throat and open my mouth with no idea of what might come out. "Ha . . . ha . . . yeah. You know. Gotta be prepared." I'm awkward.

"Well, just don't go off to Harvard without me." He smiles brightly with his perfectly straight white teeth. "Us Blakely Farms kids have to stick together, right?" A small nudge against my shoulder. "Just like old times." He obviously sees my dreadlocks and pimples. He can probably smell my breath. He knows the rumors. Everyone does. Is he trying to comfort me? Is he trying to be nice?

I'm so taken aback that I don't react when he slaps me on the back and throws a "Catch ya later, neighbor" over his shoulder as he walks away.

Yeah, he commented on my appearance. He saw the

obvious. But he also talked to me like I'm a real human. I see him round the corner with a knot of friends and finally feel myself unglue from the pavement. Walking to Civics and Ethics, back to counting and tiptoeing, I realize he is the only person I've actually *talked* to, besides Dr. Nelson, in weeks.

And suddenly I'm feeling a wave of motivation. One day, every conversation could be like this. At some point, with Dr. Nelson and after a few more appointments, I could talk to Sara, or Jenny. Or Sam. Maybe I'll find a way to start eating real meals again. Maybe one day I'll pick out an outfit from my closet and not worry that it's going to kill me and all those I care about.

Or maybe I'm getting ahead of myself. Maybe these are unrealistic goals to shoot for. But imagine! The possibilities!

I'm settled into my desk in Civics and Ethics, these radical ideas still speeding through my mind. Brushing my teeth, wearing makeup. Doing my homework, making A's on tests. Talking with my friends, complaining about Coach Millings between breaths during cross-country practice. All the things that the former Allison used to do. It feels like I could get some of them back.

And it's then, as Mr. Roberts squeaks off the top of his whiteboard marker, that I know what I need to do. It's time. And I'm ready.

I slowly unzip the front pouch of my book bag with the care of an archaeologist dislodging a piece of pottery from the arid ground. Although I know pencils are safe, I feel like I should try to keep my plan a secret from the universe, if possible. Just in case.

With a sizzle and a violent jump to a six, which quickly fades to a five, four, three, I've got a pencil in my hand and I carefully inch it up toward the desk. And there is the notebook paper. Blue horizontal lines daring me, staring at me like they know I won't do it. They're saying I'm too weak. Too far gone.

But I'm holding the pencil. And it's poised over the paper. My head is pounding. As much from excitement and adrenaline as anxiety. Pencil, paper. Pencil, paper. They go together. For my whole life, they've been partners. It makes sense. It's natural.

And I'm writing. I see the black lines spell out *Civics and Ethics: January 10.* Instantly, I'm a student, just like everyone else around me. Despite my clothes and face and thoughts, I'm just a girl taking notes in class. Nothing to see here, nothing strange about this situation. A high school sophomore trying to get through another day. I look around the room, half expecting a standing ovation. Can anyone else see what's happening? Does anyone else understand the importance of this?

At least for these few seconds, I'm *normal.* And it's amazing.

Although Mr. Roberts says nothing of real importance during the class, I write down his every syllable. My pencil whips across the paper, and with it a tension deep inside me unspools like a ball of tightly wound yarn. The lead smears across the side of my hand, and a wide smile smears across my face. I can smell the sharp edge of the graphite. Smells like hope.

What an incredible day! I exclaim to myself, over and

320

over, as I take notes through the day in Spanish, precal, and chemistry. I run out of paper in all three classes (only two sheets of notebook paper allowed per class), but it doesn't even matter. I'm *writing*. I'm taking notes. I'm . . . functioning.

By the time I get home from school, I'm almost exhausted with happiness. I've spent the whole afternoon grinning to myself. And thinking about the future and all the things I might be able to do. I'm padding up the stairs, leaning forward to use my hands against the carpet, when I feel a lump underneath my foot. It's not hard like a rock or stick but soft and forgiving. Almost squishy.

My mind still consumed with my plans to eventually use blue pens and eat apples, I've almost forgotten there's danger in the world. Danger that just weeks ago was the sole focus of my life. Until I look down and watch my naked foot slowly rise from the stair. And there, lying flat, looking almost innocent, is a sock. A gray-toed, Hanes brand, cotton sock.

We stare at each other for a few moments as I feel my body preparing to react. It must have fallen out of the laundry hamper last night when my mom was doing laundry. *Mom*, my brain screams, *you ruin everything*. This day was perfect. This day was progress. This day was *hope* until now. Until you doomed me to cancer and death and hospital beds . . .

My brain shoots forward into a tirade. All my work with pencils, all those appointments with Dr. Nelson. They're done. Over. Pointless. Now I have cancer. And after all I've done for my mom, *this* is how she repays me? After all my sacrifices? *This* is what I get? This is how I'll die? A lone sock on the stairwell?

But when I stop to take a breath, I realize that the world is silent. No alarms, no bees. No dark clouds on the horizon, no pounding in my head. It's just me and my foot and a crumpled sock lying on the carpet. Huh. I stand there for twenty more seconds, my eyes scanning the walls around me, waiting for an attack. I mean, it's a *sock*. I still remember the afternoon when my monster seized it in the kitchen. It's definitely dangerous. It definitely causes cancer. Except, it seems, it doesn't.

Huh. I stare at it for another five seconds and look around, giving the storm one last chance to appear over the horizon. But it's quiet. This sock is safe. And, looking at it, I somehow know that, from now on, all socks are safe.

"My, my, you're a chatty Cathy today," my mom says, glancing at me with a smile over the center console on our drive to Dr. Nelson's. I'm in a good mood, the winter sun blaring in through the front window, and I've been telling her about the play we're reading in English. She reaches her arm over and tickles me quickly in the stomach. "I missed talking with you like this!"

I move to continue my story, but as soon as I process her words, my muscles tense up. Why does she have to point that out? Why must we bring attention to this? "Yeah, uh, I don't know. I mean, yeah," I grunt, leaning forward to turn up the radio as an escape. My mom's favorite Beatles song is on, and after she gives me a few overly enthusiastic nudges in my arm, I give in and wiggle around a little bit in my seat, a halfhearted attempt at a dance. My mom laughs with glee and she belts the rest of the song out loud. Humoring her, I begin to gently mouth the words. I'm singing almost as loud as my mom by the time the song ends and we pull into Dr. Nelson's parking lot.

I'm feeling boisterously happy. Pencils! Socks! What more could a girl ask for? This is incredible! When plastered against the dark backdrop of the past three months, the past few days have been the best of my life. And I'm going to show Dr. Nelson just how much progress I've made. She's going to be so amazed! I rustle in my backpack, pull my well-used pencil out of the front pouch, and stick it behind my ear.

I wince briefly as if I've got a cramp in my neck. The pencil is so close to my brain. So close to the tumors. But I wipe the thought away like steam on a mirror. *It's just a pencil.* Just a pencil. Wood. Lead. Nothing.

Vibrating with anticipation, I try to sit calmly across from Dr. Nelson. Every few minutes a small thought in the back of my head pipes up, *Um, excuse me, miss. Um, yes, did you know pencils cause cancer?* I smash it hard with my fist. Shut up.

I can't believe she hasn't caught on yet. We've been talking, looking at each other across the carpet, for five minutes now and she hasn't said a thing! As she tells me about the "incredible" cucumber she grew in her garden last summer, I turn my head pointedly to the left so the pencil behind my ear is directly in her eye line. I sway back and forth slightly, hoping it will catch her attention. *Come on!*

She's looking at me strangely, her story halted, trying to figure out what kind of message I'm sending her. Maybe Dr. Nelson isn't as quick as I thought. I roll my eyes at her and jerk my hand up, pointing at the pencil tucked behind my ear.

"What's this?" She mimics my hand gesture. "What are you showing me?"

"Dr. Nelson! Come on! Pencil! A pencil behind my ear!" I hear it coming out, and it sounds like a whine but . . . but . . . a pencil behind my ear! How can she not *see?*

"Well, look at that! Now, if that's not impressive!" She claps her hands together loudly. "When did you find out you were able to do that?"

"Just now, in the car." I shrug, trying to sound nonchalant in a way that tells her I still want more compliments on my bravery. "I also took notes in class almost all day yesterday *and* today."

"You took notes? On notebook paper? With a pencil?"

"Yes!" I flail my hands at her in excitement.

"*What!*" She throws my folder into the air, papers flying everywhere. "That's *amazing!*"

"I *know!* I've been so excited to tell you! And it wasn't even *that* bad, you know? I mean, now that I'm okay with pencils, using one to actually write wasn't a big deal."

She's shaking her head at me, her eyes gleaming. "This is incredible work, Allison. Absolutely incredible. I'm so very proud of you. Wow." She is still shaking her head as she bends down and quickly gathers all her notes on me off the floor.

"And I have one more thing to show you." I wiggle my toes inside my running shoes.

"Something else? Really? Oh my, okay. Let's see it!"

"Well, remember how you said that some things would just get better on their own? Like, once I started getting over a few, some other fears I haven't even targeted will just go away?" I rustle in my seat, bending down toward my shoes. I'm wearing socks. I've been wearing them all day. And nothing has happened! No anxiety. And they're so comfortable.

"Yes, yes, I remember talking about that." She tilts her head, her voice questioning.

I adjust myself in my seat and pull up my pants leg. "I'm wearing socks."

"Yes, so you are." She nods, sticking up her leg at me, raising her khakis. "So am I!"

"No, I'm *wearing socks.*" I roughly pull both my shoes off and wave my white-cottoned feet at her, staring at her hard across the carpet.

"Oh! *Socks!* Oh my, you're wearing socks! How very wonderful!" She gazes at me in amazement, pouring out an endless stream of enthusiasm. "How did this come about? Did you work on them on your own?"

"No, I didn't work on them at all! And I don't know! Like, I have no idea! I just accidentally stepped on one yesterday on the stairs, and it didn't scare me at all, even though it's on the list. Even though for months socks caused cancer. So"—I shrug at her—"I decided to wear some today. To show you."

"Well, I'm certainly glad you did! Quite the surprise!"

We smile at each other across the carpet for a long time. "So. It really seems like you're doing well. Like you're getting a handle on this thing."

"Yeah, definitely. I agree. It's hardest at the beginning, but once you get going and get past the first few exposures, things get much better."

"Yep. Exactly. That's ERP in action, my girl!" We nod at each other. "And speaking of ERP, I think it's time we choose another victim, right? What do you say? You're clearly well on your way to defeating pencils," she says with a laugh, raising her arm up to gesture toward my ear. And before I respond, she is in her manila folder, flipping through papers. She hands me a copy of my danger list and looks down at her own. "Okay, well, I think we need to still be focusing on school." Eyes on the paper, she is intentionally not giving me time to interrupt. "Let's see: notebook paper for homework, *not* the computer"—she looks up and winks at me—"your pile, putting binders in your locker. Or, oh. Here we go." She taps the papers with the end of her pen. "Calculators."

We do three rounds of ERP, and by the last one, ears ringing, I peak at a seven, finding my way to relative calm in less than a minute. And I'm exhausted. The calculator is lying on my hand, and although it is no longer screaming at me, I'm looking at the ceiling to ensure I don't accidentally glance at it.

"Okay! Very good, very good! You did some great work today, Allison. Truly great." She looks up at me cheerily, expectantly. But I don't have the energy to respond. "So, and I'm sure you're expecting this, your homework is to try to expose yourself to calculators as much as possible. As you've seen, the more you do it, the faster you start to become desensitized, right?"

I nod at her but my head hurts. The weight of the calculator on my arm takes up about half my brain.

"Also, in addition to working on calculators, I think you—"

Whipping my head toward her, mouth open, I let out a half cough, half gasp. Is she serious? *More?*

"Don't balk at me like that! Of course there's more!" She wiggles her eyebrows. "But I think it's time you got a fun one, hmm? Don't you?"

"Fun?" My voice is flat, and I scrunch my nose at her, head still buzzing.

"Yes, there is such a thing as fun homework, believe it or not. And it's called shopping. How does that sound?"

"Shopping? My homework is to go shopping?"

"Yes! Your Christmas gifts! You have a mini fortune waiting for you in all of the gift cards that you haven't been able to use." She underlines the entry on the list with her pen. Oh, right! I exclaim to myself. Through the family grapevine, and to my complete embarrassment, most of my relatives were informed long before Christmas that I was going through some sort of emotional crisis. As a result, I was deluged with gift cards to all my favorite stores over the holidays. It was my family's not-so-subtle way of trying to lift my spirits. But as soon as I opened them, of course, they were moved to the danger list, never to be seen again. I remember stashing them furtively under my bed, tucking them under a pile of contraband clothing for extra protection.

Oh my gosh, Dr. Nelson, you're a genius! My face lights up at her. Gift cards.

"But we're going to need to involve someone else," she continues. "Given that you can't drive yourself yet."

We walk down the carpeted hall together toward the waiting room. "Momzilla, we've got some homework for you," I call out in a singsong voice. My mom is gazing down at her computer, mouth slightly open.

"Pardon me?" It's difficult for her to pull herself from her work, but she looks up at us after saving whatever it is she is working on. "I'm sorry, I missed that." Sliding her computer to the adjacent chair, she stands up, runs her hands down the front of her business slacks, and approaches the desk.

"Homework. For this weekend." Dr. Nelson says. "I've got an assignment that involves both you and Allison."

"Ohh, I see. Sounds interesting. I haven't had homework in years!" My mom smiles at me and, nodding, nudges me gently with her elbow, as if we've got some sort of secret now. "I'm ready for whatever you got!" With her hand in a fist, she swings her arm into the air. "Go, team!" I cringe, scrunching my eyebrows together, but I shoot her a small grin when she looks my way.

"Yes, yes, I think you will both enjoy it." Dr. Nelson cuts her eyes at me quickly. "It seems Miss Allison here is in possession of some very valuable gift cards from the Christmas holidays. And this weekend, both of you are assigned to spend them. All of them."

My mom nods again, with even more enthusiasm than before. "Oh my gosh, yes! That's right. What ever happened to those, Allison? There were some *good* ones, if I remember. American Eagle, J.Crew, Anthropologie. What else was there?"

"Nordstrom."

"Oh! Nordstrom. Faaancy." Something in the way she carries out the last word, or maybe the sassy flick of her wrist, suddenly, unexpectedly, draws out a loud snort from my nose. One loud burst of a guffaw that then hangs in the air like a rainbow over the reception desk. It sounds like a loud awkward hiccup, but it's a laugh. As close as I've come to one in front of my mom for as long as I can remember. They both look at me, startled, and I bring my hand up to cover my open mouth. I see Dr. Nelson and my mom make eye contact, and my mom's face is stretched into a huge smile.

CHAPTER 27

I'm leaning down over my desk, scrawling out notes, when a movement catches my attention and I look up. It's Jenny, two rows over and one seat up. She's slamming her hand against a plastic binder, trying to force it down into her book bag.

In a moment of either very good or very bad timing, she lifts her head and looks toward me. We make instant eye contact. It's for less than a second, but long enough that I know she has seen me. That I have crossed her mind. As soon as she realizes who she is looking at, it seems, she jerks her body back to the front and sits rigidly in her seat.

Craning my neck, I stare for a few more seconds at the slice of her striped T-shirt that I can see through the desks and bodies. I raise two fingers and wave at her back.

It's Jenny who I've missed, even more than Sara, over the past few months. The way she shuffles slightly when she walks, her ridiculous laugh, even her long-winded stories. Dr. Nelson said that we need to focus on the important things first. Pencils, my grades, Bed, Bath, and Beyond. But a warmth has risen in me just from catching her eye, just from thinking about her. And I realize she might be one of the important things.

Maybe I could explain. And then she wouldn't be so mad. She would understand, hopefully, why I yelled at her. Twice. I'll just tell her the truth. I'll tell her everything.

But I know that's not an option. There's too much to say and not enough words. It would take a book to really summarize what's happened here. I tell myself to remember to bring this up with Dr. Nelson.

In the time since I discovered socks were okay a few days ago, my mind has been bombarded by a meteor shower of safe items falling back into my life. At breakfast, my mom's glass of milk and my cup of orange juice sit placidly on the counter. The cancer waves that usually surround them are gone. When I go to dig the Christmas gift cards out from under the bed, I find a benign pair of khakis. And somehow the gray sweatshirt with the cartoon horse trots its way back as well. Breathing out a sigh of relief, I grin at myself in my new outfit as I rotate in front of the mirror.

It's Saturday afternoon and it's our first trip back to our old stomping grounds since my nightmare. The mall is packed, so my mom and I are in the very last row of spots, at least a five-minute walk across a treacherously cracked slab of pavement.

I'm not going to be able to make it in one breath, I know this from the start. And about one hundred steps in, as usual, the fuzziness creeps into the edges of my mind. My heart pounds as the blood vessels in my face and neck bulge outward. My mom is talking incessantly, and I don't think she notices when I lunge forward slightly, exhaling two lungfuls of old air. Leaning back, dizzy, I take a few normal breaths against my will. And, as I glance up at the wispy clouds above, the typically green-contaminated air feels strangely pure in my lungs. Even though I can see green-leaved bushes dotting the medians and tall evergreens planted along the edge of the mall itself, there don't seem to be any cancer fumes polluting the parking lot. I slow, sniffing gently at the air. Huh.

And I breathe normally, stepping over cracks in the asphalt, walking by green patches of grass and green cars, until we reach the main entrance of the mall. As I open the door, a wave of comforting heat blows forward, along with the distant sound of classical music playing over the speakers. We pass illuminated stores, gumball machines, photo booths. Without words, we know the familiar route, the loop we always follow that connects the handful of my favorite stores.

"After you, my darling." My mom dons a fake British accent and gestures toward the escalator.

Inside American Eagle, the music is blaring loudly through a thick layer of perfume. I poke tentatively through the stacks of clothes, wary of getting too close, wary of triggering the alarm system that is on the brink of explosion. I know there's nothing real to be scared of, but that doesn't make it any less scary. I tiptoe aimlessly around the circular tables covered in mounds of perfectly folded, color-coded piles.

"*Ohhh!* What about *this*?" My mom appears out of nowhere, barely containing her excitement. In her hand is a pink button-up with tiny flowers sewn over stripes. It's terrible. Really terrible. But as I begin to shake my head, I look at her face and she's so happy. She's moving sideways from foot to foot. So I lie.

"How pretty! Didn't even see that." I wave my hand at

her and she walks over and hands it to me. I roll my eyes slightly and quietly pat myself on the back for being such a good daughter.

There are sweaters, a wall of denim, another wall of corduroy. T-shirts, sequins, beads. And that's when I see it. A white linen blazer hanging on the second row of hooks high on the wall. Gold buttons with small engraved anchors. The inside lining is silk, white and blue stripes. Oh, it's perfect. It will look so good with my . . . *brain cancer brain cancer brain cancer. Braincancerbraincancerbraincancer.*

No! I scream to myself, stomping my foot against the cement floor. It's beautiful. My hands clench into fists, preparing for a fight. It's a blazer. Just a jacket. Just pieces of cotton sewn together. It's a blazer. Nothing more.

"Excuse me, sir?" I wave over the sales associate who is folding polo shirts on a wooden table, talking over the sound of my brain. "Could you please get one of those white blazers down for me? Extra small."

I'm wearing my newly safe pair of khakis as I slide a navy blue shirt off its thick wooden hanger. My hip bones are protruding sharply outward, and the notches in my sternum climb upward like a ladder. Looking in the mirror in the tight, oblong dressing room, I see that I'm still bones and sharp curves and ribs, but my skin has lost its sickly yellow tone. Despite my knotty hair, if I'm at the right angle, if I catch the right light, I look a little bit like myself.

The floor of the dressing room is hardwood, so I tightrope-walk my way sideways down the hall and pose on

333

tiptoes in front of my mom. She stares at me, nods twice, and comments, "Very nice," before bringing her hand up to her mouth. There's more going on in her head than I can probably imagine. Dr. Nelson has told me, a few times, that my parents are deeply worried and intensely curious about my progress. But I don't want to talk to them. Not about this. And I make Dr. Nelson promise she won't share anything either. I don't want them to know about this part of me. At all. This is my problem, my secret.

After about twenty seconds of her silent, emotional gaze, I'm getting uncomfortable. There are tears welling in her eyes as she watches me rotate in front of the mirror. Oh, for goodness' sakes. "Really, Mom?" I jerk my head around the dressing room, moving my arms to show her that we're in public. "Really?"

She immediately looks up at me, as if expecting it. "I know, I know." Wiping underneath her eyes, she adds, "I'm just a mom. You're going to have to give me a second." I roll my eyes at her as my heart swells. I love you, too.

I tiptoe back to the dressing room and slip into the white linen blazer, adjusting it in the mirror. The shoulders are crisp, the sleeves are the right length. The seams cinch in at my sides. It's perfect. I take it off and throw it onto the seat without even showing my mom. I'm getting that blazer.

But I cause cancer! it screams.

I reach down and fold it over onto itself. Shut up.

We settle down on a wooden bench, our shopping bags tucked between our legs, sharing a hot pretzel from an Auntie

Anne's. It's our routine. I don't think my mom and I have ever entered a mall without splitting a buttery, salty, delicious, hot pretzel. I pull and she pulls and two rounded arches tear off into our fingers. I've already decided that mall pretzels are a different species from normal, small, hard pretzels, which are prominent members of the danger list. They're totally different things, I assure myself.

"You know, it's really been remarkable how much progress you have made in such a short time with Dr. Nelson. It's like you're—"

"Mom!" I bark at her. "Don't, okay? Just, please, don't." The walkways are crammed with people, their legs buffeting against ours, but I'm alone. And trapped. I can't talk about this with her.

"Allison Marie. Enough of this attitude and enough of shutting me out. I'm worried about you, damn it!" Pretzel gripped between her two fingers, she slams her hand down on her thigh. My eyes spread wide. She never curses at me. With a small noise, I move to speak—

"No. Allison, no. For just a second. I am your mother. And I love you. And I want to help you. That's my job. That's what I'm here for. So stop shutting me out. You can trust me, and I *want* to be here for you." She isn't crying, but I can hear the pain oozing out of her voice. Months' worth of pent-up frustration and concern. Weeks' worth of silent waiting rooms. "I'm your mother. This is my job. Please let me help you. Let me be a part of this."

I take a deep breath and shoot my eyes to the ceiling. "It's not you, Mom." The sentence comes out with a long, meaningful exhale. "It's just that, I don't know, this stuff is embarrassing. It's *weird*. Even I don't really understand it." I shrug at her and we make eye contact. I take a bite of pretzel to buy a few seconds, but I don't really have anything else to say. "It's not you." I shake my head for emphasis. "I promise."

I'm on my way to chemistry and I'm strutting like I'm on a catwalk. Today I've got on my safe khakis, a *bra!*, the pink button-up shirt my mom picked out (which, surprisingly, isn't that bad), and the new white blazer. I look awesome. I feel awesome.

I can do anything. Me. This girl. I can overcome pencils and calculators and spend gift cards. I can take notes in class and drink milk and wear socks. I've got my chin up and I'm trying my best not to tiptoe while still avoiding the sidewalk cracks. Humming to myself, I push my way into the heated sciences building. Eyes up, shoulders relaxed, I've blossomed out of Hunchback of Notre Dame and into a normal, upright position.

I'm a few steps into the classroom when I realize Ms. Matthews is calling my name. I turn to her, and it's obvious from the look on her face that she repeated herself multiple times before I heard. "Allison. Thanks for joining us. You've been missing a lot of class recently."

I freeze like a frightened deer, and I begin to tremble like one too. "What's that?" I had heard her but I don't have a response. Stall, stall, stall.

"I *said* that you've been missing a lot of class recently." She pauses for five long seconds, during which every head in the class turns to look at me. I feel my right leg rising into the air. I take a gulp of breath and hold it in. "And this is a very important chapter we're on. It's really the foundation for the rest of the semester."

There's no question here, but apparently, her bulging eyes insist, I'm supposed to respond. A warm nausea rises in my stomach. My appointments with Dr. Nelson. We meet twice a week in the afternoons. Before the start of the semester, Dr. Nelson and my mother quietly coordinated with school administrators so I would be granted excused absences for all my appointments. Under my adamant input, however, they did not contact any of my teachers directly. I don't want them to know what's going on. I'm a straight-A student in their eyes—or at least I hope they still see me that way—and I want to keep it like that.

"So?" She throws her flabby arms into the air, and her collection of bracelets and bangles clinks loudly together

I look back up at her. "Right, yes. I've had appointments."

"So many? In the first weeks of school?"

I nod, tight-lipped, and let out a small "mm-hm." Pivoting on my planted foot and coming down from the flamingo stance, I move to march in between tiles to the lab table in the back.

"Do you even eat?" Her voice hits the back of my tangled head.

"What?" It comes out like a croak, and I whip around to face her.

"Your pants. They're falling off you! It's all bones and"— she crinkles her face—"skin."

The room is silent. Twenty-five curious heads await my answer.

"Yes, I eat." I suddenly wish I had my pile to hide behind. My shoulders begin to slope forward under my new jacket, returning to their default position. "I mean, I've lost some weight, I guess. But I definitely eat. It's just . . . that . . ." I'm flailing. Rambling. My mouth opens and closes like a fish slapped on a dry wooden dock.

"She sits with me at lunch, Ms. Matthews." The voice comes from nearby. It's Jenny. She's got her hand raised, and she's pushing up off her desk with her arms so she can look the teacher in the eye. "The girl eats like she's starving. Trust me. It's actually impressive."

I look at Jenny, who is staring straight ahead, and then up at Ms. Matthews. A few seconds of silence. "Well, coulda fooled me." She moves her arm in the air, pointing at my head, then lowering her finger down my body. And with that she turns to the blackboard and picks up a stick of chalk.

Jenny sits in the fourth seat of the outside row. When I move by her, I focus all my energy on looking as normal as possible. Maybe she'll notice my new blazer. I can't resist a glance. Just one furtive look in between steps. I can't be sure—I am trying so hard to be subtle—but I think she might be smiling at me. Not a usual Jenny smile, only the tiniest of movements around the corners of her lips. A small raise of her cheeks. But I'll take it. *Thank you, Jenny.*

CHAPTER 28

After we spent the better part of my appointment deciding how to explain my OCD to Jenny, Dr. Nelson had the idea for me to give her a pamphlet just like the one I first found in Dr. Adams's display. I wouldn't have to tell Jenny face-to-face. I could just give her the information and let her absorb it on her own. The pamphlet, now crinkled and folded, has been weighing down my book bag all day. Since I got it yesterday, I have carefully picked my way through the words and bulleted lists, circling things and making small notes. Highlighting certain sentences and scribbling examples that Jenny may have noticed. It is a CliffsNotes version of my OCD. And I'm going to give it to Jenny. Today. If I ever work up the nerve.

I almost did it after art, but it just felt too ambitious. Too early in the day. And I thought about sliding it across our table at lunch, but that didn't seem right either. I hadn't been to the cafeteria since last semester. Plus, Rebecca would be there. The afternoon whirs by until I'm in chemistry. Seeing Ms. Matthews, remembering how Jenny stood up for me, I know now is the time.

"Jenny, wait!" I yell at her at the end of class, reaching forward before the bell has finished ringing. She might hear me, because she turns slightly, almost glancing at me, but then keeps walking forward. I snatch up my binder, throw my book bag onto my back, and tiptoe toward her. "Jenny!"

She stops and pauses for a few seconds, recognizing my voice. "I have something for—"

But my voice catches in my throat as I see Ms. Matthews rise from her desk in the corner. Jenny looks at me and moves her head just an inch, asking me to meet her in the hallway. We both shuffle out. She clears her throat before turning around.

The pamphlet is in my hand, and I'm rubbing the paper between my thumb and forefinger. "Look." I take a deep breath. "I'm really sorry for the way I—"

"Are you anorexic?" Her voice cuts into me. It hits me like an unexpected punch, and my head jerks physically backward.

"What?" I am so surprised by her question that I fumble around for words before sputtering, "M-me? What?"

She clenches her face at me, shoving her hand forward. "Yes, you," she mimics. "I mean, it's obvious. You've lost so much weight. You seem depressed. Are you anorexic? Is that what has been wrong this whole time? Is that what you're hiding?" They're accusations as much as they are questions.

"No, I—I—"

"You could have just told me, you know. I could have helped you. Or at least tried, somehow. I could have done something so you didn't turn into . . ." But she stops, realizing what she is about to say. Her eyes finally meet mine and she shrugs. "Why didn't you *tell me*?" She seems upset by my secrets, not by the times I yelled at her, like I thought. "I could have been there for you."

My heart floods with warmth as my muscles soften and I shake my head. "I'm not anorexic, Jenny." I briefly fidget with a hangnail, working up my last bit of courage, before quickly extending the now-warm pamphlet. "I have OCD." She takes it, looks down at the paper and then back up at me with a completely blank face, unsure what to do. "Well, I thought you could read this and then you would know what has been going on the past few months. Why I've been acting this way." I've got my mouth pushed to the side, a scalding wave of heat creeping up my neck.

She quietly flips through the pages. "This is why you count your steps?" She points at a scribbled note in the margin, and I nod at her. She reads further but doesn't say anything else. I can tell she doesn't know how to react. This is completely foreign.

I interrupt her thoughts, trying to steer her in the right direction. "But I'm getting better now. I've made so much progress. My doctor has been really impressed." I try to say it casually, gesturing at my khakis. "I just wanted you to know. I just . . . I wanted to explain."

It feels good to talk to Jenny again, even for just a few minutes, even if it's about this. She deserves an explanation for the way I treated her last semester. Somehow she is different from my parents. It's like I owe her the courtesy of telling the truth. She flips the pamphlet over quickly, looks at me through slightly squinted eyes, and nods, mostly to herself. "OCD. Obsessive-compulsive disorder." She gestures at me with her head, and we walk together down the hallway. "I thought this was when you washed your hands all the time? And were scared of germs or something?"

"No, it's not always—"

"*Yeah!* That's for sure!" She forcefully interrupts me. "You are not afraid of germs. Your bedroom is *gross!*" We laugh, and she nudges me playfully with her shoulder.

"No, not all OCD is like that. I mean, some is, definitely. There are lots of different kinds." We push through the double doors into the sunshine. "Mine is mostly about worrying something terrible is going to happen to me or my family. And then doing all sorts of weird stuff to try to prevent it." She is silent for a few seconds and we continue to walk toward seventh period.

"Hey," she almost whispers as she nudges me softly with her shoulder. I turn quickly toward her and we make eye contact as a sea of students filters around us. Her face warms into a smile. "Thanks for telling me."

I stare at her, even after she has turned to look away, and it takes a few seconds to register: I've got a friend again. A friend who knows the truth. And I'm surprised how easy it was to tell her, how naturally I labeled the past few months with the letters *OCD*. Almost like I've accepted it.

That night I allow my book bag to collapse to the floor of the den, sending reverberations through the house. I crouch down to the carpet, on the opposite side of the room from the cancer desk and computer, far from the reach of their dangerous cloud of carcinogens. The binder I've been using for all my classes is splayed open in front of me. I pull a wooden yellow pencil out of my book bag and, with a small zap of electricity in my brain, begin scribbling away on homework.

But something's off. There's that itch on the back of my brain. That tension growing in my temples. And my skin. It's burning. I start to squirm around on the carpet, still half focused on my homework, when I hear it. Or maybe feel it. An invisible sneer: *You thought I was safe, but I'm your worst nightmare.* I jerk up straight, trying to tune my body in to the source of the anger. It's not the pencil, not the notebook paper, not the desk. I look down and feel my chest growing hotter, the skin on my arms screaming against the heat. My shirt. My new gift-card shirt. It's furious. Glowing. It hates me.

I throw my pencil down and grab the bottom hem of the shirt to pull it over my shoulders. To save myself. Get it off, get it off, get it off before it can hurt me. *Allison, where are you now?* Dr. Nelson's voice echoes in the back of my mind and I stop, the shirt frozen half on my body, half draping over my head. Dr. Nelson. I see us in her office, the beige chair sitting on the beige carpet. And I'm reminded of who I am. This is OCD, I tell myself. The room is silent. This is OCD. Just like pencils and calculators. Just like socks and sidewalk cracks.

Guided by these thoughts and Dr. Nelson's invisible presence, the shirt still buzzing with cancer rays around my head, I slowly lower my arms, allowing the fabric to fall back onto my body. My brain clenches and a knot is forming deep under my shoulder blade and there's a screeching inside my ear and I'm an eight. My heart is pounding. My pointer finger is digging aggressively at a bleeding hangnail on my thumb. It's just OCD. It's just OCD. It's just OCD. And I'm a seven.

And as I sit rigidly on the carpet, my anxiety falls to a six, a five, a four. Until, just two minutes after almost stripping off my shirt, I'm able to breathe again. I roll my head slowly around in a circle. All the happiness I felt about reconnecting with Jenny filters away. Yes, I've made progress. And compared to where I was a few weeks ago, I'm an entirely new person. But it's clear I'm still a prisoner. I still jump at my mind's beck and call. With a deep sigh, I know I'm no longer the old Allison. As much as I wish I could be. And I'm not sure I'll ever be that person again. I can't stick to my five-year plan if I can't even get through a homework assignment. I can't make honor roll if I'm cowering from my own mind.

But if I'm not that girl, who am I? If I can't be an overachiever, if I can no longer stake my pride on my sparkling straight A's, then . . . then . . . then I don't know.

After the shirt incident, I become more aware of all the times I'm attacked by angry thoughts. I'm no longer proud that I can write, that I can wear khakis and socks. Because there is so much that I *can't* do. I'm still miles away from normal. Gray clouds hover over my head through the next day until my afternoon appointment with Dr. Nelson. It's like she can sense my frustration, because her tone is a little more subdued than usual as we sit down across from each other.

"So, how have the past two days been?" Her head is tilted to the side, concern and sympathy on her face.

"Fine." I look at her like I do my mom, challenging her to pry information out of me. But she only nods, her hands folded on her lap, smiling gently. And we sit in silence. Until I can't hold it in anymore. "It's just that . . . I still have so many thoughts!" I fling my arms forward in frustration. "I know I've gotten over a lot of things, but it's just *constant*. It's like I'll never get better. I'll always be like *this*." I gesture with my hand toward my knotted hair, feeling sorry for myself.

Dr. Nelson doesn't move and continues to nod gently, as if she knows there's more.

"I don't know. I guess . . . I guess I'm just upset. About this. All of it. Like, I know I'm doing well but . . . I'm still . . ." Lost for words, I lift my arms in the air and flop them down loudly on top of my thighs. Warm tears well in the corner of my eyes.

"Okay, okay." She adjusts in her chair. "It seems like you've had a tough few days, hmm? What brought this on?"

"My *life* brought this on!" I say dramatically, trying to feel annoyed at her. "I'm ready to be over this! I get it. I have OCD. I need to fight against my thoughts. But it's not helping! Nothing is helping!"

"Allison, I think you're forgetting what incredible progress you've made thus far and"—I move to interrupt her, but she raises her voice and talks over me—"*and* you will continue to improve. I think you know that. In fact, I know you know that. But you can't expect magic. You need to be patient with yourself."

"I *have* been patient. And it sucks." I lean back in the seat with my arms crossed. "I'm tired of this." Saying it out loud, I realize how frustrated I've felt, even if I haven't allowed myself to admit it. "Will I ever be all the way . . . you know. Like I was before?"

We make eye contact, and she lets out a long sigh.

"You will probably always have some level of OCD thoughts. Some days it will be worse than others. It will ebb and flow. And you'll learn to control it better. But OCD tends to be for life." The clock on the wall ticks into the quiet room as I look down at my hands, trying to figure out how I feel. Dr. Nelson clears her throat. "I know this is hard. And as you said, it sucks. It really, really sucks. You didn't ask for this. You had no idea what OCD was really about until a month ago, right?" As much as I want to pout, my eyes are drawn to her face, and I feel myself nodding, agreeing with her. "But here's the thing: that doesn't matter." We stare at each other as her words settle on the room. "You have obsessive-compulsive disorder. For richer or poorer, for better or worse." She shrugs at me. "That's just how it is."

I'm tempted to be angry. Or maybe start crying. But I know she's right. She's always right.

"So, you've got to do the best you can with what you've got. You're a smart girl. You're determined." She's smiling at me now, and it's so genuine, and I know I'll never forget her and what she's done for me. What she's saved me from. "You're going to be fine, Allison Marie. We just have to keep working for it. Like boxing."

My heart swells as I look at her, and I'm filled with a

wave of motivation. I'll never be the old me . . . but I can be the new me. A girl who, despite the buzzing of angry thoughts in her head, slaps on a smile and trudges forward, always forward. It will never be easy. It will never be clean and simple. It's going to be a fight. Just like boxing. And I'm determined to win.

NOTE TO READERS

As Dr. Nelson predicted, my OCD continued to play a major role in my life throughout the rest of high school. With ERP, we were able to chisel away at my danger list, but it seemed like my mind found new threats as quickly as I overcame the old ones. While I sometimes still felt out of control, with Dr. Nelson's help I learned how to better handle my thoughts and anxieties in daily life. I was able to do well in school (the special testing allowances ended up being a huge help after all) and rejoin the cross-country team, eventually being named captain my senior year. I had fewer friends after my OCD explosion, but they were real ones. And that's what matters. I was an honor graduate from Samuelson and went on to an idyllic undergraduate experience at Wake Forest University. There, I was able to start fresh in a place unfamiliar with the legacy of my sophomore year, though I made sure to keep in touch with Dr. Nelson to help me through the transition. After earning a BA and an MA, I began a career in marketing and eventually married my college sweetheart. Although obsessive-compulsive disorder will always be a part of my life, I would not be anywhere close to the person I turned out to be if I hadn't finally asked for, and accepted, help. It is loved ones, friends, and a handful of dedicated physicians who have helped me find happiness and stability in my mental illness. There are many online resources available to those affected by obsessive-compulsive disorder, and I hope you will engage with them if you or someone you know is affected by OCD or other mental health issues:

ACTIVE MINDS
activeminds.org

MENTAL HEALTH AMERICA
mentalhealthamerica.net

THE NATIONAL ALLIANCE ON MENTAL ILLNESS
nami.org

THE NATIONAL INSTITUTE OF MENTAL HEALTH
nimh.nih.gov

THE INTERNATIONAL OCD FOUNDATION
iocdf.org

ACKNOWLEDGMENTS

This book would still be a handful of pages saved on a laptop if my husband hadn't constantly badgered me to "work on the OCD book." Gavin, you believed in me, and this book, long before I took either seriously. Thank you for making my life a Taylor Swift song and for being exactly the person you are.

Endless gratitude to Lauren Galit and Caitlin Rubino-Bradway of LKG Agency for picking me out of a crowded inbox and taking a chance on a complete newbie. Your guidance, hard work, and support made this dream a reality. I couldn't have hoped to be part of a better team.

To Liesa Abrams and the incredible team at Simon Pulse: you all have transformed this book into something more than I could have ever imagined. Liesa, thank you for your thoughtful advice, sensitivity, and enthusiasm. It has truly been a pleasure.

And to my parents, my original support system, thank you for always accepting me for the person I am and encouraging me to embrace it as well.

Last but not least, lots of head pats to Ranger the dog for long, long walks through the Upper West Side when I was feeling stuck. And for being so cute.

ABOUT THE AUTHOR

Allison Britz graduated with her BA and MA from Wake Forest University. When not spending all of her money on books, she enjoys cooking, three-day weekends, arguing with her OCD, and extensive Netflix binges. She lives in Colorado with her husband and their dog. *Obsessed* is her first book.